Culturally Diverse Library Collections for Youth

Herman L. Totten

Carolyn Garner

Risa W. Brown

Neal Schuman Publishers, Inc.
New York   London

Published by Neal-Schuman Publishers, Inc.
100 Varick Street
New York, NY 10013

Printed and bound in the United States of America.

Library of Congress Cataloging-in-Publication Data

Totten, Herman L.
    Culturally diverse library collections for youth / by Herman
L. Totten, Carolyn Garner, and Risa W. Brown.
        p. cm.
    Includes bibliographical references (p.) and index.
    ISBN 1–55570–141–8 (alk. paper)
    1. Minorities—United States—Juvenile literature—Bibliography.
2. Young adults' libraries—United States—Book lists. I. Garner,
Carolyn. II. Brown, Risa W. III. Title
Z1361.E4T677 1996
[E184.A1]
305.8'00973—dc20   96-1020

 CONTENTS

❈ INTRODUCTION ❈

Culturally Diverse Library Collections for Youth, an annotated bibliography of multicultural literature for secondary students, was the brainchild of Dr. Herman Totten, Professor of Library Science at the University of North Texas. This volume is a companion piece to his earlier work *Culturally Diverse Library Collections for Children* produced in collaboration with Risa Brown.

The scope, organizational scheme, and selection criteria of this volume are identified below.

Purpose and Scope.

Culturally Diverse Library Collections for Youth is designed to help librarians broaden and diversify their print and video collections with materials written both for and about America's four largest emerging majorities. The arrangement and indexes are intended to help librarians develop specific parts of their collections as well as identify recommended works on specific subjects. Materials included in these pages are intended for middle, junior high, and senior high school libraries as well as young adult collections in public libraries.

Organizational Scheme.

Culturally Diverse Library Collections for Youth is divided into five sections:

- Materials about African Americans;
- Materials about Native Americans;
- Materials about Hispanic Americans;
- Materials about Asian Americans;
- Multiethnic Materials.

Each of these five sections lists recommended books followed by recommended videos. Entries within each section are arranged alphabetically by title. Recent but unreviewed video titles are separated from recommended and reviewed videos and are clearly labeled as such. The Multiethnic Materials category lists works covering two or more ethnic groups.

Books within each ethnic category are further subdivided by genre: biographies, folklore, literature, and poetry; young adult fiction; reference and scholarly works; and nonfiction. Because of the diversity of groups covered in the Asian American section, reference, scholarly, and nonfiction, titles are broken into sections covering Cambodian Americans, Chinese Americans, Japanese Americans, Korean Americans, Pacific Islanders, and Vietnamese Americans. Titles covering more than one Asian American group are listed in a final category labeled Asian Americans–Multiethnic.

Author, title, and subject indexes to all titles appear at the end of the volume.

Selection Criteria

All of the books and videos listed here meet one or both of the following selection criteria:

- They have been personally reviewed by the compilers and/or used successfully in Dr. Totten's multicultural classes;
- They were favorably reviewed in such professional journals as *School Library Journal* or *Booklist* between January 1993 and October 1995.

A broad selection of new and reprinted materials is being marketed under the multicultural umbrella. Librarians should stick to their selection standards and not alter their selection process simply to accommodate any multicultural title. Some criteria that may help the multicultural material include the following:

1. Is the character a unique individual? Watch out for a character purportedly representing an entire racial or ethnic group.
2. Is the culture of the character accurately and respectfully portrayed?
3. Does the character solve his or her own problem? Avoid titles in which the protagonist's problems are solved by a member of the larger culture.
4. In a biography, is the character overly glamorized? An oversimplification may present an unrealistic portrait of a famous ethnic person.
5. Is the setting authentic and fair to the ethnic group?
6. If historical, are the facts accurate? Watch out for the perpetuation of historical distortions and pertinent omissions.
7. Does the presence of dialect have a legitimate purpose?
8. Watch out for offensive descriptions.
9. Are illustrations accurate?
10. Are females portrayed realistically?

About this Book

The citations in this book were verified in *Books in Print CD-Rom* using the July 1995 update. In those instances where information was not available in *Books in Print,* the primary source was used when possible. In some cases, the primary source did not have data such as LC numbers, and the standard library cataloging sources were used to gather that data. Every attempt was made to make the entries as complete as possible.

We know, as in our previous book, *Culturally Diverse Library Collections for Children,* that librarians will find this book a great asset in helping to expand the diversity of materials in their collections as well as guiding students, teachers, and other library patrons to materials that meet specific multicultural needs and interests.

✦ AFRICAN AMERICANS ✦

Biographies

Alvin Ailey, Jr.: A Life in Dance. Julinda Lewis-Ferguson. New York: Walker and Company, 1994. 64 pp. ISBN 0–8027–8239–6. LC 93–17906. Junior high and up.

This work tells not only the story of the life of dancer/choreographer Alvin Ailey, but the story of his company and its works. The author discusses Ailey's creations, giving the background and history of each. Small black-and-white photos throughout. Good for studies of notable African Americans.

Aretha Franklin: Lady Soul. Leslie Gourse. Danbury, CT: Franklin Watts, 1995. 160 pp. ISBN 0–531–13037–1. LC 94–29074. Junior high and up.

Well written, detailed, and worth the purchase. Gourse tells the story of Aretha Franklin, a minister's daughter, who made her first gospel recording at the age of 14, signed a contract with Columbia Records at 18, and became famous as "Lady Soul." Good for units on notable African Americans.

Arthur Ashe: Against the Wind. David R. Collins. Morristown, NJ: Silver Burdett Press, 1994. People in Focus Series. 128 pp. ISBN 0–87518–647–5. LC 94–17853. Junior high.

Arthur Ashe grew up in a segregated neighborhood and learned to play tennis at Brook Field Park in Richmond, Virginia. By the time he reached his teens, he was already recognized as a superior player. Finally, he was offered the opportunity to finish high school in St. Louis and enter a special tennis program. He received a scholarship to UCLA and went on to worldwide fame. He beat Jimmy Connors at Wimbledon in 1975. Ashe was a sports champion, a civil rights activist, a humanitarian, and an inspiring man to the end of his life. Good for units on notable African Americans.

Black Cowboy: The Life and Legend of George McJunkin, 3rd Edition
Franklin Folsom. Niwot, CT: Roberts Rinehart, 1992. 162 pp. ISBN 1–879373–
14–9. LC 91–66680. Junior high and up.

George McJunkin was born a slave in Texas. Having no name of his own, he took
that of his master. George became a cowboy by watching and practicing. Being a
cowboy was not his only interest; he also discovered the "Folsom points," flint
weapons proving that humans had inhabited the North American continent long
before anthropologists and historians of the day had believed. Useful for American
history units and African American studies.

**Buck Leonard, the Black Lou Gehrig: The Hall of Famer's Story in His
Own Words**. Buck Leonard and James Riley. New York: Carroll and Graf, 1995.
304 pp. ISBN 0–7867–0119–6. LC 94–26563. Young adults.

Buck Leonard played first baseman for the Homestead Grays during the Negro
Baseball League days of the 1930s and 1940s. He was finally inducted into the
Baseball Hall of Fame in 1972. Writing with his son, Buck Leonard tells more
about his games and fellow players than his life. Should appeal to his fans and fans
of baseball with an interest in the Negro Leagues.

Charlie Parker: Musician. Ron Frankl. New York: Chelsea House Publishers,
1992. Black Americans of Achievement Series. 112 pp. ISBN 0–7910–1134–8. LC
92–12126. Grade 5 and up.

Introduction by Coretta Scott King. Brief, authoritative biography of Charlie
Parker, noted jazz musician. Traces his tragically short life and professional rise.
Selected discography and black-and-white photos. Good for units on notable
African Americans.

Clarence Thomas: Supreme Court Justice. Norman L. Macht. New York:
Chelsea House Publishers, 1995. Black Americans of Achievement Series. 144 pp.
ISBN 0–7910–1883–0. LC 94–44353. Grade 5 and up.

A somewhat uneven account of the life of Supreme Court Justice Clarence Thomas.
The author begins with Thomas's childhood in Georgia and describes the experiences that influenced him, but leaves out most of the details of his legal career. His
ideas and opinions are explored in depth. His confirmation hearings and Anita
Hill's accusations are addressed only as they affected him and his family. Tends to
ramble in spots. Black-and-white photos. Useful only to have something on the
subject. Watch for better.

Coming Home: From the Life of Langston Hughes. Floyd Cooper. New York: The Putnam Publishing Group (Philomel Books), 1994. 32 pp. ISBN 0–399–22682–6. LC 93–36332. All ages.

A picture book about the childhood and life of Langston Hughes. Dreamy, earthtone pictures. Expresses the child's longing for a "real" home with his parents and portrays scenes from his foster homes. Cooper's story expresses and confronts Hughes's sadness without becoming maudlin. Gives a good sense of the noted author. Good for author studies and studies of notable African Americans.

Dancing Spirit: An Autobiography. Judith Jamison and Howard Kaplan. New York: Doubleday and Company, 1993. 256 pp. ISBN 0–385–42557–0. LC 93–25480. Junior high and up.

Dancer, choreographer, and teacher Judith Jamison tells the story of her life, her career, her devotion to dancing, and her position as artistic director of the Alvin Ailey American Dance Theater. Over 60 black-and-white photos. Much use of technical terms and jargon with no explanation. Of interest to dance students. Useful for studies of notable African Americans.

Deion Sanders: This Is Prime Time. Aaron Klein. New York: Walker and Company, 1995. 144 pp. ISBN 0–8027–8369–4. LC 94–44793. Junior high and high school.

Disjointed and idealized account of the career of Dallas Cowboy cornerback and wide receiver Deion Sanders, the former San Francisco 49er who also plays baseball for the Cincinnati Reds. He gets better and better. This book doesn't. Wait for a better one if possible.

Duke Ellington: A Life of Music. Eve Stwertka. Danbury, CT: Franklin Watts, Inc., 1994. 160 pp. ISBN 0–531–13035–5. LC 93–21267. Junior high and up.

Edward Ellington Kennedy, also known as Duke Ellington, was a band leader who developed a style of jazz uniquely his own. Stwertka traces Ellington's life from early childhood through his career and acceptance as one of the world's great jazz musicians and composers. Of interest to music students. Of use to units on notable African Americans. (Impact Biographies Series)

Eddie Murphy: Entertainer. Deborah Wilburn. New York: Chelsea House Publishers, 1993. 112 pp. ISBN 0–7910–1879–2. (Paper: ISBN 0–7910–1908–X). LC 92–31310. Junior high and high school.

The story of the life and career of Eddie Murphy, one of Hollywood's biggest stars.

Somewhat outdated, but fun. Shares the problems as well as the fame of the star. Of interest to fans and in units on notable African Americans. Introduction by Coretta Scott King.

The Emmitt Zone. Emmitt Smith. New York: Crown Publishing Group, 1994. 275 pp. ISBN 0–517–59985–6. LC 94–20939. Junior high and up.

Autobiography of Emmitt Smith, renowned running back for the Dallas Cowboys. Modern Horatio Alger story. Smith tells of his very traditional upbringing, his consciousness of being a role model, and the importance of values. Sure to please Cowboy and Emmitt Smith fans.

Frederick Douglass: In His Own Words. Frederick Douglass. Milton Meltzer, ed. Orlando, FL: Harcourt, Brace & Company, 1995. 240 pp. ISBN 0–15–229492–9. LC 94–14524. Junior high and high school.

Not an autobiography. Meltzer has compiled articles and speeches by Douglass, giving a clear picture of his views on abolition, "happy slaves," the condition of free blacks, Lincoln's presidency, the manner in which the Civil War was conducted, and more. Linocut prints. Excerpts arranged chronologically. Brief notes on historical context for each section. Profiles of several of Douglass's contemporaries. Illustrated by Stephen Alcorn. Good for history units.

Guts: Legendary Black Rodeo Cowboy Bill Pickett. Cecil Johnson. June Ford, ed. Arlington, TX: Summit Publishing, 1994. 223 pp. ISBN 1–56530–162–5. LC 94–38591. Junior high and up.

Biography of Bill Pickett, the champion rodeo rider known as the "Dusky Demon." Pickett performed with various rodeos for over 40 years and was recently honored by having his face placed on a U.S. postage stamp. Of use for units on notable African Americans.

Hang Time: Days, Dreams, and Destinations with Michael Jordan. Bob Greene. New York: St. Martin's Press, Inc., 1993. 416 pp. ISBN 0–312–95193–0. LC 92–26494. Junior high and up.

Highly subjective, intimate biography of basketball star Michael Jordan. Gives insight into his character, his childhood, his determination, and his sports successes. Primarily for fans' reading pleasure.

I Have a Dream: The Life and Words of Martin Luther King, Jr. Jim
Haskins. Brookfield, CT: Millbrook Press Incorporated, 1992. 112 pp. ISBN 1–
56294–087–2. LC 91–42528. Junior high.

The story of King's life and achievements is told in very readable prose. Haskins
covers personal details as well as King's importance to the Civil Rights movement.
Excerpts from King's speeches are interspersed with text. Features an introduction
by Rosa Parks and a number of black-and-white photos of King and others, clearly
reflecting the mood and flavor of the time. Good for junior high or reading-
challenged high school students.

I Know Why the Caged Bird Sings. Maya Angelou. New York: Random
House Incorporated, 1970. 256 pp. ISBN 0–394–42986–9. (Paper: ISBN 0–553–
27937–8.) Junior high and up.

Autobiography of well-known black poet Maya Angelou. Ms. Angelou has written a
frank, moving account of her years growing up in Arkansas, St. Louis, and San
Francisco. She spares no details of events that combined to make her the strong
woman she is today. Suggested for more mature readers. Also made into a movie.
(See video section.) Useful for units on notable African Americans overcoming
adversity.

In My Place. Charlayne Hunter-Gault. New York: Farrar, Straus & Giroux, 1992.
256 pp. ISBN 0–374–17563–2. LC 92–16331. Junior high and up.

Charlayne Hunter-Gault was the first black woman to graduate from the University
of Georgia. This is the story of a young black woman growing up in the 1950s and
1960s under the guidance of loving parents. They taught her that there was nothing
she couldn't do if she put her mind to it, and helped build in her the strength of
character to face and fight the racism and bigotry of those who tried to stand in her
way. Good for women's studies and units on notable African Americans.

Jackie Joyner Kersee: Champion Athlete. Geri Harrington. New York:
Chelsea House Publishers, 1995. Great Achievers: Lives of the Physically Challenged Series. 112 pp. ISBN 0–7910–2085–1. LC 94–038230. Junior high and
high school.

Jackie Joyner Kersee has asthma. Despite the fact that she is unable to take many
prescription drugs that could help control her condition because they contain
substances forbidden by the Olympic Committee, Jackie Joyner Kersee has worked
to become a four-time Olympic champion. She won the silver medal for the
heptathlon in 1984, the gold medal for the heptathlon and the long jump in 1988,
and the gold medal for the heptathlon in 1992. The book contains black-and-white

photos, bibliography, chronology, and list for further reading. Will appeal to young readers.

The Kidnapped Prince: The Life of Olaudah Equiano. Adapted by Ann Cameron. New York: Knopf, 1995. Alfred A. Knopf Books for Young Readers. 144 pp. ISBN 0–679–85619–6. LC 93–29914. Junior high.

The true story of Olaudah Equiano, who was kidnapped from his home in Benin at the age of 11 and sold into slavery in England, the United States, and the West Indies. Equiano was eventually able to buy his freedom. Based on his autobiography published in 1789. Details the horror of slave ships, slavery, auctions, and forced labor. Good for African American history units. Introduction by Henry L. Gates.

Langston Hughes. S. L. Berry. Mankato, MN: Creative Education, Inc., 1994. Voices in Poetry Series. ISBN 0–88682–616–0. LC 93–741. Junior high and up.

Moving blend of biography, poetry, and photographs of the life of Langston Hughes. Personal details of his life, including his awareness of his homosexuality, are described along with their effects on his work. Of use for units on notable African Americans.

Louis Armstrong: A Cultural Legacy. Marc H. Miller, Richard A. Long, Dan Morgenstern, and Donald Bagel. Seattle, WA: University of Washington Press, 1995. 248 pp. ISBN 0–295–97382–X. (Paper: ISBN 0–295–97383–8.) LC 94–21134. Junior high and up.

Photos, drawings, and illustrations trace the career of the incomparable Satchmo, one of the twentieth century's greatest musical innovators. Miller discusses Armstrong's cultural impact, his struggles against segregation and his trips to Africa; surveys his music; and describes his movie appearances. Includes an index. Good for units on notable African Americans.

Louis Armstrong: Swinging, Singing, Satchmo. Sanford Brown. Danbury, CT: Franklin Watts, Inc., 1993. Impact Biography Series. 124 pp. ISBN 0–531–15680–X. LC 92–43192. Junior high and up.

Life of Louis Armstrong from his childhood in Louisiana to his success as a musician. Brown emphasizes Armstrong's musical ability, his career, his contribution to the world of music as the musician most instrumental in popularizing jazz. Black-and-white photographs. Good for units on notable African Americans.

Malcolm X: A Force for Change. Nikki Grimes. New York: Fawcett H. Book Group, 1992. Great Lives Series. 177 pp. ISBN 0–449–90803–8. LC 92–90414. Junior high and up.

Biography of Malcolm X from his youth to his rise as a Civil Rights leader. Emphasizes his positive qualities, contributions, and aspirations rather than the negative facets of his personality. Black-and-white photographs add little. Use for content; look for better.

Malcolm X: By Any Means Necessary. Walter Dean Myers. New York: Scholastic, Inc., 1994. 224 pp. ISBN 0–590–48109–6. LC 92–013480. Junior high.

Biography of the famous African American Civil Rights leader. Useful for reports and units on notable African Americans.

Maya Angelou, Author. Miles Shapiro. New York: Chelsea House Publishers, 1994. Black Americans of Achievement Series. 112 pp. ISBN 0–7910–1862–8. (Paper: ISBN 0–7910–1891–1.) LC 93–3249. Junior high and up.

Frank, well-written story of the life of Maya Angelou. Material is taken from interviews and her autobiographical works. Spares no details of Angelou's early life and dysfunctional family. Liberal use of black-and-white photos accurately shows life during segregation. Traces Angelou's rise as a writer, poet, and professor. Good for units on notable African Americans. Introduction by Coretta Scott King.

The Memphis Diary of Ida B. Wells. Miriam DeCosta-Willis, ed. Boston: Beacon Press, 1995. Black Women Writers Series. 222 pp. ISBN 0–8070–7064–5. LC 94–9087. High school and up.

Not a complete autobiography. The diary covers three primary phases of Wells's life. The first section covers her life in Memphis; the second covers her passage to England; and the third covers her campaign for Illinois state senator shortly before her death. Well corroborated by her autobiography. Good for units on notable African Americans. Foreword by Mary H. Washington. Afterword by Dorothy Sterling. Illustrations.

Michael Jackson: Entertainer. Lois P. Nicholson. New York: Chelsea House Publishers, 1994. Black Americans of Achievement Series. 103 pp. ISBN 0–7910–1929–2. (Paper: ISBN 0–7910–1930–6.) LC 93–39777. Junior high and up.

Limited story of Michael Jackson's life and rise to fame. This book, shorter and easier to read than his autobiography, *Moonwalk*, tells of his career but downplays his eccentricities, his troubled childhood, and barely mentions his sexual molestation charges. Offers little insight into his unusual lifestyle. Black-and-white photos of the Jackson Five, Jackson himself, and other recording stars. Some errors in the index. Short and readable. Illustrations.

Michael Jordan: A Shooting Star. George Beahm. Kansas City, MO: Andrews and McMeel, 1994. 160 pp. ISBN 0–8362–8048–2. LC 93–046005. Junior high.

Biography of basketball star Michael Jordan. Articles and photographs tracing the star's meteoric career. Does not mention his retirement to play baseball. Published in 1994, it does not cover his return to basketball. Of interest to fans. Of possible use for units on notable African Americans.

My Life With Martin Luther King, Jr. Coretta Scott King. New York: Henry Holt and Company, Inc., 1993. 352 pp. ISBN 0–8050–2445–X. LC 92–23525. High school and up.

Revision of the 1969 edition. Coretta Scott King relates the details of her girlhood, her courtship and marriage to Martin Luther King, Jr., their work for the Civil Rights movement. Her story is naturally somewhat one-sided and does not address allegations made about Dr. King by the FBI and many of his critics. No substantial changes from the earlier work. Sixteen pages of black-and-white photographs. Good for units on African American history, civil rights and notable African Americans.

Nelson Mandela: Voice of Freedom. Libby Hughes. Morristown, NJ: Silver Burdett Press, 1992. People in Focus Series. 144 pp. ISBN 0–87518–484–7. LC 91–31543. Junior high and high school.

Perceptive biography of the noted South African Civil Rights leader. The author covers Mandela's life, his imprisonment, his leadership of South African blacks, and their ultimate victory over Apartheid. Extensive background information. Gives the reader a personal look at an important political figure. Black-and-white photographs. Includes bibliography and index. Good addition to any library.

One More River to Cross: The Stories of Twelve Black Americans. Jim Haskins. New York: Scholastic, 1994. 215 pp. ISBN 0–590–42897–7. LC NA. Junior high and up.

This group biography includes stories of Malcolm X, Crispus Attucks, C. J. Walker, Eddie Robinson, and nine other notable African Americans who have left their indelible stamp on American culture and politics. Good source for short reports.

Order Out of Chaos: The Autobiographical Works of Maya Angelou. Maya Angelou. Dolly A. McPherson, ed. London, England: The Virago Press, 1992. 176 pp. Studies in African and Afro-American Cultures Series. ISBN 1–853812–13–7. LC 89–36377. Junior high and up.

Noted African American author and poet Maya Angelou's life is revealed in her autobiographical works.

Ray Charles: Musician. David Ritz. New York: Chelsea House Publishers, 1994. Great Achievers: Lives of the Physically Challenged Series. 112 pp. ISBN 0–7910–2080–0. (Paper: ISBN 0–7910–2093–2.) LC 93–30224. Junior high and high school.

Biography of Ray Charles. Includes index and illustrations. Tells of Charles' boyhood, the childhood glaucoma that took his sight, his determination to succeed in the world of music, and his rise to fame. Good for units on overcoming adversity and notable African Americans.

Rosa Parks: Civil Rights Leader. Mary Hull. New York: Chelsea House Publishers, 1994. Black Americans of Achievement Series. 110 pp. ISBN 0–7910–1881–4. (Paper: ISBN 0–7910–1910–1.) LC 93–17699. Junior high and high school.

Contains black-and-white photographs. Details the adult life of Rosa Parks, her fateful decision not to give up her seat on the bus to a white passenger, and her meetings with and influence on the rise to fame of Dr. Martin Luther King, Jr. and the Reverend Ralph Abernathy. Highlights her achievements, but gives few personal details. Good for units on notable African Americans and civil rights.

Shaquille O'Neal. Ken Rappoport. New York: Walker and Company, 1994. 128 pp. ISBN 0–8027–8294–9. LC 93–38561. Junior high.

Well-documented biography of basketball star Shaquille O'Neal. Full of details of Shaq's life and career, examining the forces that work on a young athlete of promise. Twenty pages of glossy black-and-white photos. Six pages of source material. Of interest to basketball fans.

Spike Lee: Filmmaker. Bob Bernotas. Springfield, NJ: Enslow Publishers, Inc., 1993. People to Know Series. 112 pp. ISBN 0–89490–416–7. LC 92–41234. Junior high and high school.

Spike Lee's life, dedication, drive, and determination to present black issues are detailed in this book. His films are presented and examined in chronological order.

Black-and-white photos. Worthwhile addition to any collection. Good for units on notable African Americans; film students.

Toni Morrison: Author. Douglas Century. New York: Chelsea House Publishers, 1994. Black Americans of Achievement Series. 103 pp. ISBN 0–7910–1877–6. LC 93–31166. Junior high and high school.

Details the life and career of Toni Morrison. Discusses each of her novels, explaining their literary expression and themes. Contains captioned photographs and chronology. No source quotes. Illustrations. Of interest to fans. Good for African American studies, women's studies and units on African American authors.

We Shall Overcome: Heroes of the Civil Rights Movement. Fred Powledge. New York: Charles Scribners Sons Books for Young Readers, 1993. 224 pp. ISBN 0–684–19362–0. LC 92–25184. Junior high and up.

Brief history of slavery, followed by the stories of ten individuals—both black and white, most well known to the public, who were key figures in the Civil Rights movement. Each person is presented in a separate chapter. Research material, black-and-white photographs, extensive chronology and index included. Good starting place for reports.

We Were Always Free: The Story of The Maddens, a Free Negro Family of Virginia. Anne Miller and T. O. Madden, Jr. New York: W. W. Norton and Company, Inc., 1992. 256 pp. ISBN 0–393–03347–3. LC 91–30200. Junior high and up.

Genealogy of the Madden family, one of whom traveled from Ireland to Virginia as an indentured servant. She gives birth to Sarah Madden, whose father is a slave to James Madison, Sr. According to Virginia law, children take on the status of the mother, so Sarah and all of her children had to serve as indentured servants for 31 years. The family stayed together in spite of all odds and miserable treatment of blacks at the time. Good for African American studies.

Folklore, Literature, Poetry

Celebration: Visions and Voices of the African Diaspora. Roger and Patra Sevastiodes, eds. New York: Rosen Publishing Group, Inc., 1994. Icarus World Issues Series. 167 pp. ISBN 0–8239–1808–4. (Paper: ISBN 0–8239–1809–2). LC 93–4713. Junior high and up.

Features ten selections by different authors. Nine are nonfiction; one is fiction. Nowhere does the book explain what the Diaspora is. Selections feature African religions, art, excerpts from a diary, black-and-white photos, and a glossary. Possibly useful as supplementary material.

Children of Promise: African-American Literature and Art for Young People. Charles Sullivan and Mary S. Campbell, eds. Bergenfield, NY: Harry N. Abrams, Inc., 1991. 128 pp. ISBN 0–8109–3170–2. Junior high and up; professional use.

Art and literature conveys the feelings, images, and lives of African Americans over the last 200 years. Useful for studies on African American art and literature. Foreword by Mary S. Campbell. Illustrations. Good selection tool for junior high and high school libraries.

Children of Yayoute: Folktales of Haiti. Francois Turenne Des Pres. New York: Universe Publishing, Inc. and California Afro-American Museum Foundation, 1994. 96 pp. ISBN 0–87663–791–8. LC 93–50605. Junior high.

Published by the Turenne Des Pres family with collaboration by the California African American Museum. Traditional Haitian tales told to the author by his grandmother, nursemaid, and others. Useful to round out folklore collections.

Christmas Gif': An Anthology of Christmas Poems, Songs, and Stories Written By and About African-Americans. Charlemae Hill Rollins, ed. New York: Morrow Junior Books, 1993. 128 pp. ISBN 0–688–11667–1. LC 92–018976. All ages.

This nostalgic holiday collection contains poetry, prose, and recipes by illustrious African American authors such as Langston Hughes, Zora Neale Hurston, Booker T. Washington, Frederick Douglass, Lawrence Dunbar, and many others. The original contents are unchanged except for a new introduction by Augusta Baker and block-print style black-and-white illustrations replacing the original line drawings. A worthy addition for any collection.

Daughters of Africa: An International Anthology of Words and Writing by Women of African Descent from the Ancient Egyptian to the Present. Margaret Busby, ed. San Francisco: Thorsons, 1992. 1152 pp. ISBN 0–679–41634–X. LC 92–54116. Young adults; professional use.

Busby has collected over 200 writings from women spanning over four centuries. The anthology features well-known writers and many obscure ones. The arrangement is chronological by the author's birth date. Wide variety of genres, styles, and countries of origin. Contains an extensive scholarly bibliography. Of interest to librarians; instructors; and students of women's studies and women authors, particularly students of African American women's studies and authors.

Grandmothers: Poems, Reminiscences, and Short Stories by the Keepers of Our Traditions. Nikki Giovanni, ed. New York: Henry Holt and Company, 1994. 168 pp. ISBN 0–8050–2766–1. LC 94–6144. Junior high and high school.

An anthology of poems, stories, and memories on the theme of grandmothers. All but one are written by women. Includes works by blacks, southerners, and Asians. Sentimental, but not maudlin. Answers questions about the lives, memories, and experiences of grandmothers and those who know them. For reading pleasure or possible use in social studies or sociology.

Heinemann Book of African Women's Poetry. Stella Chipasula and Frand Chipasula, eds. Oxford, England: Heinemann, 1995. 256 pp. ISBN 0–435–90680–1. LC 95–44227 High school and up.

The editors, both African American poets, have collected an anthology of poetry dating from the time of Hatshepsut, the first woman pharaoh of Egypt, to the present. The poems express the women's feelings about repression, sexism, racism, tyranny, and everyday life. Useful for students of African American women's studies or writings, or just for pleasure.

I Hear a Symphony: African Americans Celebrate Love. Compiled by Paula L. Woods. Felix H. Liddell, ed. New York: Doubleday & Co., Inc. Anchor Books, 1994. 352 pp. ISBN 0–385–47502–0. LC 94–006742. Junior high and up.

Anthology of poetry, fiction, essays, love letters, and color illustrations in which African American artists express their impressions of love and loving. For pleasure reading and to demonstrate that humans of every race share common feelings and expressions of love.

Lift Every Voice and Sing. James Weldon Johnson. New York: Walker and Company, 1993. 36 pp. ISBN 0–8027–8250–7. LC 92–27333. All ages. LCCN 92–032283.

Known as the African American National Anthem, the song was written for an Abraham Lincoln birthday celebration in 1900. The book places a couple of lines of the song on each double-page spread, borders it with turquoise and black geometric designs, and faces it with a black-and-white print of a well-known African American, such as Harriet Tubman, or an anonymous African American. Sheet music is given at the end. Attractive. Illustrated by Elizabeth Catlett. Good for pleasure reading and units on African American studies.

Many Thousand Gone: African Americans from Slavery to Freedom. Virginia Hamilton. New York: Alfred A. Knopf Books for Young Readers, 1992. 160 pp. ISBN 0–394–82873–9. LC 89–19988. Junior high.

The story of slavery in America to the end of the Civil War. Many slaves escaped to freedom, some by their own wits, some by underground railroad. Hamilton presents a collection of stories of nearly three dozen slaves. The stories are fresh, lively, and readable—far superior to many collective biographies available for young people. Some of the stories covered include that of a prince captured and sold into slavery, a slave who had himself nailed into a box and mailed north, and a mother whose story of her escape over the ice with her baby was fictionalized by Harriet Beecher Stowe in *Uncle Tom's Cabin*. An enthralling read and recommended for reluctant readers. Good companion piece to *The People Could Fly* by the same author. Illustrated by Leo Dillon and Diane Dillon.

Swing Low: Black Men Writing. Compiled and edited by Rebecca Carroll. New York: Crown Publishing Group, 1995. 266 pp. ISBN 0–517–59981–3. (Paper: ISBN 0–517–88324–4.) LC 94–33373. Young adults.

Sixteen living black men contributed to this collection of drama, poetry, prose, autobiography, and nonfiction on the theme of the common experiences of black men. An introductory essay and black-and-white photograph accompanies each selection. For more mature students. Good for African American studies.

Fiction for Young Adults

AK. Peter Dickinson. New York: Dell Publishing Company, 1994. 240 pp. ISBN 0–440–21897–7. Junior high.

An African boy, orphaned by war in his country, has learned to trust no one but himself. Eventually he learns to trust a commando leader who trains him as a warrior. With the war coming again, he sets out to find his AK47 rifle, which he buried with the coming of peace.

The African Mask. Janet E. Rupert. Boston: Houghton Mifflin Company, 1994. 125 pp. ISBN 0–395–67295–3. LC 93–7726. Junior high.

Set in Yoruba 900 years ago, *The African Mask* is the story of Layo, a 12-year-old girl, who is one of a family of potters. She has exceptional talent and longs to take her place as a respected craftswoman instead of merely an apprentice. Rupert is faithful to the times, the social customs, the treatment of women, and the family structure, and tells a compelling coming-of-age tale.

Ajeemah and His Son. James Berry. New York: HarperCollins, 1992. Willa Perlman Books. 96 pp. ISBN 0–06–021043–5. LC 92–006615. Junior high and up.

Ajeemah and his 18-year-old son Atu are captured on their way to Aru's wedding and sold into slavery in Jamaica. When they finally realize that they will never again be free, Atu kills himself. Ajeemah copes by marrying and raising a new family. He survives until slavery is outlawed in Jamaica many years later.

And Do Remember Me. Marita Golden. New York: Doubleday and Company, 1994. 208 pp. ISBN 0–345–38271–4. LC 91–43566. Junior high and up.

Jessie, a young black woman, runs away from home to escape her sexually abusive father and finds herself participating in "Freedom Summer." She is intelligent, but is kept from reaching her full potential because she is black. The author clearly shows the oppression of women and blacks who are treated as property. For more mature readers. Explicit sexual content.

The Autobiography of Miss Jane Pittman. Ernest J. Gaines. New York: Bantam Books, Inc., 1982. 256 pp. ISBN 0–553–26357–9. Junior high and up.

Jane Pittman was born a slave in Louisiana before the Civil War. She lives to witness the struggle for equality and civil rights during the 1960s. Her life story reflects the fortitude, courage, and determination of American blacks. Also written into a stage play and a screenplay.

Beyond the Horizon. Amma Darko. Oxford, England: Heinemann, 1995. African Writers Series. 139 pp. ISBN 0–435–90990–8. LC 95–24228. High school and up.

Darko tells her fact-based story of South African women forced into prostitution in Europe through the eyes of Mara, a beautiful young woman from Ghana. Mara leaves her rural village to be sold as a wife. Her husband eventually immigrates to Germany and sends for Mara. She is then forced into prostitution, but eventually comes to terms with her fate and her place. For older YAs.

Brothers and Sisters: A Real Love Knows No Boundaries. John Ballard. Mill Valley, CA: World Citizens, 1993. MacBurnie King Soul to Soul Adventure Series. 273 pp. ISBN 0–932279–11–2. LC 93–12119. Junior high and up.

Second in the series. A group of young African Americans are touring Africa when one member of their group disappears. They travel from country to country, becoming involved in the political scene wherever they go. Written in diary format. Variety of print styles. Black-and-white illustrations, maps of the countries, and encyclopedic information are included throughout. Two books in one. Introduction by Nelson Mandella.

The Captive. Joyce Hansen. New York: Scholastic, Inc., 1994. 128 pp. ISBN 0–590–41625–1. LC 93–083134. Junior high and up.

Based on the true story of Kofi Kwame, a slave born in Africa in the early nineteenth century who traveled to this country on a slave ship, then eventually back to his village in Africa. Illustrated.

Cezanne Pinto. Mary Stolz. New York: Knopf, 1994. 256 pp. ISBN 0–679–84917–3. LC 92–046765. Junior high and up.

Taken from his mother in early childhood, Cezanne Pinto, 12-year-old slave, runs away just before the Civil War in an attempt to find his mother. Told from the point of view of Cezanne Pinto at age 90.

Christmas in the Big House, Christmas in the Quarters. Patricia C. McKissack and Frederick L. McKissack. New York: Scholastic, Inc., 1994. 68 pp. ISBN 0–590–43027–0. LC 92–33831. Grade 2 and up.

The McKissacks tell a moving story of preparations for the Christmas of 1859 as seen from the point of view of the white residents of the plantation house as well as from the point of view of the black slaves in the quarters. Poems, songs, and recipes of the times are included. Contrasts between the two celebrations are starkly shown by the daughter of the plantation owner requesting her "own personal slave" for Christmas while a young slave promises his mother a "store-bought" present. Winner of the 1995 Coretta Scott King Award. Strongly recommended for school and public libraries. Illustrated by John Thompson.

The Color Purple. Alice Walker. Orlando, FL: Harcourt, Brace, and Co., 1992. 290 pp. ISBN 0–15–119154–9. LC 81–048242. Junior high and up.

Cele is oppressed by her husband and trusts no one but her sister and her god. Her feelings and experiences are entrusted to her sister in a series of letters. Another woman brings a healing love into her life. Also a movie starring Whoopie Goldberg. Tenth Anniversary Edition.

Colour Me Blue. Gaele Sobott-Mogwe. Portsmouth, NH: Heinemann, 1995. African Writers Series. 119 pp. ISBN 0–435–90971–1. LC 95–24232. High school and up.

This collection of short stories was collected by an Australian-born English professor who is now a citizen of Botswana. He uses his series of stories to dispel old stereotypes and reverse the idea of female passivity. Some heavy–handedness with messages about gender, race, class, and one's "place."

Come a Stranger. Cynthia Voigt. New York: Fawcett Book Group (Juniper), 1991. 240 pp. ISBN 0–449–70246–4. LC 86–3610. Junior high and up.

Eleven-year-old Mina Smiths, a talented, intelligent, and popular black girl, wants to be a ballet star, but a growth spurt at puberty renders her so awkward that she is dismissed. From remarks made at her dismissal, she realizes that her scholarship may have been granted to her so the federal government would continue to fund the school's artistic programs. Mina learns to deal with her anger and reach out through her own hurt to help the local minister on whom she has an unrequited crush.

The Contender. Robert Lipsyte. New York: HarperCollins Children's Books, 1987. 176 pp. ISBN 0–06–447039–3. LC 67–019623. Junior high.

A club where boxing champions work out becomes a haven for Alfred Brooks, a 17-year-old high school dropout, when he flees from several street gangs bent on doing him harm.

The Creation. James Weldon Johnson. New York: Holiday House, 1994. 32 pp. ISBN 0–8234–1069–2. LC 93–003207. All ages.

Illustrator James E. Ransome won the Coretta Scott King Award for his outstanding artwork for Johnson's well-known poem, "The Creation." Strongly recommended for school and public libraries.

Creole Folk Tales. Patrick Chamoiseau. New York: New Press, 1995. 113 pp. ISBN 1–56584–185–9. LC 94–21475. High school and up.

Chamoiseau calls himself a "wordmaker," but "picturemaker" might be more accurate. In his book of Creole folktales from Martinique, the author manages to conjure up word pictures of his culture. His stories contain the well-known Brer

Rabbit, wise children, and all the elements that make folktales enduring. Translated by Linda Coverdate from French to English.

Crossing Over Jordan. Linda Beatrice Brown. New York: Ballantine, 1995. 320 pp. ISBN 0–345–40231–6. LC 94–94558. Junior high and up.

"Crossing over Jordan" is a metaphor describing the difficulties in the lives of four black women from the immediate postbellum years to the twenty-first century. Hermine's mother, Story Temple McCloud, has raised her to believe that she is an orphan and that Story is her aunt. She must find her own way to understand and forgive her mother, then forge her own future as a strong black woman. A challenging read.

Daddy Was a Number Runner. Louise Meriwether. New York: Feminist Press at the City University of New York, 1986. 240 pp. ISBN 0–935312–57–9. LC 86–009019. Junior high and up.

Francie's father is a number runner in Harlem in the 1930s. Francie has to cope with adolescence, poverty, and finding her own identity as a young black woman.

The Ear, the Eye, and the Arm. Nancy Farmer. New York: Orchard Books, 1994. 320 pp. ISBN 0–531–06829–3. LC 93–11814. Junior high and up.

A combination of science fiction and fantasy, this tale is set in Zimbabwe in 2194. Society is terribly regulated. Tendai and his younger sister, Rita, set off on a cross-city trek to earn a Scouting merit badge. This results in their being kidnapped and used as pawns against their father, who is Chief of Security.

Edgar Allen. John Neufeld. New York: S. G. Phillips, Inc., 1968. 95 pp. ISBN 0–87599–149–1. Paper: ISBN 0–451–15870–9. LC 68–031175. High school and up.

A white minister and his wife agree to adopt a three-year-old black boy. Their family and the community are appalled by their actions, and when the couple enrolls Edgar Allen in nursery school, long-smoldering prejudices erupt. Their oldest daughter threatens to run away from home; a cross is burned on their lawn. Even their decision to return the child to the agency precipitates a crisis, and their own children learn that even their parents have flaws. Illustrated by Loren Dunlap.

Fragments of the Ark. Louise Meriwether. Edited by Jane Rosenman. New York: Washington Square Press, 1995. 352 pp. ISBN 0–671–79948–7. LC 93–29504. Junior high and up.

A Civil War story told from the point of view of Peter Mango, a slave who has been trained as a navigator. Based on the true story of former slave Robert Small, Mango steals a steamboat and takes it north to work for the union. After the war, he returns to the south as the owner of his former master's plantation.

The Friendship. Mildred D. Taylor. Illustrated by Max Ginsberg. New York: Dial Books for Young Readers, 1987. 56 pp. ISBN 0–8037–0418–6. LC 86–29309. Junior high.

Four black children are sent on an errand to the store in Mississippi in the 1930s. They are taunted because of their race and threatened by local whites. Tom Bee, an old black man, addresses the store's proprietor by his first name without using the title, "Mister," a liberty unheard of at the time. In spite of the fact that Tom Bee saved his life at one time, the man insists on being addressed properly. Tom Bee refuses and is beaten severely. The title is ironic.

The Glory Field. Walter Dean Myers. New York: Scholastic, Inc., 1994. 333 pp. ISBN 0–590–45897–3. LC 93–43520. Junior high and up.

Reminiscent of *Roots*. An African American's family is traced through time from Muhammad Bilal, who was brought from Africa on a slave ship, to Malcom Lewis, a contemporary Harlem youth who is offered a scholarship as a "token black" to participate in sports for an all-white college.

The Good Negress. A. J. Verdelle. Chapel Hill, NC: Algonquin Books of Chapel Hill, 1995. 312 pp. ISBN 1–56512–085–X. LC 94–40889. Junior high and up.

Denise has been living in rural Virginia with her grandmother. Her mother, living in Detroit, has another baby and needs Denise's help, so Denise moves north. She is dismayed to find that her father and brothers leave all the housework to her and deride her efforts to get a good education, learn to speak standard English, and pull herself up by her bootstraps. She wants to educate herself, to be more than the "good negress" some people expect her to become—that is, never to "look above her station in life." Her mother expects her to quit school and take care of the baby, but one of Denise's teachers encourages her to "jump to the moon," and she continues to study at home.

Having It All. B. B.Calhoun. New York: Random House, 1994. Ford Super Models of the Year Series. 176 pp. ISBN 0–679–86368–0. LC 94–66353. Junior high and up.

Taira is an overachiever. She is bright, talented, and accustomed to getting what she wants whenever she puts her mind to it. Adding modeling to her already overly full schedule may just be too much.

Hold Fast to Dreams. Andrea Davis Pinkney. New York: Morrow Junior Books, 1995. 112 pp. ISBN 0–688–12832–7. LC 94–32909. Junior high.

Dee Willis, a strong, confident, intelligent girl, is the only black student at the suburban middle school she attends when her family moves following her father's promotion. She doesn't know how to act or how to be accepted by her white peers. She quickly finds out that "acting white" isn't the answer. She seeks guidance from successful black authors, whose advice is to show people that you won't tolerate disrespect and to "stand proud and show everyone what you've got." Influencing Dee is the fact that her father is facing the same problems at his new job. The book does a good job of showing that an outsider is a person, too.

How Many Spots Does a Leopard Have and Other Tales. Julius Lester. New York: Scholastic, 1989. 72 pp. ISBN 0–590–41973–0. All ages.

This is a beautifully illustrated collection by David A. Shannon of 12 folktales: ten African and two Jewish. This book could be used as an excellent read-aloud source.

I Am the Darker Brother: An Anthology of Modern Poems by Negro Americans. Arnold Adoff, ed. New York: Simon & Schuster Children's, 1970. 128 pp. ISBN 0–02–041120–0. LC 68–12077. Junior high and up.

These 64 poems by 29 African American poets have been thematically arranged by sections titled: "Like I Am," "Genealogy," "Shall Be Remembered," "If We Must Die," "I Am the Darker Brother," and "The Hope of Your Unborn." Poems by well-known writers, and some whose names are less familiar, explore how African Americans feel about themselves and about their roles in a wide range of emotions, making this anthology valuable for classroom use. Explanatory notes about the background of several poems are given; brief biographies of the poets are included; and indexes to authors and first lines are appended. Illustrated. Also in Trade Paper (Collier Books for Young Adults)

I Been in Sorrow's Kitchen and Licked Out All the Pots: A Novel. Susan Straight. New York: Doubleday, 1993. 368 pp. ISBN 0–385–47012–6. LC 92–45887. Young adults.

Marietta Cook, a young black girl, leaves her home in Pine Gardens, SC, when her mother dies and moves to Charleston to live with her uncle. During the course of the story, Marietta returns to Pine Gardens to bear her twin sons, then returns to

Charleston to earn a living for her family. The story spans her life from age 14 in Pine Gardens to her settling down as a homeowner and, possibly, bride-to-be. Strong female protagonist.

I Hadn't Meant to Tell You This. Jacqueline Woodson. New York: Delacorte Press, 1994. 128 pp. ISBN 0–385–32031–0. LC 93–8733. Junior high and up.

Marie, an eighth grader at a predominantly African American school, befriends Lena, a white girl. During the course of their friendship, Lena reveals that her father is molesting her. Marie is unable to cope with such news, blames Lena, and the friendship nearly falls apart. But the girls' friendship and common problems bring them back together.

If Beale Street Could Talk. James Baldwin. New York: Dell Publishing Company, Inc., 1986. 224 pp. ISBN 0–440–34060–8. Junior high and up.

Tish and Fonny are in love. When Tish finds herself carrying Fonny's child, they decide to marry. Before they can do so, Fonny is accused of raping a Puerto Rican woman and is sent to prison. Tish and her family work tirelessly to find the evidence they need to free him. The story is told through Tish's point of view.

Is Your Heart Happy? Is Your Body Strong? Stella Fabian. Costa Mesa, CA: Brighton and Lloyd, 1992. 165 pp. ISBN 0–685–52888–X. LC 92–70361. Junior high.

Ahmed, a 14-year-old boy in North Africa, anxiously awaits the day that his father asks him to be his fishing partner—one of the rites of passage into manhood. Before this can happen, his father is drowned. His father and uncle had made a pact that if either of them were to die, the other would take care of the deceased one's children and make them partners. Instead, his uncle tries to rob Ahmed of his inheritance. The villagers find out and banish the uncle. Ahmed's grandfather encourages him to forgive his uncle and agree to be his partner.

The Jasmine Candle. Christina A. Botchway. New York: Chelsea House Publishers, 1994. 132 pp. ISBN 0–7910–2932–8. LC N/A. High school and up.

Zenobia is a young woman from Kenya whose parents are members of warring tribes. When the secret is revealed, Zenobia is condemned to death. The young man assigned to kill her falls in love with her and rescues her instead.

Kehinde. Buchi Emecheta. Oxford, UK: Heineman, 1994. African Writers Series. 192 pp. ISBN 0–435–90985–1. LC N/A. Junior high and up.

Kehinde and Albert have lived in England for many years. Albert decides to move the family back to Nigeria and pressures Kehinde to abort the baby she is carrying. He then leaves her to do so and to sell the house. He returns to Nigeria, marries again, and has another family by the time Kehinde gets there. His family pressures her to accept the role of subservient wife and accept his will. She comes to her own conclusions and decision.

Kindred. Octavia E. Butler. Boston: Beacon Press, 1988. Black Women Writers Series 288 pp. ISBN 0–8070–8305–4. LC 87–047897. High school and up.

Dana, a young African American woman married to a white man, finds herself whisked back into the past and into slavery on a plantation in Maryland in the early 1800s. She has been "called" back to this time by a threat to the life of young Rufus Weylin, her great-great-grandfather. Young Rufus is the plantation owner's son and is accident-prone. Can Dana keep him alive and out of danger until he gets old enough to father her great-grandmother? Introduction by Robert Crossley.

Like Sisters on the Homefront. Rita Williams-Garcia. New York: Dutton Children's Books (Lodestar Books), 1995. 176 pp. ISBN 0–525–67465–9. LC 95–3690. Junior high and up.

Fourteen-year-old Gayle is black and pregnant for the second time. Against her will she is sent south to stay with relatives she has never met and to do some growing up. Streetwise, angry, and resentful, she is not a pleasant addition to the family. Gradually, she comes to know and respect her great-grandmother, learn something about her family and herself, and gain an understanding of family love and the power of friendship.

Living, Loving, and Lying Awake at Night. Sindiwe Magona. Brooklyn: Interlink Publishing Group, Inc., 1994. Emerging Voices New International Fiction Series 208 pp. ISBN 1–56656–147–7. Junior high and up.

An anthology of stories of the lives of women in South Africa. Some are mundane, some are tragic; all reflect the lives of women today.

The Longest Memory. Fred D'Aguilar. New York: Pantheon Books, 1995. 144 pp. ISBN 0–679–43962–5. LC 94–028276. Junior high and up.

The story of a slave in antebellum Virginia who escapes, then dies during the course of his punishment, is told through the eyes of the master who beats him to death, his foster father on the plantation, the cook in the big house, the master's daughter, and the slave's mother.

Losing Isaiah. Seth J. Margolis. New York: Jove Publications, Inc., 1994. 400 pp. ISBN 0–515–11539–8. LC 92–38301. Junior high and up.

What is best for Isaiah? His black mother gave him up for adoption to a white couple for $25,000. Isaiah's adoptive mother has raised him to childhood, seen him through a difficult infancy, and loves him with all her heart. His biological mother kicked her drug habit, joined a literacy program and turned her life around. Now she wants her son back. A made-for-TV movie.

Mississippi Chariot. Hariette Gillen Robinet. New York: Simon and Schuster, 1994. 128 pp. ISBN 0–689–31960–6. LC 94–11092. Grades 4 and up.

Twelve-year-old Shortnin Bread Jackson's father has been wrongfully convicted of a crime and sent to work on a chain gang. Shortnin Bread does his best to help him escape. In doing so, Shortnin Bread saves the life of a white boy whose family helps him and his father escape.

The Mouse Rap. Walter Dean Myers. New York: HarperCollins, 1992. 192 pp. ISBN 0–06–440356–4. LC 89–35419. Junior high.

Gangster Tiger Moran is rumored to have hidden treasure in an abandoned building in 1930. True or not, Harlem teenager Mouse and his buddies spend their summer searching for the missing treasure as well as for themselves. Contribution and edited by Andy Badra.

The Moves Make the Man. Bruce Brooks. New York: HarperCollins, 1996. 256 pp. ISBN 0–06–440564–8. LC 83–049476. Junior high and up.

Jerome, a young black basketball player, and Bix, a young white baseball player, become friends. Jerome teaches Bix his skills as a basketball player. As their friendship grows, the game becomes a reflection of their lives.

Nightjohn. Gary Paulsen. New York: Dell Publishing Company, 1995. 96 pp. ISBN 0–440–21936–1. LC 92–1222. Junior high and up.

Sarney is only 12 and has not yet begun menstruating, so she is allowed by her master to stay a child and is not sent to be bred. She encounters Nightjohn, a new slave, who is naked and shackled in a hut. Nightjohn teaches Sarney to read. When she is discovered writing words in the dirt, she is beaten and two of Nightjohn's toes are cut off with a hammer and chisel. The two continue their lessons in spite of threat of punishment. A strong commentary on the evils of slavery.

Ninety-Two Queen's Road. Dianne Case. New York: Farrar, Straus & Giroux, 1995. 164 pp. ISBN 0–374–35518–5. LC 94–009483. Junior high.

Partly autobiographical, *Queen's Road* tells the story of a family of mixed blood in South Africa. Kathy learns about apartheid, bigotry, and racism as she hears a white man forbid his children to associate with her. Her uncle and cousin, passing as white, pretend not to recognize her when they see her in public. There is no political emphasis, just the heartfelt story of a family facing bigotry on a daily basis.

No Surrender. James Watson. London, England: Collins Educational, 1994. 160 pp. ISBN 0–003–30082–X. LC 94–13517. High school and up.

Malenga Natale, daughter of an Angolan resistance leader, returns to her country from England to work as a medic. She is kidnapped by a South African army unit and imprisoned with Hamish, a nonathletic intellectual. They attempt to escape, and Hamish is killed. Clearly shows the inhumanity of the South African soldiers and the close relationship between them, the CIA, and the Angolan rebels.

One Dark Body: A Novel. Charlotte Watson Sherman. New York: HarperCollins, 1994. 224 pp. ISBN 0–06–092466–7. LC 92–53342. Junior high and up.

Raisin's mother, Nola, who turned her over to a foster mother at birth, comes to claim her and take her away. She then meets Sin-Sin, a 14-year-old boy, and Blue, a shaman who helps Raisin and Sin-Sin to grow up, accept themselves, and reach their full potential. Rich language and characterizations. Good addition to any library.

Othello: A Novel. Adapted by Julius Lester. New York: Scholastic, 1995. 160 pp. ISBN 0–590–41967–6. LC 94–12833. Junior high and up.

Novelization of Shakespeare's *Othello*. Lester states that his book is not a substitute for the original, but merely a "re-imaging" of the story. Lester changes the races of some of the characters. Notably, Iago and Emilia are now black Africans who have come to England together. Lester sees his novelization as a bridge to the play. Useful for introducing the original.

Plain City. Virginia Hamilton. New York: Scholastic, 1995. 208 pp. ISBN 0–590–47365–4. LC 93–019910. Junior high.

Bulaire Sims is having a hard time making the transition from child to young woman. Like most girls her age, she is concerned with her looks, her changing body, and her family—with one major difference. She discovers that her family has lied to her about her father's having been killed in Vietnam. She finds him living under a bridge, the victim of mental illness and prejudice because of his racially mixed heritage. Bulaire experiences similar problems and is able to overcome them.

The President's Daughter. Barbara Chase-Riboud. New York: Ballantine Books, 1995. 480 pp. ISBN 0–345–38970–0. LC 93–042499. Junior high and up.

Fictionalized story of the life of Harriet Hemings, who is supposedly the illegitimate daughter of Thomas Jefferson and quadroon Sally Hemings, who travels to Philadelphia and passes for white.

Promises to Keep. James Lincoln Collier and Christopher Collier. New York: Delacorte Press, 1994. 233 pp. ISBN 0–385–32028–0. LC 93–37655. Junior high.

Even though Johnny has promised his father that he will stay home and run the family farm, the lure of battle is too great and he joins a wagon train carrying food to the Confederate army. He is captured by Cush, a black Union soldier, who insists that Johnny teach him to read, then saves him from imprisonment when they reach the Union camp. The friendship develops believably; the battle scenes are well done. WARNING: The word "nigger" is used, but is discussed in a two-page foreword. Should be popular with young readers.

Rite of Passage. Richard Wright. New York: HarperCollins, 1994. 128 pp. ISBN 0–06–023419–9. LC 93–2473. Junior high and up.

By the author of *Native Son*. Johnny Gibbs discovers he is a foster child. The discovery drives him to find his "family" in the streets of Harlem—in a street gang.

Rites of Passage: Stories About Growing Up by Black Writers From Around the World. Tonya Bolden, ed. New York: Hyperion, 1994. 240 pp. ISBN 1–56282–688–3. LC 93–31304. Junior high.

Seventeen coming-of-age stories by black authors from the United States, Africa, Australia, the Caribbean, and Central America. Each story is told in the expressive language of its country of origin, but reflects universal themes such as love, heart-break, betrayal, and friendship. The book includes brief biographical information on each author. Edited by Tonya Bolden. Foreword by Charles Johnson.

Scorpions. Walter Dean Myers. New York: HarperCollins, 1990. 224 pp. ISBN 0–06–447066–0. LC 85–045815. Junior high and up.

Jamal is having a very hard time getting along. The principal is always on his case, and the leader of the Scorpions, a local gang, wants Jamal to take his place until he gets out of jail. Then someone produces a gun. Jamal is afraid, but attracted to the idea of having a gun. The inevitable tragedy ensues. Illustrations by Vince Natale.

The Shark Callers. Eric Campbell. New York: Harcourt, Brace & Company, 1994. 232 pp. ISBN 0–15–200007–0. (Paper: ISBN 0–15–200010–0.) LC 93–044881. Junior high and high school.

A tsunami resulting from a violent volcanic eruption destroys the island village of Rabaul. Andy Thompson and his parents have been travelling aboard their boat, the "Quintana," and Kaleku and his family have been preparing for his initiation as a shark caller. The tsunami results in both boys heading out to sea, pursued by a pack of sharks. The two boys' stories are told in alternating chapters.

Skin Deep and Other Teenage Reflections. Angela Shelf Medearis. New York: Simon & Schuster Children's, 1995. 48 pp. ISBN 0–02–765980–1. LC 94–19928. Junior high and high school.

Angela Shelf Medearis presents forty poems which sensitively, poignantly, and accurately reflect the hopes, dreams, and anxieties of teens in America. She ponders report cards, personal identity, attitude, friendship, divorce, getting good grades, and many other themes which will resonate with teens. Excellent addition to any school or public library. Illustrated by Michael Bryant.

Something Terrible Happened: A Novel. Barbara Ann Porte. New York: Orchard Books/Richard Jackson, 1994. 224 pp. ISBN 0–531–08719–0. LC 94–6923. Junior high and high school.

Twelve-year-old Gillian's West Indian mother contracts AIDS, and Gillian is sent to live with her white father and his family. The story is told in a mixture of family parables, letters from the perspective of a family friend, and some folklore. Moving but not overwhelming.

Somewhere in the Darkness. Walter Dean Myers. New York: Scholastic, 1992. 168 pp. ISBN 0–590–42412–2. LC 91–19295. Junior high.

Jimmy Little's father, accused of a crime and in hiding, is dying. Before he dies, he wants to prove his innocence. He returns to take Jimmy on a cross-country journey in hopes of finding evidence to prove his innocence.

The Song of Be. Lesley Beake. New York: Puffin Books, 1995. 81 pp. ISBN 0–14–037498–1. LC 94–044587. Junior high and up.

Be, a young Namibian bushwoman, has been bitten by a snake and is dying. In this story, told in flashbacks, Be and her mother are taken in by a Boer farmer and his wife. But tragedy strikes and Be feels responsible, so she leaves and attempts to return to the home of her childhood. She finds it empty. The book traces the history of the bushmen and the difficulties in trying to make them into farmers and offers the hope that the bushmen will once again come together in pride and independence.

Sound the Jubilee. Sandra Forrester. New York: Lodestar, 1995. 183 pp. ISBN 0–525–67486–1. LC 94–32664. Junior high and up.

Based on a true story. A group of runaway slaves makes it to the north and establishes a colony on Roanoke Island during the Civil War. The story deals with Maddie's coming of age, but it is not a "happily ever after" story. It deals with the harsh reality of the times and the fact that northerners can be as bigoted as southerners.

Spite Fences. Trudy Krishner. New York: Delacorte Press, 1994. 288 pp. ISBN 0–385–32088–4. LC 94–8665. Junior high and up.

Fourteen-year-old Magnolia Pugh witnesses the brutal beating of her young black friend, Zeke, for violating a segregation policy. She doesn't dare tell her abusive mother that she recognized her sadistic next-door neighbor as one of the gang. Zeke gets Magnolia a job as housekeeper to a well-educated black man who has come to town to organize nonviolent protests against segregation, racism, and bigotry. Through her association with him, Magnolia gains the courage to speak about what she saw and to recognize the importance of facing up to the truth.

Standing Tall, Looking Good. Gloria Miklowitz. New York: Dell Publishing Company, 1992. ISBN 0–440–21263–4. ISBN 0–385–30162–6. LC 89–25865. Junior high.

Three teenagers join the army to "be all you can be." David joins to escape his stepfather. Carver joins to get out of a Pasadena ghetto. Paula joins to pay for her college education. Can they make it through the army's grueling basic training?

Taste of Salt: A Story of Modern Haiti. Frances Temple. New York: HarperCollins, 1994. 192 pp. ISBN 0–06–447136–5. LC 92–6716. Junior high and up.

Based on real people and events. Djo is a street urchin in Haiti. He becomes one of "Aristide's boys," a group of boys taken in by a priest. He is beaten up by the Tonton Macoute and ends up in a hospital. Jeremie is a young girl from a convent school working at the hospital. She gets Djo's story on tape and adds her own. Very expressive of the miserable conditions in Haiti.

Tears of a Tiger. Sharon M. Draper. New York: Simon and Schuster, 1994. 192 pp. ISBN 0–689–31878–2. LC 94–10278. Junior high and high school.

Four young basketball players get drunk while celebrating a team victory. One is killed in a car accident, and the driver, overcome with guilt, commits suicide. The story is told through newspaper articles, homework assignments, journal entries, letters, and conversations. Contemporary idiom is effective and well done. The racism endured by young blacks is revealed through the eyes of Andy, the driver. Also good for units on alcohol abuse, racism, and teen suicide.

Timothy of the Cay: A Prequel-Sequel. Theodore Taylor. New York: Harcourt, Brace & Company, 1993. 192 pp. ISBN 0–15–288358–4. LC 93–7898. Junior high.

Sequel to *The Cay*, by the same author, in which Timothy sacrifices his life to save Philip Enright from a hurricane. In *Timothy of the Cay*, the author traces Timothy's life up to the point where he meets Philip, then on Philip after his rescue and his operation to restore his sight.

Where Do I Go From Here?. Valerie Wilson Wesley. New York: Scholastic, Inc., 1993. 138 pp. ISBN 0–590–45607–5. LC 92–36628. High school and up.

Nia and Marcus, the only two black students at snobbish Endicott Academy, are thrown together by their shared ethnicity and become friends. Then one day Marcus disappears. When Nia overhears a white student making racial remarks, she gets into a fight and gets suspended. At first, she is glad to be home; then she looks around and sees that most of her friends are on destructive paths. When she finds out what has happened to Marcus, she returns to Endicott determined to be all she can be.

Wolf by the Ears. Ann Rinaldi. New York: Scholastic, Inc., 1993. ISBN 0–590–43412–8. LC 90–40563. Junior high and up.

It is a time for decisions. Harriet Hemmings is rumored to be the daughter of Thomas Jefferson by his mistress, Sally Hemmings. Will she choose to pass as a white, or will she remain a slave in her relatively sheltered, but restrictive life at Monticello?

Yoruba Girl Dancing. Simi Bedford. New York: Viking Penguin, 1993. 192 pp. ISBN 0–14–023293–1. LC92–53783. Junior high and up.

Remi is a Yoruba girl from Nigeria. Tradition dictates that the oldest child be reared by the elders, so Remi grows up with her grandparents. She is a member of a rich, cultured family, but when her grandfather dies and Remi is sent to England to school, she faces prejudice and bigotry for the first time. She is the only black student enrolled, and the white students react as though she were a "jungle savage." After struggles and pain, Remi rises to the top of her class, and convinces the other girls that "the black doesn't rub off," and continues to grow into a strong woman.

Your Blues Ain't Like Mine. Bebe Moore Campbell. New York: Ballantine Books, 1995. 331 pp. ISBN 0–345–38395–8. LC 95–8920. Junior high and up.

Emotional story of a 15-year-old black boy who unwittingly crosses the generally accepted and understood line of conduct for blacks in early 1950s Mississippi and is murdered by a poor white. Everyone in the town is affected. Not for younger readers. Contains sexually explicit scenes. Good for readers who enjoyed Mildred Taylor's books and *The Color Purple.*

Reference and Scholarly Works

Biographical Dictionary of Afro-American and African Musicians. Eileen Southern. Westport, CT: Greenwood Publishing Group, 1981. Encyclopedia of Black Music Series. 478 pp. ISBN 0–313–21339–9. High school and up.

A thoroughly researched and comprehensive volume, this work includes over 1,400 musicians of African American or African descent, born between 1640 and 1955, who have made significant contributions to folk, popular, jazz, religious, and classical music. Many of the entries include evaluative comments, bibliographies, and discographies. Good for music students and units on African American studies.

Biographical Encyclopedia of the Negro Baseball Leagues. James A. Riley, ed. New York: Carroll and Graf Publishers, 1994. 1280 pp. ISBN 0–7867–0065–3. LC 94–1380. Junior high and up.

Lengthy narratives on both well- and lesser-known figures in the Negro leagues. Short narratives on the significance of the leagues and their history. Good for baseball fans, units on African American studies. Illustrated. Introduction by Monte Irvin.

Black American Colleges and Universities: Profiles of Two-Year, Four-Year, and Professional Schools. Levirn Hill, ed. Detroit: Gale Research, Inc., 1994. 800 pp. ISBN 0–8103–9166–X. LC 94–3898. High school and up; professional use.

Contains profiles of 118 two-year, four-year, and professional schools whose students are predominantly African American. Schools are arranged by state. Entries are three to seven pages in length and include admission requirements, total enrollment, type of school, cost per year, average GPA for freshmen, student-teacher ratio, degrees available, and financial information. Appendixes include lists of land-grant schools, state-supported schools, two-year schools, professional schools, and Thurgood Marshall Scholarship Fund Member schools. Useful for high school and junior college counselors and social workers. Recommended for high school, junior college, and public libraries.

Black American Reference Book. Mabel M. Smythe, ed. New York: Prentice Hall, 1976. 1,026 pp. ISBN 0–13–077586–X. LC 75–26511. High school and up. Out of print.

This comprehensive volume, one of the best of its kind, is a source of historical material on all aspects of the African American experience in lengthy essays contributed by prominent writers and subject experts. A new edition is in preparation.

Black American Writers Past and Present: A Biographical and Bibliographical Dictionary. Compiled by Theresa R. Rush, Carol Fairbanks Myers, and Esther Spring Arata. Metuchen, NJ: Scarecrow Press, 1975. 2 vols. 865 pp. ISBN 0–8108–0785–8. LC 74–028400. Professional use.

These volumes provide brief biographical information and bibliographies of some 2,000 authors from the eighteenth century to the present who wrote for adults and children. African American anthologies and/or African American literature courses usually contain these authors' works. Valuable to a librarian, instructor, or serious researcher.

Black Americans Information Directory, Third Edition. Darren L. Smith, ed. Detroit, MI: Gale Research, Inc., 1993. 425 pp. ISBN 0–8103–8082–X. Young adults.

This directory is a comprehensive "source of information on organizations, programs, facilities, publications, and other resources for and about black Americans." Areas covered include religious organizations, library collections, awards, honors, prizes, and publications as well as several others. This volume includes a master name and a keyword index. Useful for research on the college level.

Black Children and American Institutions: An Ecological Review and Resource Guide. Valora Washington and Velma La Point. Source Books on Education. New York: Garland Publishing, 1988. 464 pp. ISBN 0–8240–8517–5. LC 88–16490. Professional use.

This book deals with topics such as the status of African American children, developmental issues, African American children in the educational system, family support, public assistance and child welfare services, African American children and youth in the criminal justice system, and physical and mental health. Also included is a resource guide for advocacy of African American children and a listing of community institutions and public action committes. The book concludes with a lengthy reference and annotated bibliographic section. A good book for those seeking an insight into understanding African American children. Of use to librarians, instructors, and serious researchers.

Black Elected Officials: A National Roster, 17th Edition. Washington, DC: Joint Center for Political and Economic Studies Inc., 1991. 570 pp. ISBN 0–941410–79–X. Young adults, professional use.

Compiled in this volume are statistics and information about all of the African American elected officials in the United States. The roster is divided by state and broken down by level of office—state, county, municipal, etc. Of possible use to serious researchers.

The Black Experience in Children's Literature. Barbara Rollock. New York: New York Public Library, 1994. 64 pp. ISBN 0–87104–726–8. LC N/A. Professional use.

Coordinated and supervised by Barbara Rollock, former coordinator of Children's Services in the New York Public Library System. This edition, prepared by The Black Experience in Children's Books Committee, provides access to a wide variety of quality children's books, both fiction and nonfiction. Emphasis is on the African American experience in the United States, although works by authors and illustrators of all ethnic and racial groups are included. An additional feature is a special index indicating which contributors are black. Of use to school and public librarians wishing to build an African American collection.

Black Genesis: An Annotated Bibliography for Black Genealogical Research. James M. Rose and Alice Eichholz, eds. Genealogical and Local History Series, vol. 1. New York: Gale Research, Inc., 1978. 326 pp. ISBN 0–8103–1400–2. LC 77–74819. Young adults. Out of print.

The editors of this unique work have demonstrated that a wealth of material exists, but that conventional research methodology in tracing ancestry does not apply to

African American genealogy. Sources are identified, described, and located. Useful to those interested in tracing family trees.

The Black Resource Guide. Tenth Edition. Compiled by R. Benjamin Johnson and Jacqueline Johnson. Washington, DC: Black Resource Guide, Inc., 1992. 390 pp. ISBN 0–9608374–8–5. LC 85–91077. High school and up.

This work is divided into two areas: topical lists of businesses and organizations directly involved with or developed by African Americans, and statistical information of interest to or about African Americans. The businesses and organizations cover areas such as adoption, law, media, politics, education, and celebrities. Entries include name, address, and telephone number. Statistical information includes African American population distribution, revenues of businesses, and health and mortality figures. Of use for research for African American studies units.

The Black Student's Guide to College Success. Ruby D. Higgins, et al., eds. Westport, CT: Greenwood Press, 1994. 392 pp. ISBN 0–313–29431–3. LC 94–027944. High school and up; professional use.

This comprehensive guide, written especially for African American students, is a must for public and high school libraries and high school counselors. It includes information on more than 900 colleges and universities as well as essays by well-known African Americans on the importance of education and how they handled various problems and succeeded in college. Included valuable information on how to prepare for college, select the right college, and how to succeed once there. Good resource for high school counselors. Contributions by William J. Ekeler.

Blacks in American Films and Television: An Encyclopedia. New York: Garland Publishing, Inc., 1988. 510 pp. High school. Out of print.

Divided into three main sections—movies, television, and profiles—this volume provides information about film and television productions and about individual performers. Useful for reports and for general interest.

The Color Line and the Quality of Life in America: The Population of the United States in the 1980s. Reynolds Farley and Walter R. Allen. New York: Oxford University Press, Inc., 1989. 520 pp. ISBN 0–19–506029–6. LC 86–10079. Professional use.

Written in report form with the use of graphs and charts. Ambitiously attempts to give meaning to data obtained in the 1980 census. Contains a bibliography. Of possible interest to instructors interested in statistics.

Contemporary Black American Playwrights and Their Plays: A Biographical Directory and Dramatic Index. Bernard L. Peterson, Jr. Westport, CT: Greenwood Press, 1988. 651 pp. ISBN 0–313–25190–8. LC 87–017814. High school and up.

This directory provides a source of information "on more than 700 contemporary Black American and U.S. resident dramatists, screen writers, radio and television script writers, musical theater collaborators, and other originators of theatrical and dramatic works written, produced and/or published between 1950 and the present." The brief entries include information about the artists as well as their works. In addition to the full entries, there are two appendixes which list other African American playwrights. There is a title index as well as a general index in this volume. Useful for those wishing to produce African American drama.

Dictionary of Afro-American Slavery. Randall M. Miller and John David Smith, eds. Westport, CT: Greenwood Publishers Group, 1988. 882 pp. ISBN 0–313–23814–6. LC 87–37543. High school and up.

Arranged alphabetically to cover topics dealing with slavery in individual states and terms and occupations associated in some way with slavery. Each short article is followed by a selected bibliography. Of use to students of the ante- and post-bellum periods and to readers who find unfamiliar terms when reading about slavery.

Dictionary of American Negro Biography. Rayford W. Logan and Michael R. Winston, eds. New York: W.W. Norton and Company, 1983. 680 pp. ISBN 0–393–01513–0. LC 81–9629. High school and up.

This volume includes biographical information about African Americans who are no longer living. The cutoff date for inclusion was set at 1970 by the editors, as the purpose of the book is to evaluate and assess the historical significance of the careers of the individuals selected to be included in this work. Many entries in this volume include suggested readings for further information. Useful for reports and general interest.

Dictionary of Literary Biography Series, Vol. 33: Afro-American Fiction Writers After 1955. Thadious M. Davis and Trudier Harris, eds. New York: Gale Research, Inc., 1984. 368 pp. ISBN 0–8103–1711–7. LC 84–18724. High school and up.

This work includes 49 African American writers. Compiled in essay form, each entry includes a biography of the writer and a brief discussion of the work. At the end of each article, sources for interviews, papers, a bibliography, and references are given. At the conclusion of the volume, there is an introduction to African American Literary Critics as well as a list of books for further reading and a cumulative index. This is an excellent source for high school students seeking information on lesser-known African American writers.

Dictionary of Race and Ethnic Relations, Revised edition. E. Ellis Cashmore, ed. New York: Routledge, 1993. 320 pp. ISBN 0–415–10291–X. LC 93–31203. Junior high and up.

Alphabetically arranged. The dictionary covers historical, political, and social aspects of race and ethnic relations. Also included with each entry are suggested additional readings. Cross references provided. Useful for race relations units.

Directory of Blacks in the Performing Arts. Second Edition. Edward Mapp. Metuchen, NJ: Scarecrow Press, Inc., 1990. 612 pp. ISBN 0–8108–2222–9. LC 89–30477. High school and up.

Biographical and career information for 800 African Americans who have made significant contributions to the performing arts—dance, film, music, radio, television, and theater are included. Of interest to drama, music, and film students. Of possible use in African American studies. Foreword by Earle Hymen.

Encyclopedia of Black America. W. Augusta Low and Virgil A. Clift, eds. New York: De Cappo Press, Inc., 1984. 941 pp. ISBN 0–306–80221–X. LC 80–13247. High school and up.

Despite the uneven quality of its essays and lack of balance, this work is a good ready–reference tool. Its 1,700 entries provide comprehensive coverage of African American history, life, and culture. The majority of entries are brief: the remaining entries are thematic essays on a broad spectrum of topics. Good for research.

Famous First Facts About Negroes. Romeo B. Garrett. North Stratford, NH: Ayer Company Publishers, Inc., 1978. 224 pp. ISBN 0–405–01987–4. LC 75–172613. High school and up.

This book records famous firsts in African American history. The book is arranged in categories alphabetically. An informative and valuable read. Good for book reports.

Famous Firsts of Black Women. Martha Ward Plowden. Gretna, LA: Pelican Publishing Co., Inc., 1993. 112 pp. ISBN 0–88289–973–2. LC 93–13837. Junior high.

As indicated in the title, the author profiles briefly the accomplishments and lives of 20 African American women who were the first to establish themselves in their fields. The author explores each woman's childhood, background, personality, and other factors which led to her accomplishments. A full-page pen-and-ink sketch accompanies each entry. Good starting point for reports. Illustrated by Ronald Jones.

From Afar to Zulu: A Dictionary of African Cultures. Jim Haskins with Joann Biondi. New York: Walker and Company, 1992. 212 pp. ISBN 0–8027–8291–7. LC 94–11545. Junior high and up.

Thirty of Africa's best-known cultures are outlined here. The daily lives, traditions, and religions of pre-Islamic and pre-colonial history as well as modern times are detailed with illustrations, maps, and photographs. Good starting point for research; general interest reading.

In Black and White, fifth edition. Mary Mace Spalding, ed. New York: Gale Research, Inc., 1980. 2 vols. 1,312 pp. ISBN 0–8103–0438–4. High school and up.

These volumes index biographies found in some 450 books (exclusive of individual biographies), 50 magazines, 25 newspapers, and 12 miscellaneous sources. Entries identify the biographee and cite references. An occupational index also includes specific categories, e.g., child prodigies. Good starting point for reports.

Index to Black Poetry. Compiled by Dorothy H. Chapman. New York: G. K. Hall, 1974. 541 pp. ISBN 0–8161–1143–X. LC 74–8835. High school and up, professional use. Out of print.

Poems by African Americans and non-African Americans writing on the African Americans experience, found in 125 collections (1,000 poets and 5,000 poems) are indexed by title, first line, author, and subject. An update is needed since some collections indexed are out of print and numerous others have appeared since the early 1970s. Useful for reports, pleasure reading, and as a selection tool for high school and public libraries.

Index to the Schomburg Clipping File. New York Public Library, Schomburg Center for Research in Black Culture Staff, eds. Alexandria, VA: Chadwyck-Healy, Inc., 1986. 176 pp. ISBN 0–89887–035–6. LC 86–20707. High school and up; professional use.

The Clipping File at the Schomburg Center for Research in Black Culture of the New York Public Library, which holds the largest collection of materials related to African American history in the world, is composed essentially of periodical and newspaper clippings. This enormous body of information has been transferred to microfiche. The index lists nearly 7,000 subject headings with the corresponding microfiche serial number. Useful for research.

Juba to Jive: The Dictionary of African-American Slang. Clarence
Major, ed. New York: Viking Penguin Books, 1994. 432 pp. ISBN 0–670–85264–
3. (Paper: ISBN 0–14–051306–X.) LC 93–11748. High school and up.

Based on *The Dictionary of African-American Slang* by the same author. Each entry
has an explanatory note describing the culture in which it arose and the geographic
area of use. Most sources are documented. The author's claim to exclusivity on
some terms is weak. Many can be traced to other sources. Useful for special
collections on African Americans or slang and unconventional English; public and
academic libraries.

Living Black American Authors: A Biographical Dictionary. Ann Allen
Shockley and Sue P. Chandler. New York: Bowker, 1973. 220 pp. ISBN 0–8352–
0662–9. LC 73–17005. High school and up; professional use. Out of print.

A listing of some 450 African American authors who have written books and have
been published in anthologies, magazines, newspapers, and journals. Also includes
authors of plays, television scripts, and filmstrips. The information includes name
and occupation, place and date of birth, family, professional experience, memberships, awards, publications, and mailing address. Some respondents listed only their
publications. Written in data style, this makes an excellent source for detailed facts
that might otherwise be difficult to find. Good addition for public or school
libraries.

Modern Black Writers. Compiled and edited by Michael Popkin. New York:
Continuum Publishing, Co., 1978. A Library of Literary Criticism. 400 pp. ISBN
0–8044–3258–9. LC 76–15656. Professional use.

Like others patterned after Moulton's Library of Literary Criticism, this work
reprints salient excerpts from criticisms which appeared in a wide variety of sources.
Eighty significant African American authors from both the U.S. and abroad
(novelists, poets, and dramatists) are treated. Useful for librarians, instructors, and
students of African American writers.

Negro Almanac: A Reference Work on the Afro-American, Fifth edition.
Compiled by Harry A. Ploski and James Williams. Bronxville, NY: Bellwether
Publishing Co., 1989. ISBN 0–913144–09–6. LC 86–72654. High school and up.

The current edition of this important ready-reference source manifests considerable
updating. The profusely illustrated text consists of a chronology of African American history since 1600, a section on social and cultural life, numerous biographical
sketches, statistical and historical tables and charts, and much more that is useful
for history, sociology, and African American studies classes; also useful for librarians
and class instructors.

Quotations in Black. Edited and compiled by Anita King. Westport, CT: Greenwood Publishing Group, 1981. 334 pp. ISBN 0–313–22128–6. LC 80– 1794. High school and up.

More than 1,100 quotations (from more than 200 individuals) and more than 400 proverbs reflect the rich heritage of African American contributions to our culture. Emphasis is on quotations of historical figures. The volume is a worthy expansion of quotations appearing in standard works such as *Bartlett's Familiar Quotations*. Useful for African American studies. Illustrated.

Timelines of African-American History: 500 Years of Black Achievement. Jack Mcguire, Richard Newman, and Emory J. Tolbeth, eds. New York: Berkeley Publishing Group, 1994. 368 pp. ISBN 0–399–52127–5. LC 94–12771. High school and up.

Detailed chronology of the African American experience dating from 1492 to 1993, beginning with the first African Americans who came to America as explorers. Events of each year are subdivided into categories such as politics, civil rights, sports, literature, journalism, the visual arts, the military, and more. Contains an index of proper names, but no subject index. Bibliography. Good for American history and African American history units. Recommended for high schools, public libraries, and undergraduate and community college libraries.

Who's Who Among Black Americans, Eighth edition. William C. Matney, ed. Detroit: Gale Research, Inc., 1994. 1793pp. ISBN 0–8103–5461–6. LC N/A. High school and up.

Over 13,000 persons who have attained distinction in many fields—government, law, medicine, civil rights, sports—are covered in data-type entries. This work is the most comprehensive of its type. Good starting point for reports. Useful for units on African American studies.

Nonfiction

The African-American Kitchen: Cooking From Our Heritage. Angela Shelf Medearis. New York: UAL Dutton, 1994. 320 pp. ISBN 0–52593834–6. LC 94–1323. Junior high and up.

More than 250 recipes from Africa, the Caribbean, the United States, and others. Medearis includes African American celebrations with the appropriate foods. Includes index. Good for home economics and multicultural units.

African Americans: Voices of Triumph Series. Alexandria, VA: Time-Life Books. Three-volume set. Includes free teacher's guide for each volume. High school and up. (Volumes listed individually in Books in Print.)

Perseverance. Time-Life Books, 1993. 256 pp. ISBN 0–7835–2250–9. LC 93–19566. Brought to America as slaves, African Americans have persevered, survived, and struggled to attain freedom and equality. This volume chronicles this facet of African American history.

Leadership. Time-Life Books, 1994. 256 pp. ISBN 0–7835–2254–1. LC 93–21147. This volume traces the progress, education, and major contributions of African Americans since the time of slavery.

Creative Fire. Time-Life Books, 1994. 256 pp. ISBN 0–7855–2258–4. LC 93–31616. Evolution of American music as influenced by African Americans. Contributions to the arts include drama, music, literature, and fine arts. Excellent for American history and African American studies units.

African American Voices. Michele Stepto, ed. Brookfield, CT: Millbrook Press, Inc., 1995. Writers of America Series. 160 pp. ISBN 1–56294–474–6. LC 94–10681. Junior high and high school.

The author provides insight into the African American culture in an introduction explaining the literary traditions and dominant themes of the culture. The collection contains work by such noted authors as W. E. B. DuBois, Toni Morrison, Ralph Ellison, and James Baldwin. Source notes and bibliography provided. Valuable addition to libraries and classroom collections. Illustrations.

African Arms and Armor. Christopher Spring. Washington, DC: Smithsonian Institute Press, 1993. 192 pp. ISBN 1–56098–317–5. LC 93–84191. Junior high and up.

Comprehensive work on the history, religious significance, creation, and use of African weapons. Maps of territories and peoples discussed. Full-color pictures as well as black-and-white photographs to accompany the detailed text. Good for African American studies units.

African Journey. John Chiassom. New York: Bradbury Press, 1986. 64 pp. ISBN 0–02–718530–3. OCLC 86–8233. Junior high and up.

The text describes the culture and habitat of the people in six distinctly different regions of Africa: The Sahel, the plains of Benin, the city of Dakar, the Atlantic coast, river ports along the banks of the Niger, and Ethiopia. The text is fascinating, albeit skimpy; the pictures, by John Chiassom, make this book truly unique. The photo essays of the regions and the peoples are a stark, compelling documentation of the continent. Good for multicultural and geography units.

Africans in America. Ayanna Hart and Earl Spangler. Minneapolis: Lerner, 1995. In America Series. ISBN 0–8225–1952–6. ISBN 0–8225–3476–2. LC 94–33873. Junior high.

Hart and Spangler tell the stories of African slavery, the Civil War, and the civil rights struggle as well as outline African American achievements in a number of fields; however, the authors cover nothing in depth. This book might be good for a short report, but other sources are necessary for a more detailed look at African American history.

The Antislavery Movement. James T. Rogers. New York: Facts on File, Inc., 1994. Social Reform Movements Series. 128 pp. ISBN 0–8160–2907–5. LC 93–40960. Junior high and up.

History of slavery from 1619 to after World War II. Details how slaves began as indentured servants, then became slaves as the southern economy came to depend on the free labor. Contains numerous quotes and biographical information; black-and-white photos; chronology; notes; and careful documentation. Good for units on American history and African American history.

Baseball & the Color Line. Tom Gilbert. New York: Franklin Watts, Inc., 1995. The African American Experience Series. 176 pp. ISBN 0–531–11206–3. LC 94–23935. Junior high and up.

Gilbert deals less with the Negro Baseball Leagues than with the men who played baseball in the late ninteenth century, before the "color line" was totally enforced. He emphasizes the efforts of those who fought to integrate the all-white sports field. Numerous photographs and source notes. Appendixes are included. Good for sports fans and units on African American studies.

Before the Mayflower: A History of Black America, Sixth Edition. Lerone Bennett Jr. New York: Penguin Books, 1993. 720 pp. ISBN 0–14–071822–8. LC 82–82391. High school and up. Out of print.

This history begins with a look at "The African Past." In addition to an extensive, comprehensive history, this volume contains several special features: (1) a thorough chronology covering 1619 through 1987 in nearly two hundred pages; (2) a list of African American firsts in many areas including politics, entertainment, and sports;

and (3) a very detailed index. Good for American history and African American studies units. Recommended for high school and public libraries.

Between Two Fires: Black Soldiers in the Civil War. Joyce Hansen. Danbury, CT: Franklin Watts, 1993. The African American Experience Series. 160 pp. ISBN 0–531–11151–2. LC 92–37381. Junior high and up.

During the Civil War, nearly 10 percent of the Union troops were African American. These men fought not only for their country and for their freedom, but against racism, hatred, and bigotry. They were given low pay, inferior equipment, poor food, and were not permitted to attain officer rank. This book is a tribute to the character and spirit of those men in the preintegration armed forces. Useful for social studies, American history, and African American studies units. Illustrated.

The Black Americans: A History in Their Own Words 1619–1983. Milton Meltzer. New York: HarperCollins, 1987. 320 pp. ISBN 0–06–446055–X. LC 83–046160. High school.

This is a revision of the author's three-volume work, *In Their Own Words*. Each of the earlier volumes was designated an ALA Notable Children's Book. This volume is comprised of excerpts from many African Americans covering a time period of more than 350 years. An extensive index allows for ready access to the text. Good for units on African American studies and American history units.

Black Confederates and Afro-Yankees in Civil War Virginia. Ervin L. Jordan, Jr. Charlottesville, VA: University Press of Virginia, 1995. A Nation Divided Series. 403 pp. ISBN 0–8139–1544–9. LC 94–016923. University, professional, educational use.

Virginia had a large free African American population as well as a large slave population before the Civil War. As the war approached, Virginia didn't know which way to turn—toward the confederacy or toward the north. Even the African American population was divided, though all favored freedom. Jordan has written a detailed and meticulously researched work on the Virginia of the Civil War. Contains an index and illustrations. An excellent addition to any collection on the Civil War.

Black Diamond: The Story of the Negro Baseball Leagues. Patricia C. McKissack and Frederick McKissack, Jr. New York: Scholastic, 1994. 192 pp. ISBN 0–590–45809–4. LC 93–22691. Junior high.

Covers the history of baseball and the introduction of blacks into the sport. Text describes the teams of the Negro Baseball League, the players, organizers, and owners and the prejudice they faced. Numerous black-and-white photographs. Good for baseball fans and African American studies.

Black Eagles: African Americans in Aviation. Jim Haskins. New York: Scholastic, 1995. 192 pp. ISBN 0–590–45912–0. LC 94–018623. Junior high.

Many people think that African Americans in aviation began with World War II. Haskins tells the stories of African Americans who flew during the period before World War II. Eugene Bullard flew with the Lafayette Escadrille, and Bessie Coleman was a stunt pilot in the 1920s. Tells the story of black aviation from earliest times to the present. Contains a bibliography and chronology. Useful for American history units and studies of notable African Americans.

Black Journals of the United States. Walter C. Daniel. Westport, CT: Greenwood Publishing Group, Inc., 1982. Historical Guides to the World's Periodicals and Newspapers Series. 432 pp. ISBN 0–313–20704–6. LC 81–13440. High school and up.

Profiles of black newspapers and other periodicals are the focus of this volume. Entries run to several pages in length, including footnotes. Each entry also includes information about title changes, circulation, and editors. This volume contains an index as well as a selected chronology, which also places initial dates of publications of important black journals among other important dates in black history. Useful for journalism, American history, and African studies units.

Black Judges on Justice: Perspectives from the Bench. Linn Washington. New York: New Press, 1995. 288 pp. ISBN 1–56584–104–2. LC 94–027447. Junior high and up.

Is there really "justice for all"? Fourteen black justices from either the trial or appellate levels give their views and relate their experiences with the American judicial system. Each interview gives the subjects' legal background, why each chose law as a career, goals and reflections, and a discussion of the conflict between race and justice. No index. Good for social studies and racism units.

Black Misery. Langston Hughes. New York: Oxford University Press, 1994. The Iona and Peter Opie Library of Children's Literature Series. 64 pp. ISBN 0–19–509114–0. LC 93–49590. Junior high and high school.

Published as a picture book, but not for children. Hughes deals with bigotry, racism, misery, and hard times with wit and humor. Some of the jokes are those that African Americans tell among themselves, but the bite of pain comes through.

Useful for discussions and units on racism. Illustrated by Arouni. Introduction by Jesse Jackson. Afterword by Robert G. O'Mealley.

Black Music. Dean Tudor and Nancy Tudor, eds. Littleton, CO: Libraries Unlimited, 1979. American Popular Music on Elper Series. 262 pp. ISBN 0–87287–147–9. LC 78–15563. Professional use. Out of print.

This excellent selection tool is designed to aid in building a record collection of African American music. The 1,300 entries (blues, rhythm 'n' blues, gospel, soul, reggae) were chosen for their popularity and artistic merit. First choices are starred. Jazz (Littleton, CO: Libraries Unlimited, 1979. 302 pp. ISBN 0–87287–148–7, LC 78–11737), a companion volume, supplements this work. Of value to librarians or to serious collectors.

Black Music in America: A History Through Its People. James S. Haskins. New York: HarperCollins Children's Books, 1987. 224 pp. ISBN 0–690–04462–3. LC 85–47885. Junior high and up.

This illustrated book covers the major eras of African American music as it evolved in the United States, starting with early slave music to ragtime and blues to jazz to soul and through the 1970s and 1980s. This book contains concise biographies of various African American musicians as well as supplies enough historical background for the book to read like a narrative history. A very complex index is included, making the book an excellent reference tool. Useful for music students and for general use in any junior high school, high school, academic, or public library.

The Black Press and the Struggle for Civil Rights. Carl Senna. Danbury, CT: Franklin Watts, 1993. The African American Experience Series. 176 pp. ISBN 0–531–11036–2. LC 93–17558. Junior high and up.

This history of the African American press from its beginning in 1827 to the present. Contains excerpts from the early African American papers. It contains information on John Brown, W. E. B. DuBois, Ada B. Wells, Carl Rowan, Frederick Douglass, John Harold Johnson, and others. Good quality black-and-white photos. Of interest to journalism students. Useful for American history and African American studies. Illustrated.

Black Talk: Words and Phrases from the Hood to the Amen Corner. Geneva Smitherman. Boston: Houghton Mifflin Company, 1994. 242 pp. ISBN 0–395–67410–7. (Paper: ISBN 0–395–69992–4) . LC 94–591. High school and up.

Less formal than *Juba to Jive*. The language is more contemporary and emphasizes hip-hop culture. Smitherman has collected language through the early 1990s from "primarily oral" sources. The author's approach stereotypes European-Americans in some areas and suggests that European-Americans lack oral tradition and use African American language to "spice up" their otherwise dull language. Arranged in dictionary style. There is no phonetic key, but examples of usage are given. Incomplete bibliographic information on scholarly works mentioned. Some strong language. For more mature readers. Useful for general interest and African American studies and linguistics studies.

Black Women's Health Book: Speaking for Ourselves. Second Edition. Evelyn C. White, ed. Seattle, WA: Seal Press-Feminist, 1993. 396 pp. ISBN 1–878067–40–0. LC 93–28901. Junior high and up.

Reissue of book published in 1990. Expanded edition adds eleven additional essays by such notable black authors as Lucille Clifton, Marian Wright Edleman, and Toni Morrison on topics that include domestic violence, sexual abuse, suicide, pregnancy, midwives, politics of black women's health, skin color, menopause, HIV, AIDS, and much more. Useful for health units.

Blackface: Reflections on African Americans and the Movies. Nelson George. New York: HarperCollins Publishers, Inc., 1994. 224 pp. ISBN 0–06–017120–0. LC 94–10686. Junior high and up.

Music critic, novelist, and film maker George Nelson shares his memories of his involvement with the cinema. Nelson covers underrepresentation, stereotypes, "blaxploitation," and how far the industry has come. The author includes a time line of milestones in the making of African American films for the last 30 years as well as memories, anecdotes, and commentaries on those films. Of interest to film students and for units on racism.

Body and Soul: The Black Women's Guide to Physical Health and Emotional Well-Being. Linda Villarosa, ed. New York: HarperCollins Publishers, Inc., 1994. 576 pp. ISBN 0–06–095085–4. LC 94–13140. High school and up.

A health guide especially for African American women. It includes such topics as fibroids, keloids, diabetes, AIDS, pregnancy, mental and sexual health, masturbation, diet, and living in a violent world. May be too intense for younger readers. Useful for health units.

The Buffalo Soldiers. Catherine Reef. New York: 21st Century Books, Inc., 1993. African American Soldiers Series. 80 pp. ISBN 0–8050–2372–0. LC 92–34412. Junior high.

Shows the important roles African American soldiers played in American history from the Civil War to the present. Demonstrates their dedication to duty in the face of racism, bigotry, and hatred from those they were sworn to protect. Includes bibliography, chronology, index, photographs, and reproductions. Good for history reports and for general interest. Illustrated

Centuries of Greatness, 1750–1900: The West African Kingdoms. Philip Koslow. New York: Chelsea House Publishers, 1994. Milestones in Black History Series. 118 pp. ISBN 0–7910–2266–8. LC 91–40667. Junior high.

Beginning with eighth century Ghana, the book traces the West African Kingdoms through the fall of the Asante kingdom in 1900. The book contains maps, black-and-white photos, chronologies, and bibliographies. Koslow discusses the rulers, cultures, religions, major social events, and the slave trade. Useful for African American history units and geography units.

Civil Rights Leaders. Richard Rennert. New York: Chelsea House Publishers, 1993. Profiles of Great Black Americans Series. 63 pp. ISBN 0–7910–2051–7. (Paper: ISBN 0–7910–2052–5.) LC 92–37655. Junior high.

Introduction by Coretta Scott King. Profiles of eight well-known African American figures. Black-and-white photographs. No documentation. Some minor inaccuracies, but well written and interesting nonetheless. Useful for short book reports. Illustrated.

The Civil Rights Movement. Sanford Wexler. New York: Facts on File, 1993. 368 pp. ISBN 0–8160–2748–X. LC 92–28674. Junior high and up.

Covers the Civil Rights movement from 1954 to 1965 in letters, speeches, newspaper articles, and many other primary sources. Chronologically arranged text, plus maps of sites and events. Appendixes include historical documents and sketches. Primary sources add a feeling of being there, rather than simply reading about the topic. Good for American history units and African American studies. Illustrated.

Crossings: A White Man's Journey into Black America. Walt Harrington. New York: HarperCollins Publishers, Inc., 1993. 480 pp. ISBN 0–06–092462–4. LC 92–53379. Young adults.

Harrington, a white journalist, travelled more than 25,000 miles across the country and back—to small towns, large cities, and rural areas—talking to such diverse people as welfare mothers and film makers. The author interviewed people everywhere about their experiences with segregation, jobs and their scarcity, military service, and life in general. Includes an index, photos, and maps. Valuable to students of American culture and sociology.

The Day They Came to Arrest the Book. Nat Hentoff. New York: Dell Publishing Company, 1982. 160 pp. ISBN 0–440–91814–6. LC 82–71100. Junior high and up.

Brings the problem of censorship into the foreground. Students at George Madison High School object to reading *Huckleberry Finn* on the grounds that it is racist, sexist, immoral, and not fit to be read. The editor of the school paper does his best to battle censorship by anyone, but it may be too late. Of value to those interested in the issue of censorship.

Days of Sorrow, Years of Glory, 1831–1850: From the Nat Turner Revolt to the Fugitive Slave Law. Timothy J. Paulson. New York: Chelsea House Publishers, 1994. 112 pp. ISBN 0–7910–2263–3. (Paper: ISBN 0–7910–2552–7). LC 93–40851. High school and up.

Covers the history of African Americans beginning, as stated in the title, with the Nat Turner Revolt and ending with the Fugitive Slave Law. Contains an index, illustrations, black-and-white photos. Chapters outline such topics as slave life, the Underground Railroad, slave resistance, help by the Seminole Indians, and the abolitionist movement. Uses many original sources. A good addition to any social studies or African American studies collection.

The Dred Scott Case: Slavery and Citizenship. D. J. Herda. Springfield, NJ: Enslow, 1994. Landmark Supreme Court Cases Series. 104 pp. Grades 6–9. ISBN 0–89490–460–4. LC 93–22402. Grade 6 and up.

Details of the famous Dred Scott case in which a black slave sued his master for his freedom. The case ranks among the most important to be heard by the Supreme Court. Black-and-white photos. Good for African American studies and American history units.

Ebony: Pictorial History of Black America. The editors of *Ebony.* Introduction by Lerone Bennett, Jr. Chicago: Johnson Publishing, 1974. Three volumes. Vol.1: ISBN 0–318–53789–3. Vol.2: ISBN 0–318–53790–7. Vol.3: ISBN 0–318–53791–5. LC 71–151797. High school.

This is an extensive attempt to present a total visual experience of the African American experience. More than 1,000 pictures (along with written summaries) present the story from the Golden Age of Africa to the Civil Rights movement and the Black Revolution. Sections are also included on religion, sports, and the New (Cultural) Renaissance. A summary index is included at the end of Volume III. This is an excellent addition to a high school library where visual presentation of history is very important.

The First Passage: Blacks in the Americas. Colin A. Palmer. New York: Oxford University Press, 1994. 128 pp. ISBN 0–19–509905–2. LC 94–17335. Junior high and high school.

The first of an 11-volume series of African American history. Traces the presence of African Americans on the American continents from the earliest accounts. Describes what slavery meant to the 10 to 20 million blacks shipped to the New World in the sixteenth century. Describes the cultures that developed in the Americas, including the Caribbean, Mexico, Peru, and Brazil. Valuable for social studies and history units.

Forever Free. Christopher Henry. New York: Chelsea House Publishers, 1995. Milestones in Black American History Series. 119 pp. ISBN 0–7910–2253–6. (Paper: ISBN 0–7910–2679–5.) LC 94–33636. Junior high and up.

Henry describes the Civil War, the feelings and resistance of many northerners to the war, the reluctance on the part of many whites to allow African Americans to enter the armed forces, resistance to the draft, and the discrimination African Americans experienced once they enlisted. Presented from an African American perspective. Interesting as a perspective not generally found in history books. Useful as additional material for reports.

The Forgotten Heroes: The Story of the Buffalo Soldiers. Clinton Cox. New York: Scholastic, Inc., 1993. 176 pp. ISBN 0–590–45121–9. LC 92–36622. Junior high and up.

After the Civil War, a regiment of African American soldiers, called "Buffalo Soldiers" because of their appearance and bravery, was sent west to protect settlers and "maintain order." They were given the worst equipment and most dangerous duties. In spite of the fact that they were United States soldiers, they were still subject to ridicule, racism, and bigotry. Useful for units on the Civil War and on African American studies.

The Forgotten Players: The Story of Black Baseball in America. Robert Gardner and Dennis Shortelle. New York: Walker and Company, 1994. 128 pp. ISBN 0–8027–8248–5. LC 92–029618. Junior high and up.

Another worthy history of African Americans in baseball. Begins with the presegregation years of baseball and gives information on players, teams, and the problems they faced. Includes anecdotes about incidents on and off the field. Source notes are included. Twenty black-and-white photos. Interesting to the sports aficionado.

Freedom's Children: Young Civil Rights Activists Tell Their Own Stories. Ellen Levine, ed. New York: Avon/Flare, 1994. 224 pp. ISBN 0–380–72114–7. LC 93–10388. Junior high.

Sit-ins, strikes, marches, and other experiences are described by African Americans who were children or teenagers during the 1950s and 1960s. They give a firsthand look of the experiences of fighting segregation and racism during the birth of civil rights. Useful addition for history units and lessons on racism. Illustrated.

Freedom's River: The African-American Contribution to Democracy. James Steele. Danbury, CT: Franklin Watts, Inc., 1995. The African-American Experience Series. 176 pp. ISBN 0–531–11184–9. LC 94–61517. Junior high and high school.

Black-and-white photo section in the middle of the book. Index. For readers capable of handling challenging material. Traces the politics of freedom and oppression from the Civil War to the Vietnam War. Concentrates on politics rather than on individual accomplishments and contributions. Good addition to social studies collection.

From Slavery to Freedom: A History of African Americans. Sixth Edition. John Hope Franklin. New York: Knopf, 1994. 624 pp. ISBN 0–394–56362–X. LC 87–45341. Professional and educational use; research.

This book traces the interaction of African Americans and the American environment from the land of Africa through the Vietnamese War. The work concentrates on African Americans as a people rather than just a few outstanding individuals. Of possible value for comparison of attitudes and perspectives within a generation.

Historic Speeches of African Americans. Warren J. Halliburton. Danbury, CT: Franklin Watts, Inc., 1993. The African American Experience Series. 192 pp. ISBN 0–531–11034–6. LC 92–39318. Junior high and up.

The author has arranged the book into five sections covering 24 speeches on slavery, emancipation, reconstruction, segregation, civil rights, and the post-Civil Rights movement. Each section and speech has its own introduction. Sources are included.

Black-and-white photographs and reproductions. Valuable for history and social studies units.

History of the Blues: The Roots, the Music, the People—From Charley Patton to Robert Cray. Francis Davis. New York: Hyperion, 1995. 320 pp. ISBN 0–7868–6052–9. LC 94–23370. High school and up.

Essential for music library shelves. The author traces the blues from its origin to the present, saluting the genre as one of the only truly American music forms alive today, and describes the contributions of Bessie Smith, Muddy Waters, Robert Johnson, Johnny "Daddy Stovepipe" Watson, and others. Companion to a new PBS series. Valuable addition to history of music collections.

I Know What the Red Clay Looks Like: The Voice and Vision of Black Women Writers. Rebecca Carroll. New York: Carol Southern Books, 1994. ISBN 0–517–59638–5. (Paper: ISBN 0–517–88261–2.) LC 94–8342. High school and up.

Anthology of interviews with African American women writers. Each tells how she started writing, who inspired her, who influenced her, and what it's like to grow up as an African American woman in this country. Interviewees include Gloria Naylor, Rita Dove, Nikki Giovanni, J. California Cooper, Tina McElroy Ansa, Lorene Carey, Marita Golden, and many more. Useful for pleasure reading, history units and students of women's studies.

Image of the Black in Children's Fiction. Dorothy M. Broderick. New York: Bowker, 1973. 219 pp. ISBN 0–8352–0550–9. LC 72–1741. Adults; professional use. Out of print.

What authors told children about the institution of slavery, the role assigned to African Americans, and the personal characteristics attributed to African Americans are examined in this book, which covers children's literature about African Americans from 1827–1968. This is an excellent look at what white children were taught about African American children through literature. Might be of interest to mature high school students.

Interracial Dating. Elaine Landau. Morristown, NJ: Silver Burdett Press, 1993. 102 pp. ISBN 0–671–75258–8. (Paper: ISBN 0–671–75261–8.) LC 92–44814. Junior high and high school; professional use.

Landau opens with a history of interracial dating and marriage in the United States from colonial to present times, concentrating mostly on black-white and Asian-white relationships. The book features interviews with people already in interracial relationships as well as those who might become so involved. This work does not gloss over the serious problems that couples face when they cross racial, religious, and cultural lines, but remains supportive of the individual's right to personal choice. Of special interest to young people considering interracial dating and their families and counselors.

Interracial Marriage. Paul Almonte and Theresa Desmond. Morristown, NJ: Silver Burdett Press (Crestwood House), 1992. The Facts About Series 48 pp. ISBN 0–89686–749–8. LC 91–45251. Junior high and up; professional use.

The authors present the problems associated with interracial marriage in a frank and open way. While they state that a person's character is more important than his or her race, the attendant problems need to be taken into consideration. Deals primarily with African American/Caucasian marriages. Of special interest to young people considering interracial marriage and their families and counselors. Illustrated.

Into Africa. Craig Packer. Chicago: University of Chicago Press: 1994. 277 pp. ISBN 0–226–64429–4. LC 94–8428. High school and up.

Craig Packer, a field biologist since 1972, describes fieldwork, initiating newcomers into fieldwork, his work with graduate students doing research in the Serengheti, and working with Jane Goodall. Packer explores the mysteries of why lions live in groups, why male chimps band together while male baboons move from troop to troop, and how mankind and animals can better live together in a world whose resources are threatened. Good for sociology and anthropology units.

Life For Me Ain't Been No Crystal Stair. Susan Sheehan. New York: Pantheon Books, 1993. 174 pp. ISBN 0–679–41472–X. LC 93–18746. Junior high and up.

Pulitzer Prize–winning author Susan Sheehan tells a moving tale of foster care in the United States. She tells the story through the eyes of 14-year-old Crystal, who, along with her illegitimate child, was taken from her mother's home and placed in a foster home because her mother was a drug addict. The baby was placed in a separate home. Interviews with Crystal's siblings and interviews with social workers are integrated into the text. The author shows the impact of foster homes on young lives. Crystal "gets it together" and tries to help her mother and siblings as well as her own baby.

A Long Hard Journey: The Story of the Pullman Porter. Patricia and Frederick McKissack. New York: Walker and Company, 1990. American History Series for Young People 144 pp. ISBN 0–8027–6884–9. Junior high and up.

Covering a 150-year period, this sympathetic account focuses on the efforts of a small group who sought to gain recognition for the Brotherhood of Sleeping Car Porters, the first African American–controlled union. Based on primary sources (including interviews) as well as on published materials, a detailed account of the rise of the first African American union and the conditions that made it necessary. Interesting addition to African American history collections.

Masters of the Dream: The Strength and Betrayal of Black America. Allen Keyes. New York: William Morrow & Company, 1994. 288 pp. ISBN 0–688–09599–2. LC 94–028840. Junior high and up.

Keyes calls on African Americans to return to family values and self-reliance, condemning "the ideology of victimization and the 'betrayal' of the welfare system." The author encourages African Americans to remember their heritage and stand on their own two feet and not depend on anyone but themselves. Useful for African American studies.

Mississippi Challenge. Mildred Pitts Walter. Old Tappan, NJ: Simon and Schuster, 1992. 224 pp. ISBN 0–02–792301–0. LC 92–6718. Junior high school and up.

Walter tells the story of slavery, the Civil War, the formation of the Mississippi Freedom Democratic Party, the struggle to vote, and the Mississippi Challenge in the 1960s. The author covers the history of slavery and mistreatment of African Americans in only one state—Mississippi. According to Walter, conditions there were so bad for slaves that masters in other states kept their slaves in line by threatening to sell them into Mississippi if they caused trouble. Contains source notes and bibliography. Good resource for units on civil rights. Valuable addition to any library.

The Papers of Martin Luther King, Jr., Volume Two: Rediscovering Precious Values, July 1951–November 1955. Martin Luther King, Jr. Claybourne Carson, Ralph E. Luker, Penny A. Russell, and Peter Holloran, eds. Martin Luther King, Jr. Berkeley, CA: University of California Press, 1994. 800 pp. ISBN 0–520–07951–5. LC 91–42336. Young adults; instructional use.

Second of a projected 14-volume series. Introductory volume contains a biographi-cal essay, annotated letters, speeches, sermons, and other articles. The second volume covers Dr. King's doctoral studies (including his dissertation) and his term as pastor at the Dexter Avenue Baptist Church in Montgomery, Alabama. Invaluable for research.

People in Bondage: African Slavery in the Modern Era. L. H. Ofosu-Appiah. Minneapolis, MN: The Lerner Group. (Lerner Publications), 1993. 132 pp. ISBN 0–8225–3150–X. LC 91–44770. Junior high and high school.

Ofosu-Appiah paints a chilling portrait of slavery throughout the ages, in all cultures. He reveals the shame of the "might makes right" dogma and the shame of the churches in condoning slavery. He clearly shows the reasoning of many enslaved people who chose death over continued bondage. Focuses on the African slave trade. Excellent reproductions and photographs. Good for social studies, American history units and African American studies.

A Pictorial History of Black Americans. Fifth Edition. Langston Hughes, Milton Meltzer, and C. Eric Lincoln. New York: Crown, 1983. 380 pp. ISBN 0–517–55072–5. LC 83–7742 High school and up.

Originally published as *A Pictorial History of the Negro in America* in 1956. Republished in 1963, 1968, 1973, and 1983. Presented in nine parts covering African Americans in America from 1619 through slavery, freedom, and to the present. Contains a wealth of photographs depicting the lives and history of African Americans and their families. Some photographs are very graphic. Comprehensive index. Excellent for African American studies.

Racism. Volume 1. Scott Hays. Tarrytown, New York: Marshall Cavendish Corporation, 1994. Life Issues Series. 96 pp. ISBN 1–85435–615–1. LC 93–40422. High school and up.

Case studies, sections on testing attitudes, black-and-white photographs. Intended for anyone who has ever been the target of racism, bigotry, or hate crimes. WARNING: Uses strong racial epithets to make its point and get the reader involved. Good for units on racism and prejudice.

Sangoma: An Odyssey into the Spirit World of Africa. James Hall. New York: The Putnam Publishing Group, 1994. 320 pp. ISBN 0–87477–780–1. LC 94–10138. Junior high and up.

The writer describes his journey, both physical and spiritual, to Swaziland to become a sangoma (shaman). During an interview with Miriam Makeba, she tells him that he might be able to "see" as a shaman does. He journeys to Swaziland to learn the secrets of the sangoma. Of possible interest for units on personal development.

Saving Our Sons: Raising Black Children in a Turbulent World. Marita Golden. New York: Doubleday and Company, Inc., 1995. 208 pp. ISBN 0–385–47302–8. LC 94–16490. High school and up.

Sequel to *Migrations of the Heart*, in which the author describes her years in her native Nigeria and the birth of her son. *Saving Our Sons* takes the author and her son though her divorce, their journey to the United States, his childhood and adolescence, and a return trip to Nigeria. Golden decries violence in the African American community. Includes interviews with parents of children who have been killed. Of use for African American studies.

Say It Loud!: The Story of Rap Music. Maurice K. Jones. Brookfield, CT: Millbrook Press, 1994. 128 pp. ISBN 1–56294–386–3. (Paper: ISBN 1–56294–724–9.) LC 93–1939. Junior high and up.

Jones traces the history of rap music back to the traditions of the griots of West Africa. The slave trade was responsible for this particular musical form being brought to the United States. It has developed and evolved over the years into its current form. Various rap groups are profiled. Jones includes black-and-white and color photos, reproductions, and lyrics. Of interest to rap music fans, music students, units on African American studies. Illustrated.

The Seven hundred Sixty-First Battalion. Kathryn Browne Pfeifer. New York: 21st Century Books Introduction, 1994. African American Soldiers Series. 80 pp. ISBN 0–8050–3057–3. LC 93–26820. Junior high and up.

History of the 761st Tank Battalion, African American soldiers who served with distinction during World War II. Addresses the unit's battle record as well as racism and discrimination suffered by African American soldiers serving their country. Black-and-white photographs. Bibliography of books on African American soldiers during World War II. Good for American history and African American studies units.

Sickle Cell Anemia. George Beshore, ed. Danbury, CT: Franklin Watts, Inc., 1994. 76 pp. ISBN 0–531–12510–6. LC 94–015513. Junior high and high school.

History of the disease which infects primarily African Americans and those of Mediterranean descent. Describes genetic transmission of disease, screening, treatment, and symptoms. Follows two sufferers of the disease, describing how their lives have been affected. Good information on the disease. Of interest to persons with sickle cell disease and their families and friends. Good addition for junior high, high school, and public libraries.

Spreading Poison: A Book About Racism and Prejudice. John Langone. New York: Little, Brown & Company, 1993. 192 pp. ISBN 0–316–51410–1. LC 92–17847. Junior high and high school.

The author's main premise is that racism and bigotry are the results of ignorance and fear of the unknown. He maintains that anyone's attitudes and prejudices can be overcome by education. He traces the history and causes of intolerance and shows how this "poison" has affected and infected western culture. He includes racism, anti-Semitism, sexism, homophobia; and the treatment of Native Americans, immigrants, and the disabled. Good introduction to the problem of racism.

The State of Afro-American History: Past, Present and Future. Darlene Clark Hine, ed. Baton Rouge, LA: Louisiana State University Press, 1986. 301 pp. ISBN 0–8071–1581–9. LC 85–024138. High school and up.

This volume contains the proceedings of the American Historical Association Conference on the Study and Teaching of Afro-American History. Held at Purdue University in 1983, the conference boasted a group of some of the most prominent scholars, historians, and educators in the field of African American History. In this book, the contributors assess and evaluate the status of African American history, address trends, and make recommendations for the future. Of use to researchers and political science students.

The State of Black America. Janet Dewart, ed. New Brunswick, NJ: Transaction Publishers, 1990. 332 pp. Annual thru 1990. ISBN 0–914758–11–X. Professional use, research.

An authoritative analysis of the status of African Americans in American society, this annual provides an evaluation of the previous year's developments in housing, African American leadership, health, economy, and education. A comprehensive work, each volume also contains a detailed chronology of the year's events, affirmative action, race relations, and other major topics. Good for research.

The Story of Negro League Baseball. William Brashler. New York: Ticknor and Fields, 1994. 144 pp. ISBN 0–395–67169–8. (Paper: ISBN 0–395–69721–2.) LC 93–36547. Junior high and up.

Features lists of teams and their players, black-and-white photos, chapters on the major players of the era. Much of the material was gleaned from personal interviews with the players and personnel involved. Documentation is not included. Will appeal to a younger audience than will *Black Diamond*. Of interest to baseball fans.

Testimony: Black Students Naming Ourselves. Natasha Tarpley, ed. Boston: Beacon Press, 1994. 304 pp. ISBN 0–8070–0928–8. (Paper: ISBN 0–8070–0929–6.) LC 94–14362. High school and up.

Like many other young African Americans, Natasha Tarpley had many bad experiences when she enrolled as one of few African American students on a traditionally white college campus. Her experience moved her to write essays and to collect essays and poetry from other young African Americans about their experiences. The essays cover such topics as self-concept, self discovery, and African American identity. Useful for African American studies.

Till Victory Is Won: Black Soldiers in the Civil War. Zak Mettger. New York: Dutton, 1994. Young Readers of the Civil War Series. 96 pp. ISBN 0–525–67412–8. Junior high.

Photographs, paintings, maps, letters, and diaries illustrate the contributions of African American soldiers who fought and gave their lives fighting against slavery during the Civil War. Good for reports and units on American history, African American history. Illustrated.

To Be A Slave. Julius Lester. New York: Dial Books for Young Readers, 1968. ISBN 0–8037–8955–6. (Paper: ISBN 0–590–42460–2.) LC 68–028738. Junior high and high school.

Because Lester believes that one of the most overlooked sources of information about the conditions of slavery is from dialogues with actual slaves, his book introduces narratives from men, women, and children who lived through this period. Many have never appeared in print before and some interviews are extractions from sources long out of print; documentation is placed beneath quoted material. Lester ties passages together with sympathetic commentary in a historical publication that is readable and compelling. The setting is the south, beginning with the arrival of the first Africans in the colonies in 1619 and continuing into the 1900s with the formation of the Ku Klux Klan. A bibliography is included. Good for units on American history and African American history. A Newbery Honor Book. Illustrated.

Toward the Promised Land 1851–1861: From Uncle Tom's Cabin to the Onset of the Civil War. Wilma King. New York: Chelsea House Publishers, 1995. Milestones in Black American History Series. 111 pp. ISBN 0–7910–2265–X. (Paper: ISBN 0–7910–2691–4.) LC 94–42109. Junior high and up.

King presents the events leading up to the Civil War, the Civil War itself, the evolution of the Ku Klux Klan, and the reconstruction from the African American perspective. Her narrative not only tells about well known figures such as Harriet

Tubman, Sojourner Truth, and Frederick Douglass, but also about lesser-known figures such as Mary An Shadd Cary, Martin R. Delany, Henry Highland Garnett, and Henry Bibb. Well written, clear, and informative. Black-and-white photos and period drawings. Excellent for American history and African American history units.

We'll Understand It Better By and By: Presenting African American Gospel Composers. Bernice Johnson Reagon, ed. Washington D.C.: Smithsonian Institution Press, 1993. 432 pp. ISBN 1–56098–166–0. (Paper: ISBN 1–56098–167–9.) LC 91–37954. Young adults.

Reagon presents the evolution of African American gospel music through the ages and its influence on today's worship and contemporary music. Her overview and introduction give understandable definitions of the genre; then the author goes on to describe the contributions of six of the great pioneers in the field. A section on piano scores and musical analyses adds to the appeal for the music student. Interviews with composers, musicians, and their family members let the reader see their thoughts and share their experiences. Extensive index. A challenge even to competent readers. Of interest to music students.

Wouldn't Take Nothing for My Journey Now. Maya Angelou. New York: Random House, Inc., 1993. 136 pp. ISBN 0–679–42743–0. LC 93–5904. Junior high and up.

Well-known author, playwright, and poet Maya Angelou writes on a variety of subjects, including morality, friendship, manners, love, and just plain getting along. An interesting read.

Videos

Videos: Fiction, reviewed

Between Black and White. Distributed by Filmmakers Library, 1993. 26 min. Color. Preview available. VHS format. High school and up.

The adult children of racially mixed couples discuss what it's like growing up in a racially mixed family and finding their own identities in a culture that places so much emphasis on race. They discuss the problems of interracial dating and marriage such as acceptance by the families concerned and by society in general.

Thought-provoking. Good for social studies units, race relations discussions, and when such items appear in the news media.

Malcolm Takes a Shot. Produced by American Film Institute, 1990. Distributed by Carousel, 1993 release. 45 min. Color. Preview available. Junior high and high school.

Malcolm, an African American teenager, has talent as a basketball player and is popular at school. He dreams of being a professional basketball star. But his ego gets in the way of his being a team player; he is in danger of failing English because he does not study or do his homework; and his attitude is creating serious problems for him. Then he suffers an epileptic seizure during the final seconds of a basketball game. When he finds that he has epilepsy, Malcolm becomes very depressed and discouraged and engages in risky behavior until his coach, family, and friends are able to restore his confidence and help him believe in his future. Good, believable acting and action scenes. A CBS Schoolbreak Special.

Tuskegee Airmen. Produced by WCBS–TV, 1992. N.Y. Distributed by Carousel. 28 min. Color. Preview available. Junior high and up.

After emancipation, but before the Civil Rights movement, African Americans were denied the right to be a part of the American Dream. They were denied access to the schools that would have helped them become successful. When they enlisted in the military, they were denied access to career tracks that would have allowed them to become officers and instead were put in the most menial jobs. But, in 1941, Roosevelt established the training of "black and brown" airmen in the South—in Tuskegee, Alabama. These men not only wanted to serve their country, they wanted to be the best, and they worked hard to achieve that goal. No aircraft they escorted was ever lost. But after the war, they faced the same discrimination they had known before. This is the story of the Tuskegee Airmen, true role models for youth of all ethnic groups today. A valuable addition to any library and excellent for African American studies and American history units.

Videos: Fiction, not reviewed

African and African American Folktales. United Learning 1993 Niles, Ill. Narrated by Donna Washington. Junior high.

The program includes a West African tale, a "Brer Rabbit" story, and an "explanatory tale." Also available teacher's guide, 20 pps. by Barri Golbas. Cat. # 10111V

African Journey, Chicago: Public Media Video, 1990/1992. 174 min. Junior high and up.

Luke, a white boy from Canada, and Themba, an African boy from East Africa, set out together to find their fathers who have been in a mining accident, and discover how much they have in common despite their very different cultures. Wonderworks Family movies. Two video tapes + 1 guide (7pp.)

The Autobiography of Miss Jane Pittman. Charlotte, NC: United American Video. Distributed by Broadway Video Enterprises, 1991/1993. 110 min. High school and up.

Miss Jane Pittman tells the story of her birth into slavery and subsequent freedom. History of African Americans in a nutshell. Made for TV movie. Originally broadcast on CBS.

Black Like Me. Santa Monica, CA: Rhino Home Video, 1992/1964. 107 min. Black History Series. High school and up.

Made in 1964. Based on the novel written by John Howard Griffen by the same name. A white reporter dyes his skin to pass as an African American to find out firsthand about racism and prejudice. Very daring for its time.

Brother Future. Chicago: Public Media Video, 1992/1991. 116 min. Junior high and up.

T.J., a slick inner-city youth, is knocked unconscious while fleeing the police and wakes up in Charleston, S.C. in 1822, where he is taken captive as a slave. Will he ever get home? Wonderworks Family Movie.

The Color Purple. Burbank, CA: Warner Home Video, 1991/1985. 154 min. High school and up.

From Alice Walker's novel about an African American woman who grows and matures in the face of adversity to become mature and independent. Violence and profanity. Viewer discretion is advised.

Cry, the Beloved Country. Malibu, CA: Monterey Home Video, 1992/1951. 100 min. High school and up.

An African American minister in South Africa in the era of apartheid goes to the city to search for his son, who has become a criminal. Black & white. Based on a novel by Alan Paton.

The Father Clements Story. Van Nuys, CA: Live Home Video, 1993/1987, 98 min. High school and up.

Inspired by a true story. A Chicago priest attempts to adopt an African American son. Starring Louis Gossett, Jr.; Malcom-Jamal Warner; and Carroll O'Connor.

The Gift of Amazing Grace. Strand VCI Entertainment, 1991. 48 min. Junior high.

An ABC Afterschool Special. Grace Wheeler is the only member of her family, a gospel singing group, who can't carry a tune. Then she discovers her own secret talent and the key to her family's happiness.

Go Tell It on the Mountain. Malibu, CA: Monterey Home Video, 1985. 97 min. Junior high and up.

Based on the novel by James Baldwin. Covers the lives, trials, tribulations, and victories of three generations of an African American family.

Guess Who's Coming to Dinner? Burbank, CA: Columbia TriStar Home Video, 1987/1967. 108 min. Junior high and up.

A film that was startling for its time. A young white woman brings home a young African American man to dinner. Her parents don't know how to respond. Spencer Tracy, Katherine Hepburn, Sidney Poitier.

Half Slave–Half Free. Xenon Home Video. 1991. 120 minutes. High school and up.

"Solomon Northrup's Odyssey." An African American man who had been freed from slavery is captured and re-sold. He has to learn to adjust to life under a cruel master.

"Charlotte Forten's Mission." A young slave woman presents a startling and revolutionary idea to President Lincoln: let African Americans live in freedom on the Sea Islands of South Carolina. Produced in association w/KUHT Houston. For television broadcast in 1985.

Videos: Nonfiction, reviewed

African-American Artists: Affirmation Today. Produced by the National Museum of American Art, Smithsonian Institution. Distributed by Crystal Productions, Glenview, Il. 1994. 28 min. Color. Includes paperback book: *Free Within Ourselves*, 20 slides, teacher's guide. videocassette. 28 min. Junior high and up.

African American artists discuss their work, the influence on their work by their culture, African American symbolism, techniques, the origins of their ideas, the role of music in their creations, and creative processes in this beautifully filmed video, taped at the Museum of American Art. The outstanding visuals include sculptures, paintings, quilted abstracts, landscapes, portraits, Afro-Caribbean artworks, and photographs. The artists included are sculptor Leroy Almon and painters Frederick Brown, Sam Gilliam, Lois Jones, and Keith Morrison. Outstanding addition to African American and art collections.

Anchor of the Soul. Portland, ME: Portland's Abyssinian Church, 1994. 60 min. Color. Junior high and up.

Former Congresswoman Barbara Jordan narrates this history of two churches in the African American community in the Portland, Maine area. The first, the Abyssinian Church, still stands, but has been vacant since 1917. The second, the Green Memorial AME Zion Church, opened in 1920 and absorbed the membership of the older church. The video covers the origins of the two churches and the racism and bigotry their members faced. The lives of Reuben Ruby, the primary financier of the Abyssinian church, and Moses Green, for whom the newer church was named, are highlighted. The video includes interviews with current and former church members and with specialists on the history of the area. The background music consists of solo piano and singing by Jane Sapp and the Gertrude E. Brown Choir of Green Memorial Church. Will be popular in New England libraries, but is valuable to all library collections.

Black Americans of Achievement Video Collection II. Bala Cynwyd, PA: Produced by Schlessinger Video Productions, 1994. 30 min. each. Color. Junior high and up.

Adapted from and following the same format as the books published by Chelsea House. Subjects include Muhammad Ali, James Baldwin, Mary McLeod Bethune, W. E. B. Du Bois, Marcus Garvey, Matthew Henson, Langston Hughes, Elijah Muhammad, Jesse Owens, and Alice Walker. Archival photos and film footage of each subject. Some duplication of film clips and photos of general topics. Good sound quality, comments by academicians, and narration by oral historian John O'Neal. Each video tells the life story of its subject beginning with early childhood and advancing through adulthood, emphasizing the subject's contributions to society. These titles, along with Collection I, cover a broad spectrum of African American history including the arts, politics, science, sports, and history. Companion pieces to Schlessinger's *History of the Civil Rights Movement*. A must for school libraries.

Dr. Martin Luther King, Jr.: A Historical Perspective. Distributed by Xenon Entertainment Group, 1994. Black-and-white. 60 minutes. Junior high and up.

Nonprofit public performance rights included. Writer/director Tom Friedman explores King's ideas, ideals, thoughts, and activities in the Civil Rights movement. Includes seldom-seen photos and footage. Excerpts from recordings of his speeches and sermons are included. Narrated by Arthur Berghardt. Not a typical documentary. Good addition to African American collections.

The Era of Segregation: A Personal Perspective. Distributed by Knowledge Unlimited, 1993. 32 min. Color. Includes teacher's guide. Junior high and up.

Winner of the 1994 CINE Golden Eagle Award. The perspectives of Clifton L. Taulbert, author of *Once Upon a Time When We Were Colored*, combine with historical footage, photographs, and narration to create this history of segregation and its impact in the south. The film covers slavery and "legal segregation" when African Americans were shut out from white society and its advantages. Sections include "Family and Community," " The Church," "Schools Under Segregation," "The Civil Rights Movement," and "The Issues Today." And, according to Taulbert, these problems still exist. Many of today's students cannot conceive of a time when African Americans could not use the same public facilities, schools, drinking fountains, and bathrooms as whites. A real eye-opener. Good for units on American History, African American studies, and racism.

Faith Ringgold: The Last Story Quilt. Produced by Chicago, Ill. HomeVision, 1991. Portrait of an Artist Series. 30 min. Color. Junior high and up; students of children's literature; university.

One in a series on African American artists. This autobiographical film features writer/artist Faith Ringgold telling her life story in chronological order from childhood to the present. She describes the people and events in her life that influenced her work. A highlight of the film is her work in the medium of quilt paintings. Each quilt contains both narrative and visuals. Narration, interview, head shots, and segments of the artist at work. Most appropriate for high school art classes, career units, biographical studies. Appropriate for school and public libraries.

Frederick Douglass: When the Lion Wrote History. Produced by WETA, Washington, DC and ROJA Productions, 1994. Distributed by PBS Video, 1994. 90 min. Color. Junior high and up.

Outstanding presentation of Frederick Douglass's life. Comprehensive coverage of his childhood and his development as a civil rights activist, politician, public speaker, diplomat, and journalist. Narrated by Academy Award nominee Alfree Woodard. This film uses a variety of formats including live-action film, photos, drawings, artworks, and paper reprints and is complemented perfectly by the accompanying music. Better than the film on Frederick Douglass in the Black Americans of Achievement Series. Excellent for school and public libraries.

Freedom and Justice: A Salute to the Heroes of the Black Struggle. Cance, SC: Produced by CQ Television Network, 1994. Approximately 25 min. Color. Includes teacher's guide. 82 min. version on one cassette. Junior high and up.

The struggle of South Carolina with the Civil Rights movement is chronicled by photographer Cecil J. Williams. This production is divided into four parts beginning in the 1940s and ending in a discussion of the future of the Civil Rights movement. Contains interviews with civil rights workers, educators, politicians, and journalists involved in the movement. Narrated by Sony Dubose. The video focuses on Williams' photojournalism and his pictures' stories. Good for students of photography and classes in American history. Good addition to school and public libraries.

Great Black Innovators. Madison, WI: Knowledge Unlimited, 1995. 32 min. Color. Includes teacher's guide. Junior high and up.

The video is narrated by James Michael Brodie, author of *Created Equal: The Lives and Ideas of Black American Innovators*. So much emphasis is placed on the book that it would be good to have the book as a companion piece. Some of the innovators covered are Benjamin Banneker and George Washington Carver, but others such as Daniel Hale Williams, the first person to perform successful open heart surgery, are barely mentioned. Good format and appealing photos, but more emphasis is given to the fact that many African American innovators were not given due credit for their ideas and inventions than is given to what they actually contributed. Good for units on invention, inventors, and African American studies.

The History of the Civil Rights Movement. Schlessinger Video Productions. Available from Film Archives. Black Americans of Achievement Series. 30 minutes. Color. Junior high and up.

Begins with an overview of slavery, emancipation, the Jim Crow laws, the Civil Rights movement, and the movement into the 1990s. Discusses Plessy v. Fergusson, the NAACP, Brown v. the Board of Education, the Montgomery Bus Boycott, the March on Washington, and the migration of African Americans to the North. Profiles of prominent African Americans such as W. E. B. DuBois; Marcus Garvey; A. Philip Randolph; Rosa Parks; Martin Luther King, Jr.; Malcolm X; and Jesse Jackson as well as interviews with Andrew Young, James Farmer, and other prominent people involved in the Civil Rights movement are included. Good addition for any junior high or high school library.

A History of Slavery in America. Produced by Schlessinger Video Productions, 1994. Black Americans of Achievement Video Collection. 30 min. Color. Junior high, high school.

Interviews with leading scholars and historians map out the history of slavery in America, beginning with Jamestown in 1619 and continuing through the Reconstruction Period after the Civil War in 1865. Some of the areas covered are the capture and transportation of Africans to the New World, treatment of slaves, daily life on the plantations, use of slaves in textiles, industry, and agriculture, rebellion and resistance, the Underground Railroad, the Abolitionist Movement, the Emancipation Proclamation, the passing of the 13th Amendment to the U.S. Constitution, Reconstruction, and voting rights. Contributions of well-known figures such as Sojourner Truth, Dred Scott, William Lloyd Garrison, Frederick Douglass, John Brown, Harriet Tubman, and Abraham Lincoln are discussed. Visuals include period artifacts and photographs. Valuable for junior and high school collections. Useful for American history units and African American studies units.

In the Land of Jim Crow: Fighting for Civil Rights. Produced by Coronet, MTI Film and Video, Northbrook, IL: 1993. Distributed by Coronet/MTI, 1992. 22 min. Color. 1992. Preview available. Junior high and up.

The coverage of the fight for civil rights begins with a group of African American students in Greensboro, North Carolina, who decide to sit at an all-white lunch counter. Nonviolent protests soon spread over the nation and the Civil Rights movement began in earnest. African Americans, students, and "outside agitators" boycotted stores, set up picket lines, and did their best to integrate "all-white" facilities. Even the Supreme Court ruling of 1954, which declared segregated schools unconstitutional, did not guarantee that African American students would be welcomed into formerly all-white schools. Civil rights activists had to fight for every victory. The video contains interviews with civil rights activists who tell what motivated them to get involved in the fight as well as live action archival footage, still photos of events, and headlines. Warning: Some profanity, use of the word "nigger," graphic photos of lynched African Americans, and other brutalization because of race. Good for stimulating discussions of prejudice and racism. Useful for American history classes. Good for school and public libraries.

Journey Through Jazz. Two-part set. Orlando, FL: Produced by Rick Levy Associates, 1994. 20 min each. Includes teacher's guide. Junior high and high school.

Taped before a live audience of students. The Dan Jordan Trio, with the horn player as host, presents a history of jazz, showing how the notes, tempos, and sounds can evoke different emotions in listeners. They play music by Scott Joplin, Fats Walker, Coleman Hawkins, and other jazz greats. They discuss the origins of jazz and its African and European influences, particularly the African musical technique of call and response. The second part presents an overview of the influences on jazz and the different styles that have evolved. Some of the styles discussed are dixieland, bebop, swing, and progressive jazz. The message is that jazz is about communication and being creative. Useful in classes on African Americans or music.

Kwanzaa: A Cultural Celebration. Princeton, NJ: Distributed by Films for the Humanities and Sciences, 1993/1990. 30 min. Color. Junior high and up.

The African American holiday, Kwanzaa, is based on the Swahili word for harvest or first fruit. Kwanzaa was begun during the Civil Rights movement in 1966. A cultural rather than a religious holiday, Kwanzaa is held from December 26 to January 1. During this time, African American families return to their African traditions, stressing spirituality and community as they celebrate and teach the ideals of unity, self-determination, collective work, responsibility, cooperative economics, purpose, creativity, and faith. A good educational tool for discussing the holiday and how its concepts are carried over into everyday life. Good for units on African American studies.

Lost Hopes: Shattered Dreams. Produced by MTI, 1993. Northbrook, IL. Distributed by Coronet/MTI. 22 min. Color. Preview available. Junior high and up; social workers; youth workers.

A panel of mostly African American teens answer questions on what it's like to live in impoverished neighborhoods. One of the questions is: "What's the toughest thing about living in the city?" Answer: The gunshots, the random violence, the death in this war zone, the constant fights, among others. The panel discusses why so many kids drop out of school, what would make life better, who their enemies are, what's worth dying for, and their hopes for themselves in ten years. Text at the end of the video tells viewers that one boy who had said he wanted to become a lawyer was murdered shortly after the video was filmed. Good for social studies, particularly for those interested in social work or who plan to work with urban youths.

Making it Happen: Masters of Invention. Produced by Bob Oliver Communications, 1995. Distributed by Churchill Media. Van Nuys, CA. 22 min. Color. Includes teacher's guide. ISBN 0–7932–3350–X. Preview available. Junior high and up.

Narrator Glynn Turman describes inventions of African Americans and how they improved society, and how slavery and race laws affected the inventors' creativity and recogntion. Better than *Great Black Innovators*. Fast-paced and impressive. Uses period photographs and film clips. Good for units on invention and African American studies.

Malcolm X: Make it Plain. WGBH Boston, MA. Produced by Blackside, Inc. and Roja Productions, 1994. Distributed by PBS Video. 150 min. Color. Also available on three videos. High school and up.

This video biography of the famous civil rights activist uses historical black-and-white footage, speeches made by Malcolm X, and interviews with family and associates to paint a portrait of the man as well as the image. Concurrent national events are mentioned during the film. Best viewed in a group with an instructor, possibly with print material. Good for multicultural studies, American history units, social studies on the high school or college level, and for public libraries.

The Nightfighters. Produced by Fulmar TV, 1984. Falls Church, VA. Distributed by Landmark Media, Inc. 52 min. Color. Preview available. High school and up.

The story of the Tuskegee Airmen, an African American aviation group who served during World War II, is told primarily in interviews with the corps' members. This documentary covers the group's training, their recollections of their battle experiences, and the racism and discrimination they faced. The roles of their primary flight instructor, Alfred "Chief" Anderson, the first African American man to fly the United States coast to coast, and Benjamin O. Davis, their skillful and demanding commanding officer, are recounted. Includes film clips, photographs, music of the era, and songs by the Tuskegee University Chapel Choir. A valuable addition to any African American or World War II collection.

Pride and Prejudice: A History of Black Culture in America. Madison, WI: Distributed by Knowledge Unlimited, 1994. 28 min. Color. Includes teacher's guide. Junior high and up.

This video deals with the history of the inclusion of African Americans in mainline American history. It is a good companion piece for the 1968 Bill Cosby film, *Black History: Lost, Stolen, or Strayed*. A comparison of the two will show how far society's attitudes have come in nearly 30 years. It covers how African Americans have reacted to their treatment by others in their new homes. Focuses on the nineteenth and twentieth centuries. Appropriate for African American studies classes or for American history classes.

The Promised Land: Two Decades After Martin Luther King, Jr..
Produced by Otmoor Productions, 1992. Distributed by Filmmakers Library. 50 min. Color. High school and up.

What has happened in Montgomery, Alabama, in the two decades since the death of Martin Luther King, Jr.? Not much, according to this video. The city is still divided, with African Americans owning only five per cent of the businesses, having few prospects for jobs, facing growing unemployment and growing welfare rolls, and living with a disproportionate number of police in their areas. Both African Americans and whites are dissatisfied with their political leaders. Suggestions are offered for improvement, such as integration beginning at an earlier age; African American voters becoming more informed, regular, and aggressive; and desegregation being made a matter of choice rather than mandate. Well done and informative. Useful for secondary and college sociology or social problems classes.

Toni Morrison. Princeton, NJ: Distributed by Films for the Humanities and Sciences, 1994/1992. 25 min. Black and white. Preview available. Junior high and up.

Morrison discusses her writing, her inspiration, her views on American culture, the role of African American literature in America, the challenges America faces in accepting its multiculturalism, and her views of culture and race. Third in a series of conversations with African American writers. Useful for units on multiculturalism, race relations, American culture, and American authors.

Unearthing the Slave Trade. Princeton, NJ: Films for the Humanities and Sciences, 1993. Rereleased, 1994. 26 min. Color. Junior high and up.

Narrated by John Rhys-Davies. During excavation for the construction of a federal office building in New York City, a long-forgotten slave cemetery was unearthed. Work on the new building stopped amid controversy over whether to continue or to respect the burial places of former slaves. The construction was halted and the land was designated a historic landmark. The video details the unearthing of the cemetery and features maps, newspapers, drawings, contemporary photos, footage of the excavation, and interviews to relate this saga. Little attention is paid in

American history to the fact that much of New York City was built by slaves and that much of our nation's prosperity was built by slave labor. A good addition to an American history unit or African American studies unit. Originally broadcast in 1993 Series: Archaeology.

Videos: Nonfiction, not reviewed

Africa: A Musical Portrait. Media Basics Video. 56 min. Junior high and up.

Covers the music of Vangelis, Miriam Makeba, and Ladysmith Black Mambazo. Includes images of Africa from Tanzania to Mt. Kilimanjaro.

Africa: An Overview. Media Basics Video. 60 min. High school and up.

Overview of women's rights, tribal life, the AIDS epidemic, education in Zambia, the oil industry in Nigeria, and the democratic movement in Zambia.

An Evening with Sojourner Truth. Niles, IL: United Learning, 1994. 21 min. Teacher's guide. 21 pp. Junior high and up.

Dramatic presentation of the life of Sojourner Truth performed by Daisy B. Thomas-Quinnity. Includes video, teacher's guide with lesson plans, student activities, projects, discussion questions, and five Blackline Masters.

The Assassination of Martin Luther King, Jr.. Oakforest, IL: MPI Home Video, 1993. 85 min. High school and up.

Made in 1993 to commemorate the 25th anniversary of the death of Martin Luther King, Jr. Investigative report featuring news interviews with Dick Gregory, Reverend James Lawson, and Reverend Kyles.

Black American Literature. Detroit, MI: Omnigraphics, Inc., 1988. 45 min. Lecture guide available. High school and up.

Princeton professor Valerie Smith traces the history of African American literature from the 1890s to the 1930s. Covers the early African American tradition through the Harlem Renaissance.

The Black Athlete. Schoolmasters Videos, 1980. Junior high and up.

Hosted by James Mitchner. Traces the rise of African American athletes in various sports. Addresses the social, political, and economic issues, as well as the prejudice, that they have faced.

The Black Athlete in America: A Hard Road to Glory. Rochester, NY: Eastman Kodak Co., 1988. 60 min. High school and up.

Traces the careers and difficulties of African American athletes from the limited opportunities of the nineteenth century to the multimillion-dollar athletes of the present. Outlines the achievements of Jack Johnson, Jesse Owens, Joe Louis, Jackie Robinson, and others. Hosted by Arthur Ashe and narrated by James Earl Jones.

Black History: Lost, Stolen, or Strayed. BFA/Xenon Home Video, 1991/1968. 60 min. Junior high and up.

Bill Cosby narrates and examines the way in which the contributions of African Americans in the United States have been ignored, played-down, or improperly documented. Originally produced by CBS News in 1968.

Black Is My Color: The African American Experience. Bohemia, NY: Rainbow Education Video, 1993/1992. 16 min. Junior high.

The history of African Americans from slavery to the present. Colorful images and original music reveal how African Americans reacted to changes in their world, the Civil War, and the twentieth century and Civil Rights movement.

Booker T. Washington's Tuskegee America. Van Nuys, CA: Aims Media, 1981. 25 min. Junior high and up.

Story of Booker T. Washington. Study guide included. Host Hugh Downs.

Cicely Tyson is a Woman Called Moses. Santa Monica, CA: Xenon Entertainment 1992. 200 min. Junior high and up.

Featuring Cicely Tyson. Story of the woman who escaped from slavery and began the "Underground Railroad." Two video cassettes. Based on the book by Marcy Heidish.

The Civil Rights Movement. Mount Kisco, NY: Guidance Associates. 1989. 15 min. High school and up.

Interviews with Andrew Young, James Farmer, and other prominent people involved in the Civil Rights movement. VHS.

A Day to Remember August 28, 1963. Alexandria, VA. PBS Video, 1980/ 1987. 29 min. Made in 1978, color and black-and-white. Junior high and up.

Dr. King's famous "I Have a Dream" speech, plus interviews with Moe Tandler, Rep. Walter Fauntroy, and John Lewis, participants in the march on Washington.

Death of a Prophet: Malcolm X. Essenay Entertainment, 1981. 60 min. Junior high and up.

Morgan Freeman plays Malcolm X. Ossie Davis narrates this story of Malcolm X, interspersed with newsreel footage and interviews.

For Us the Living: The Story of Medgar Evans. Solar Home Video/Xenon Home Video 1992. 90 min. High school and up.

Story of the small-town insurance salesman who was instrumental in forging ahead with civil rights in Klan-supported, bigoted Jackson, Mississippi. Black History Series.

Frederick Douglass: Slavery and Prejudice. Media Basics Video. 50 min. American History Case Studies Series. High school and up.

Inspired by John F. Kennedy's *Profiles in Courage*. Story of the man who escaped from slavery, then helped others to do likewise at great risk to himself.

Free At Last. Central City Productions. Distributed by Encyclopedia Britannica Educational Corporation, 1990. 19 min. Narrated by Levar Burton. Junior high and up.

Musical tributes by Ella Jenkins and schoolchildren from around the world in memory of Martin Luther King, Jr. Guide available.

Freedom Man. Network Home Entertainment, 1989. 61 min. Junior high and up.

Story of Benjamin Banneker, patriot, writer, scientist, and engineer. Focuses on Banneker's crusade to rescue runaway slaves. Recommended by the NEA.

George Washington Carver, Botanist. Bala Cynwyd, PA: Schlessinger Video Productions, 1992. 29 min. Junior high and up.

Story of George Washington Carver, who was born into slavery and went on to become a prominent scientist. Part of the Black Americans of Achievement Video Collection.

Glory. Burbank, CA: Columbia TriStar Home Video, 1990. 122 min. High school and up.

Story of the African American soldiers who fought in the Civil War and whose courage and patriotism overcame racism, prejudice, and intolerance. Original motion picture (rated R) released in 1989.

Gordon Parks' Visions. NY: Xenon Home Video: distributed by Modern Educational Video Network. 1992/1991. 60 min. Junior high and up.

Gordon Parks tells the story of his childhood and how he grew up to be a best-selling author, award-winning photographer, composer, and director.

Gospel. Venice, CA: Bennett Video Group. 1994. Two videotapes. 120 min. Junior high and up.

Featuring the Hawkins Family and the Clark Sisters. Special tribute to a genre that is uniquely American.

Great White Hope. NY: CBS/Fox Video 1990/1970. 103 min. High school and up.

Academy Award winner. Adapted from the Pulitzer Prize–winning play by Howard Sackler. Based on the life of boxing legend Jack Johnson. Motion picture released in 1970.

A History of Slavery in America. Bala Cynwyd, PA: Schlessinger Video Productions. 1994. 30 min. High school and up.

Prominent African American history scholars discuss the history of slavery in America. Black Americans of Achievement video collection.

In Remembrance of Martin. Alexandria, VA. PBS Video. 1988. 60 min. Archival footage. High school and up.

Interviews with Coretta Scott King, Reverend Ralph Abernathy, Julian Bond, Jimmy Carter, Jesse Jackson, Edward Kennedy, Bishop Desmond Tutu, and others. Original television broadcast.

The Jackie Robinson Story. N. Hollywood, CA, Hollywood Select Video distributed by Timeless Video. 81 min. 1993/1950. Junior high and up.

Jackie Robinson plays himself in this story of his rise from the all-African American leagues to become the first African American to play major league baseball. The Black Experience Collection. Motion picture originally released in 1950.

Jazz Time Tale: The Music of Fats Walker. Van Nuys, CA: Family Home Entertainment. 1992/1991. 29 min. High school and up.

The history of jazz in New York City in 1919 and the man who made it famous. Animated story narrated by Ruby Dee.

The Jesse Owens Story. Hollywood, CA: Paramount Home Video. 1984. 194 min. High school and up.

Biography of Olympic champion Jesse Owens, the man who helped prove Hitler's theories on the inferiority of the African American race to be nonsense. Two video cassettes. Beta or VHS. Motion picture originally released in 1984.

Joe Louis—For All Time. NY: ABC Video Enterprises. 1984. 89 min. High school and up.

Documentary of the famous boxer from 1932 to 1949. 1 videocassette.

The Joe Louis Story. Xenon Home Video. 1991/1953. 88 min. Junior high and up.

Dramatized biography of boxing great Joe Louis who inspired African Americans and White Americans alike during the Great Depression. Black History Series. 1 videocassette. VHS. Original motion picture released in 1953.

King. Two volume set. Media Basics Video, 1978. High school and up.

Featuring Paul Winfield, Ossie Davis. Chronicle of the life and times of Dr. Martin Luther King, Jr. and his fight for civil rights. Contains excerpts from his most important speeches.

The Ladies Sing the Blues. New York: View Video. 1988/1986. 60 min. Junior high and up.

Footage of the women who made the blues famous—Bessie Smith, Billie Holiday, Dinah Washington, Lena Horne, Ruth Brown, and many others.

Legacy of a Dream. Chicago, IL: Films, Inc., 1989/1974. 29 min. Junior high and up.

Narrated by James Earl Jones. Examines the life and times and work in the Civil Rights movement of Dr. Martin Luther King, Jr. Originally produced by Richard Kaplan Productions.

The Life and Times of the Buffalo Soldier. Samuel Garland-Bogue, Ken Nicodemus Group, 1993. 36 min. Junior high and up.

Filmed on the actual locations where the Buffalo soldiers fought, this video traces the history of African American soldiers who fought during the Civil War.

Malcolm X. Burbank, CA: Warner Home Video. 1993/1992. 201 min. High school and up.

Spike Lee's award-winning film about the life and death of Malcolm X. Rated PG. Two VHS videocassettes.

Malcolm X. Huntsville, TX: Educational Video Network. 1988. 60 min. Junior high and up.

The life story of Malcolm X includes his boyhood in Harlem, his stint in prison, and his rise as one of the nation's most charismatic African American leaders.

Malcolm X: El Hajj Malik El Shabazz. Santa Monica, CA: United American Video, dist. by PAL Video, 1991. 60 min. High school and up.

Life of Malcolm X as seen in the 1960s. Could be useful and interesting to compare this film with one made more recently and discuss how each treats its subject.

The March on Washington Remembered. Chicago, IL: Encyclopedia Brittanica Educational Corporation. 1990. 20 min. Junior high and up.

The program highlights Dr. Martin Luther King, Jr.'s "I Have a Dream" speech on the event of the march on Washington on August 28, 1963. Interesting to contrast with the 1995 Million Man March on Washington. Guide available.

Martin Luther King Commemorative Collection. Oak Forest, IL. MPI Home Video. 1986. 115 min. Black and white and color. High school and up.

Two programs in a slip case. Celebrity interviews interspersed with footage of Dr. King's speeches and nonviolent activities. "The Speeches of Martin Luther King" includes all of his major speeches.

Martin Luther King: I Have a Dream. Oak Forest, IL. MPI Home Video. 1988. 25 min. Junior high and up.

Dr. King's famous speech given in Washington on August 28, 1963.

Separate But Equal. Film Archives, 1991. High school and up.

Sidney Poitier plays Thurgood Marshall, the NAACP lawyer who took the fight for civil rights all the way to the Supreme Court.

Voices of Sarafina. New York: New Yorker Films. 1991. 85 min. High school and up.

Director Nigel Nobel interviews cast members of the Broadway play, "Sarafina," about their experiences in South Africa. Includes scenes from the town of Sarafina and music of Mbaqanga, the street music of liberation. Videotape release of 1988 film.

We Shall Overcome. San Francisco, CA: California Newsreel: 1989. 58 min. High school and up.

This musical documentary celebrates the growth of the human rights movement all over the world.

Zora Is My Name. Beverly Hills, CA: PBS Video distributed by Pacific Arts. 1990. 90 min. High school and up.

Tribute to songwriter Zora Hurston. Theater piece starring Ruby Dee, Louis Gossett, Jr., and Paula Kelly. 1 video cassette.

✦ NATIVE AMERICANS ✦

Biographies

American Indian Leaders: Studies in Diversity. R. David Edmunds, ed. Lincoln, NE: University of Nebraska Press, 1980. 265 pp. ISBN 0–8032–6705–3. LC 80–00043. High school and up.

A collection of essays devoted to 12 Native American leaders and their methods of leadership. The studies deal with Native American political leadership within the realm of Native American–white relations, leaders who sought security for their people in accommodations or friendships with the Anglo-Americans. Useful for reports, American History units and units on Native Americans.

American Indian Warrior Chiefs: Tecumseh, Crazy Horse, Chief Joseph, Geronimo. Jason Hook. New York: Sterling Publishing Company, 1989. 192 pp. ISBN 1–85314–114–3. Junior high and up. Out of print.

Provides biography and surrounding history of four great Native American chiefs. Includes chronology of events, bibliography, and index. Useful for studies of notable Native Americans and for reports.

Arctic Schoolteacher: Kulukak, Alaska 1931–1933. Abbie Morgan Madenwald. Norman, OK: University of Oklahoma Press, 1992. Western Frontier Library Series. vol. 59. 224 pp. ISBN 0–8061–2469–5. LC 92–54129. Young adults.

Abbie Morgan Madenwald tells the story of her journey with her husband, Ed, to teach and work with the Eskimos during the depression. They endured bitter cold and severe hardship, but faced the adventure with remarkable courage, strength, and spirit. The village where they taught no longer exists, and its inhabitants have long since moved on, but this narrative brings life to a remarkable generation. Useful for units on Native Americans of the Northwest. Illustrated.

Chief Joseph. Lois Warburton. San Diego, CA: Lucent Books, 1992. The Importance of . . . Series. 112 pp. ISBN 1–56006–030–1. LC 92–28010. Junior high and up.

Life of Chief Joseph of the Nez Perce. This series is notable for its frequent quotations from primary and secondary sources such as diaries, tapes, and letters, with no fictionalized conversations. All quotes are footnoted. Each volume contains a chronology, further reading list, index, and notes. Excellent source for studies of notable Native Americans. Illustrated.

Crazy Horse. Judith St. George. New York: Putnam Publishing Group, 1994. 192 pp. ISBN 0–399–22667–2. LC 94–12329. Junior high.

St. George recounts the life and struggles of the famous Lakota chief to preserve his people's way of life during the late 1800s. Bibliography. No documentation. Consider as an additional acquisition if more material is needed.

The Deaths of Sibyl Boulton: An American History. Dennis McAuliffe. New York: Random House, 1994. 288 pp. ISBN 0–8129–2150–X. LC N/A. High school and up.

While tracing his Native American roots, McAuliffe discovered that his maternal grandmother, a beautiful, well-educated member of the oil-rich Osage tribe, was said to have committed suicide at the age of 22. He dug further into her past to uncover a shameful time in American history when Native Americans were considered incapable of managing their own affairs and frequently fell prey to dishonest lawyers. A real-life mystery. Interesting read. Useful for Native American studies.

Extraordinary American Indians. Susan Avery. Chicago: Children's Press, 1992. Extraordinary People Series. 260 pp. ISBN 0–516–00583–9. LC 92–11358. Junior high and up.

Short but thorough biographies of 60 prominent Native Americans, past and present. Excellent cross-section of talented Native Americans and their contributions. Describes seven organizations, events, or policies such as the Iroquois confederacy, Sand Creek and Wounded Knee massacres, land allotment, Navajo code talkers, the Indian Reorganization Act and citizenship, termination and self-determination, and the American Indian movement. Contains index, suggested additional readings, photographs. Useful for units on notable Native Americans. Illustrated.

Indian Lives: Essays on Nineteenth- and Twentieth-Century Native American Leaders. L. G. Moses and Raymond Wilson, eds. Albuquerque, NM:

University of New Mexico Press, 1985. 239 pp. ISBN 0–8263–0815–5. LC 85–001188. High school and up.

A biography of successful Native American men and women. Their problems varied according to historical circumstance, though each tried to create a world that allowed Native Americans to be Native Americans according to his or her particular vision. Index, bibliography, illus. Useful for studies of notable Native Americans.

The Mighty Chieftains. Volume eight. The editors of Time-Life. New York: Time-Life Books, 1993. American Indian Series. 184 pp. ISBN 0–8094–9429–9. LC 93–22395. Junior high and up.

Arranged in four chapters by region. Describes notable Native American Chieftains and what made them prominent among their respective peoples. Photo essays accompany each chapter. No chapter subheadings. No divisions. Readers must use the index to locate specific individuals. A useful reference for libraries.

Scholars, Writers, and Professionals. Jonathan W. Bolton and Claire M. Wilson. New York: Facts on File, 1994. American Indian Lives Series. 160 pp. ISBN 0–8160–2896–6. LC 93–31683. Junior high and high school.

The authors cover Native Americans from Sequoyah to contemporary scholars, writers, and professionals. Annotated bibliography, illustrations, photographs, historical drawings, and index make this a valuable reference tool. Useful for studies of notable Native Americans.

Spiritual Leaders. Paul Robert Walker. New York: Facts on File, 1994. American Indian Lives Series. 160 pp. ISBN 0–8160–2875–3. LC 93–31684. Junior high and high school.

The author introduces a number of Native Americans who were and are important to the Native American religious experience and provides an introductory overview of Native American spirituality. Annotated bibliography, illustrations, photographs, historical drawings, and index make this a valuable reference tool.

Tecumseh: Shawnee Rebel. Robert Cwiklik. New York: Chelsea House Publishers, 1994. North American Indians of Achievement Series. 112 pp. ISBN 0–7910–1721–4. LC 92–21656. Junior high and up.

Tecumseh lead the Shawnee people from 1795 to 1813. He was widely respected as a leader, counselor, arbitrator, and military man. His people lost their land to greedy whites moving westward, not because of any lack of ability on Tecumseh's part. Black-and-white period prints with short explanatory paragraphs. Good addition to school and public libraries.

Folklore, Literature, Poetry

All Roads are Good: Native Voices on Life and Culture. Washington, DC: Smithsonian Institution Press, 1994. 224 pp. ISBN 1–56098–451–1. (Paper: ISBN 1–56098–452–X.) LC 94–8236. High school and up.

Published in conjunction with the Smithsonian's opening of the National Museum of the American Indian. A collection of 23 essays by Native Americans who selected more than 300 objects displayed in the museum. Photographs of these objects accompany the text. Of use in research and units on Native American studies. Foreword by W. Richard West. Preface by Clara S. Kidwell.

Messengers of the Wind. Jane Katz, ed. New York: Ballantine Books, 1995. 352 pp. ISBN 0–345–39060–1. LC 94–21938. High school and up.

Katz has collected the writings of Native American women, most of whom are unknown outside their own tribes. They write of their history, their customs, and their desire for the independence that conflicts with the tribe's traditional values. A moving collection and look into the hearts of Native American women. Good addition to any high school or public library.

Navajo: Visions and Voices. Shonto Begay. New York: Scholastic, Inc., 1995. 48 pp. ISBN 0–590–46153–2. LC 93–31610. Junior high and high school.

The author uses original paintings and poetry to present his own view of Navajo life. His poetry speaks of the ongoing struggles involved in living in a dual society. He covers the spiritual aspects of Navajo life along with continuing life and rebirth. Honest and straightforward. Excellent expression of the complexity of Navajo life. Useful for Native American studies.

Rising Voices: Writings of Young Native Americans. Edited by Beverly R. Singer. New York: Simon and Schuster Children's, 1992. 115 pp. ISBN 0–684–19207–1. LC 91–32083. Junior high and up.

The writings of young Native Americans spanning over 100 years—from 1887 to 1990—speak of loss of cultural identity, hope, survival, and continuance, problems the young have faced in the United States. The book is divided into six sections: Identity, Family, Homelands, Ritual and Ceremony, Education, and Harsh Realities. Excellent resource for English and social studies classes or Native American collections.

Fiction for Young Adults

Bone Game: A Novel. Louis Owens. Norman, OK: University of Oklahoma Press, 1994. American Indian Literature and Critical Studies, vol. 10. 243 pp. ISBN 0–8061–2664–7. LC 94–013882. High school and up.

Professor Cole McCurtain teaches Choctaw-Cherokee-Irish-Cajun Indian Studies in Santa Cruz, California. Recently, he's been having nightmares about a priest who was murdered in 1812 by the Native Americans he abused and about a gambler, painted half white and half black, tied to bodies which wash up on the Pacific beach. He is aided by a Navajo colleague, his college-age daughter, his father, his great Uncle, and a medicine woman from Choctaw county to decipher this puzzle of past and present intersecting.

The Brave. Robert Lipsyte. New York: HarperCollins, 1991. 208 pp. ISBN 0–06–023915–8. (Paper: LC 90–025396.) Junior high and up.

Sonny Bear learned to fight when he lived on the reservation, and this ability stood him in good stead. Now he lives in New York City. His inclinations to settle things with violence could lead him into serious trouble.

The Chief. Robert Lipsyte. New York: HarperCollins, 1993. 240 pp. ISBN 0–06–021064–8. LC 92–54502. Junior high and high school.

The somewhat uneven sequel to *The Contender* and *The Brave*, *The Chief* tells of a friendship between Marty Malcom Witherspoon, a young African American man, and Sonny Bear, a half–Native American boxer. Native American politics are somewhat muddled in this story, and the plot centers on how Sonny Bear can use his fame to help his people, the Moscondaga Nation. Told from Marty's point of view.

Child of the Dead. Don Coldsmith. New York: Doubleday, 1995. 256 pp. ISBN 0–385–47029–0. LC 94–25680. Young adults.

Running Deer's husband has died an honorable death and she wishes to join him. She leaves her people to be with Grey Mouse, the only child to survive the epidemic of smallpox which wiped out her tribe. Instead of sickening and dying, Running Deer and Grey Mouse survive and return to Running Deer's people. Ten years later, Grey Mouse returns to her own land to discover if anyone knew her extended family and to find out who she really is. Slow start. Moves quickly after that. Strong characters.

A Circle Unbroken. Sollace Hotze. Boston: Houghton Mifflin Company, 1991. 244 pp. ISBN 0–395–59702–1. LC 88–2569. Junior high and up.

Rachel Porter is captured by the Oglala Souix as a small child and raised as Dakota. She has all but forgotten her life as a white person when, at the age of 17, she is captured by hunters hired by her father, a minister, to find her and bring her home. As far as Rachel, now known as Kata Wi, is concerned, she IS home. The adjustment from Dakota to white woman is very difficult, especially since she has left behind a husband and baby. Rachel tries to adjust to her new life, but eventually she returns to the Oglala Souix and to the husband and baby she loves.

The Crying for a Vision. Walter Wangerin, Jr. New York: Simon and Schuster, 1994. 279 pp. ISBN 0–671–79911–8. LC 93–48589. Junior high and up.

Mystical story of Waskn Mani, a Lakota boy who is a dreamer and a gentle soul and who does not care for hunting and making war as do his tribesmen. He embarks on a quest to find his missing mother and confronts Fire Thunder, the Lakota leader who may have had something to do with her disappearance. Rich with heavy use of Lakota language, symbolism, and lore. Glossary of Lakota word meanings.

Dakota Dream. James Bennett. New York: Scholastic, 1994. 144 pp. ISBN 0–590–46680–1. LC 93–17854. Junior high and up.

Charley Black Crow is known as Floyd Rayfield at the group home where he has been placed. When Charley decides to become a warrior and seek his vision, the authorities decide that he needs psychiatric help. A dream tells him he will become a warrior, so he runs away to the Dakota reservation, where he embarks on the hamblecheya, the fasting and vision quest. He completes the test with a better understanding of himself and of the bureaucracy which has mishandled him from the start.

Dakota Scouts. Flynn J. Ell. New York: Walker and Company, 1992. 192 pp. ISBN 0–8027–4130–4. LC 91–45384. High school and up.

Ell blends the elements of settlers in the newly opened Dakota territory and the Sioux who have lived there for centuries. John Benson, a scout for the Seventh Cavalry, wants to build his own ranch when the territory is settled and peaceful, while Lone Bear, a Souix warrior and scout, wants enough wealth to marry Little Moon. The two hate and fear each other's people, but have great respect for each other in this story about colliding cultures.

Dawn Land. Joseph Bruchac. Golden, CO: Fulcrum Publishing, 1993. 336 pp. ISBN 1–55591–134–X. LC 92–54767. High school and up.

Young Hunter, a young Abenaki living in the Adirondack Mountains, is chosen to go on a quest for wisdom and power to prevent outside forces from destroying the world. He meets flesh-eating giants, friends, enemies, and counselors with words of wisdom. The story is told with the cadence of oral tradition and deftly includes details of the Native American beliefs, traditions, and values.

For Love of Two Eagles. Barbara Riefe. New York: Forge, 1996. 384 pp. ISBN 0–614–05509–1. LC 94–46578. High school and up.

Sequel to *The Woman Who Fell From the Sky*. A tender love story bridging two cultures. Margaret had come to Boston to enter a prearranged marriage when she met and married Oneida Chief Two Eagles. Margaret continues her adjustment to life with Two Eagles. Although they are very much in love and she has borne Two Eagles a child, not everyone in the tribe accepts her. As the story opens, Margaret's father has hired an English missionary to find her and bring her home, using force if necessary. He finds her and tells her lies about Two Eagles to get her to come home to her white family. Descriptions of torture are graphic. Complicated plot. For more mature readers.

Grandfather. Tom Brown, Jr. New York: Berkeley Publishing Group, 1993. 208 pp. ISBN 0–425–13804–6. High school and up.

An Apache grandfather imparts the wisdom of his years and culture to his grandson. He exhorts the boy to forswear materialism and waste and respect the earth that gives us sustenance. The old man is still searching for ways for mankind to live in harmony with nature rather than battling with it.

In the Time of the Wolves. Eileen Charbonneau. New York: TorBooks, 1994. 192 pp. ISBN 0–812–53361–5. LC N/A. Junior high and up.

Fourteen-year-old twins Joshua and Susannah Woods are not identical. Joshua looks more like their Dutch-English mother while Susannah favors their French-Native American father. Joshua wants desperately to be white, not a "mixed breed," and to be independent from his mixed family. He nearly betrays his father to achieve this. It is a classic coming-of-age, finding one's self story set in 1825, "the year without a summer."

The Ledgerbook of Thomas Blue Eagle. Jewel H. Grutman and Gay Matthae. Charlottesville, VA: Thomasson Grant, 1995. 72 pp. ISBN 1–56566–063–3. LC 94–8966. Junior high and up.

Without the fictional disclaimer in the back, this book could well be mistaken for the real journal of a Native American boy at the Carlisle Indian School during the late nineteenth century. Thomas struggles to learn the white man's ways without losing his own culture. The pages and illustrations by Adam Civijan-Orle are convincingly aged and the research is impeccable except for a somewhat fantastic episode obviously derived from Lakota legend. Lacks cohesion in places. Interesting read.

The Light in the Forest. Conrad Richter. Cutchogue, NY: Buccaneer Books, Inc., 1991. ISBN 1–56849–064–X. LC N/A. Junior high.

John Cameron Butler was stolen as small child and raised by the Leni Lenape tribe. He grows to manhood accepting his adoptive family's ways and culture only to be thrust unwillingly back into the white man's world when a treaty demands the return of all captives. John does not consider himself a captive; he considers himself a Leni Lenape. The story deals with his difficult reassimilation. Made into a Disney movie in the 1950s.

Navajo Long Walk. Nancy. M. Armstrong. Niwot, CO: Roberts Rhinehart Publishers, Inc., 1994. Council for Indian Education Series. 100 pp. ISBN 1–879373–56–4. Junior high.

The story of the relocation of the Navajos in 1864 and their subsequent return to the lands that became their reservation is told through the eyes of young Kee and his family. The author tells of the forced surrender, the difficult and arduous journey, the lack of food and shelter, disease, homesickness, and deaths by starvation. This work has had mixed reviews. One source considers it heavy-handed, insensitive, and badly flawed; another was neutral. Yet this work is part of the Council for Indian Education Series and was selected and approved by the Indian Editorial Board for use with Native American children. The reader will have to evaluate this work carefully before including it in a collection or reading list. Illustrations by Paula Livers-Lambert.

Pigs in Heaven. Barbara Kingsolver. New York: HarperCollins Publishers, Inc., 1993. 352 pp. ISBN 0–06–092253–2. LC 92–45739. Junior high and up. Reprint.

Taylor finds her orderly life interrupted when a Cherokee lawyer, Annawake Fourkiller, comes to claim Taylor's illegally adopted child, Turtle. Taylor flees with Turtle to avoid having to give up her daughter. After a long chase and Taylor's mother going to stay with a cousin in Heaven, Oklahoma, Taylor and Turtle return to the reservation to decide Turtle's future. Rich with details of Cherokee customs and life.

The Reindeer Hunters: A Prehistoric Novel of Passion and Adventure.
Joan Wolf. New York: NAL Dutton, 1994. 352 pp. ISBN 0–525–93048–6. LC
94–14437. High school and up.

Reminiscent of Jean Auel's books. Wolf sets her story in the prehistoric time of the
Cro-Magnons living in the Pyrenees. A number of warring peoples make peace in
order to defend themselves against outside tribes. When a fierce band of "proto-
Britons" arrives, they eventually accept the outsiders as worthy warriors and useful
new blood.

The Shaman's Knife. Scott Young. New York: Viking Penguin, 1994. 288 pp.
ISBN 0–14–014353–X. LC 92–29873. Junior high and up.

Vivid details of Eskimo culture, religions, lifestyle, psychology, and relationships
enrich this mystery set primarily in the Northwest Territories of Canada. Matteesie
is a full-blooded Inuit police inspector who, during the course of investigating the
murder of a Native American teenager and his mother, finds out that his own 90-
year-old mother was injured in the same attack.

Speciman Song. Peter Bowen. New York: St. Martin's Press, Inc., 1995. 208 pp.
ISBN 0–312–11896–1. LC 94–045770. Junior high and up.

Sheriff Deputy Gabriel Du Pré, a Metis, is generally employed as a cattle inspector.
But, sometimes, he gets involved in a murder investigation. When a young Cree
woman and several other Native Americans are killed during a folk festival on the
Mall in Washington, D.C., Du Pré is on the trail.

Sweetbitter. Reginald Gibbons. Seattle, WA: Broken Moon, 1994. 440 pp. ISBN
0–913089–6. LC 94–71680. High school and up.

Reuben Saved Sweetbitter, half white, half Choctaw, is orphaned when his Choctaw
mother dies. He is taken in and raised by an old African American woman who
gives him his name. Reuben falls in love with Martha, the daughter of a prominent
white lawyer and, as might be expected, trouble ensues. Reuben muses that there
are simply "too many worlds." An absorbing read.

Thunder Rolling in the Mountains. Scott O'Dell. New York: Houghton
Mifflin Company, 1992. ISBN 0–395–59966–0. LC 91–15961. Junior high.

Historical fiction account of the tragedy of the Nez Perce. Told from the point of
view of Chief Joseph's daughter as the U.S. Army betrays and attacks the tribe as
they prepare themselves to leave the reservation.

Toning the Sweep: A Novel. Angela Johnson. New York: Orchard Books, 1993. 112 pp. ISBN 0–531–05476–4. LC 92–34062. Junior high.

Emily's grandmother Ola is dying of cancer and coming to Cleveland to be in the hospital close to her family. Emily borrows a video camera and interviews family members on tape to give a gift of "memories of her people" to her grandmother. Emily's close friend, Native American David Two Star, helps Emily accept her grandmother's impending death. Emily and her mother share in the ritual of "toning the sweep," a variation on ringing the dead to heaven. Powerful and affecting.

Vanishing Act. Thomas Perry. New York: Random House, Inc., 1994. 304 pp. ISBN 0–679–43536–0. LC 94–017413. Junior high and up.

Native American Jane Whitefield specializes in helping people disappear. Some of her clients include a battered wife seeking shelter from her abusive husband, a card shark who has fleeced one too many victims, a young boy wanting relief from a bitter custody battle, and Felker, an accused embezzler. Jane soon finds herself romantically involved with Felker. But his story begins to fall apart as she investigates further. Jane sets out to find out the truth and finds violence.

Wolf-Woman. Sherryl Jordan. New York: Houghton Mifflin Company, 1994. 168 pp. ISBN 0–395–70932–6. LC 94–7043. Junior high.

Black-haired, dark-eyed, 16-year-old Tanith was raised by wolves and later adopted by Chief Ahearn. She is very noticeable and regarded with suspicion in his light-haired tribe. Though Tanith loves wolves and is comforted by them, her adoptive tribe hates and fears them. When Ahearn is wounded and unable to function as chief and lead his tribe, Tanith must choose between her adoptive tribe, a young warrior of a neighboring tribe, and her wolf pack. Original title: *Tanith*.

Reference and Scholarly Works

The American Indian Index: A Directory of Indian Country, U.S.A.
Gregory W. Frazier; Randolph J. Punley, ed. Englewood, CO: Arrowstar Publishing, 1985. 325 pp. ISBN 0–935151–39–7. LC 85–020155. High school and up; professional use.

This is a classified list of organizations serving Native Americans at all levels—the only comprehensive one in print. Compiled primarily from official sources, it covers tribes recognized by the Bureau of Indian Affairs, "unrecognized" tribes, Native American interest organizations, government offices (federal and state), education, housing, employment, social service (both reservation-based and urban-based), publications, museums, major pow-wows, and arts and crafts traders. Although the table of contents lists all the categories and subcategories used, there is no index, making it difficult to use unless one knows what agency does which work and in which state it is located. No reviews found. Useful for school counselors, Native Americans interested in these activities and services, and those who work with Native Americans.

American Indian Novelists: An Annotated Critical Bibliography. Tom Colonnese and Louis Owens. New York: Garland, 1985. 161 pp. ISBN 0–8240–9199–X. LC 82–49135. High school and up. Out of print.

Twenty-one authors are included. Arranged alphabetically with a biographical sketch for each author as well as listings of primary and secondary sources. Author/ title index. Useful for Native American studies.

American Indian Reference Book for Children and Young Adults. Barbara J. Kuipers. Englewood, NJ: Libraries Unlimited, 1991. Data Book Series. 176 pp. ISBN 0–87287–745–0. LC 91–6880. All ages.

Contains general reference material on Native Americans on a level suitable for children and young adults. Good to introduce units on Native Americans; also a good starting place for reports.

Atlas of the North American Indian. Carl Waldman. New York: Facts on File, 1985. 288 pp. ISBN 0–87196–850–9. LC 83–9020. Junior high and up.

Provides sound introduction to seven broad topics: Ancient Indians, Ancient Civilizations, Indian Lifeways, Indians and Explorers, Indian Wars, Indian Land Cessions, and Contemporary Indians. Includes more than 100 maps; also includes illustrations, bibliography, and an index. Useful for units on Native Americans. Good addition to school and public libraries. Illustrated by Molly Brown.

A Concise Dictionary of Indian Tribes of North America, Second Edition. Barbara A. Leitch. Edited by Keith Irvine. Algonac, MI: Reference Publications, Inc., 1991. 646 pp. ISBN 0–917256–48–4. LC 90-36256. High school and up.

Aims to present knowledge on specific ethnic groups in a systematic and accessible form. Seeks to eliminate the barrier of specialists' jargon. Comprehensive index contains about 8,500 entries; also includes photographs and regional maps. Useful for reports; also a good addition for school and public libraries.

Contemporary Native American Literature: A Selected and Partially Annotated Bibliography. Angeline Jacobson. Metuchen, NJ: Scarecrow Press, Inc., 1977. 262 pp. ISBN 0–8108–1031–X. LC 77–5614. High school and up.

Brings together the literary works of Native American authors who have written and published from 1960 to mid-1976. Index to single poems and author index. Useful source of information for reports and units on Native American writings.

Dictionary of Indian Tribes of the Americas, second edition. Newport Beach, CA: American Indian Publishers, Inc., 1981. 3 volumes. 2000 pp. ISBN 0–937862–25–8. LC 93–008019. Junior high and up.

Alphabetical listing and information on Native American tribes in the Americas. Consider as an additional source of information in school and public libraries.

Dictionary of Indians of North America. Edited by Harry Waldeman. St. Clair Shores, MI: Scholarly Press, Inc., 1978. 330 pp. ISBN 0–403–01799–8. High school and up.

An alphabetical collection of biographies of Native Americans from Columbus to the present in three volumes. Somewhat dated, but still in print. Consider more up-to-date information first. Three volume set.

Dictionary of Native American Mythology. Sam D. Gill and Irene F. Sullivan. Santa Barbara, CA: ABC–Clio, Inc., 1992. 425 pp. ISBN 0–87436–621–6. LC 92–27053. Junior high and up.

This dictionary has 1,300 entries covering Native American mythology from over 100 tribes. Contains maps, an extensive index, photos, and a bibliography. Information is thorough and easily accessible. Useful for mythology units and Native American studies. A good addition to any library.

Encyclopedia of Native American Religions. Arlene Hirschfelder and Paulette Molin. New York: Facts on File, 1992. 367 pp. ISBN 0–8160–2017–5. LC 91–21145. Young adults.

Easy to read, in-depth survey on Native American religions. This volume has over 1,200 entries on Native American beliefs, major religious systems, ceremonies, sacred objects, leaders, societies, and more. Includes black-and-white photos, charts, and an extensive bibliography. Useful for Native American studies and comparative religion classes. A welcome addition to any collection.

Encyclopedia of Native American Tribes. Carl Waldman. New York: Facts on File, 1987. 308 pp. ISBN 0–8160–1421–3. LC 86–29066. High school and up.

Contains concise yet wide-ranging information for general readers on the culture and history of more than 150 tribes in North America (i.e., U.S.A., Canada, and Mexico). Articles are alphabetically arranged, covering tribes, peoples, and culture areas. Cross-references abound, leading the reader from individual tribes to cultural area and language. Entries cover tribal or cultural name, history, housing, areas lived in, migrations, early relations with colonists, wars, and current language families. Text is clear and succinct. Watercolor illustrations by Molly Brown show tools, sculpture, and an index. Excellent for Native American studies. Good addition to any library.

Great Documents in American Indian History. Wayne Moquin and Charles Van Doren, eds. New York: DaCapo Press, 1995. 458 pp. ISBN 0–306–80659–2. LC 95–20373. High school and up.

An interesting compendium of speeches and writings presenting a survey of Native American life and history from the perspectives of Native Americans from tribes throughout the United States. The book is divided into three sections: (1) general depiction of life within the tribal communities; (2) views of the confrontations with whites over land; and (3) discussions of some of the twentieth-century issues. Each section is preceded by short quotations from non-Native Americans of each era described. This gives the reader a fascinating overview of how Native Americans were seen by non-Natives. Indexed by tribe and author, the only drawback to this volume is that for pre-twentieth century speeches, the editors had to rely on translations done previously by white men so that the accuracy of the account may be suspect. Useful for units on Native Americans and American history units. Illustrated.

Handbook of the American Frontier: Four Centuries of Indian-White Relationships: The Southeastern Woodlands. J. Norman Heard. Metuchen, NJ: Scarecrow Press, Inc., 1987. 421 pp. ISBN 0–8108–1931–7. LC 86–020326. High school and up.

Reference material on Native American and non-Native American relationships. Includes topics such as Native American tribes, Native American leaders, frontier settlers, captives, explorers, missionaries, and mountain men. Will contain five volumes when completed—each covering a different area. Volume I covers the Southeastern Woodlands. Volume II covers the Northeast. Volume III covers the

Great Plains. Volume IV covers the Southwest and Pacific Coast and Volume V includes a comprehensive index, chronology, and bibliography. Entries are listed alphabetically and articles are brief. Useful for units on Native Americans.

Handbook of North American Indians, Volume Five: Arctic. Davis Damas and William C. Sturtevant, eds. New York: Gordon Press Publishers, 1995. 829 pp. ISBN 0–8490–6531–3. LC N/A. High school and up.

Authors of these 59 essays are the top scholars in their fields. Provides an overview of Arctic culture as well as a historical overview of ethnographic and archeological research work. Includes an excellent 77-page bibliography. Lists publications in all the languages in which Arctic researchers have published. Photographs, index. More up-to-date material is available. Useful for research. Three volume set.

Nations Within a Nation: Historical Statistics of American Indians. Paul Stuart. Westport, CT: Greenwood Publishing Group, 1987. 261 pp. ISBN 0–313–23813–8. LC 86–33618. College; professional use.

A well presented and easy-to-use source for a variety of statistics. Eight chapters cover such topics as land holdings, population, health care, eduction, employment, income, and economic development. Each chapter begins with a good overview of the topic and a discussion of the statistical charts presented. Includes an index and bibliography. Good source for research and serious Native American studies.

Native American Almanac: Portrait of Native America Today. Arlene Hirschfelder and Martha K. DeMontano. New York: Prentice Hall, 1993. 320 pp. ISBN 0–671–85012–1. LC 93–001057. High school and up.

This book is divided into 15 sections with five appendixes, a bibliography, and an index. The sections include Historical Overview of Relations Between Native Americans and Whites; Native Americans Today; Supreme Court Decisions Affecting Native Americans; Treaties; Bureau of Indian Affairs/Indian Health Services; Artists; Film and Video Art; Tribal Governments; Languages; Education; Religion; Games and Sports; Voices of Communication; Employment; Income; Economic Development; and Native Americans and Military Service. Appendixes include Native American Tribes by State; Reservations, Rancheras, Colonies, and Historic Indian Areas; Chronicle of Treaties; Native Landmarks; and Chronology. Gives an excellent overall view of Native Americans today. Good addition to high school, college, and public libraries.

Native American Directory: Alaska, Canada, United States. Fred Snyder, ed. Arizona: National Native American Co-operative, 1994. 366 pp. ISBN 0–9610334–0–1. High school and up; professional use.

A comprehensive directory written on Native Americans and their events and organizations. Also a guide for acquiring native art forms through galleries, Native American stores, and trading posts. Reserve land information, tribal band names, population, schools, newspapers, and periodicals are also provided. Useful for school and public libraries and librarians.

Native American Voluntary Organizations. Armand S. La Potin. Westport, CT: Greenwood Publishing Group, 1987. 204 pp. ISBN 0–313–23633–X. LC 86–025764. High school and up, professional use.

This book provides an alphabetical listing of voluntary organizations operated by and for Native Americans, spawned by their move toward personal and cultural awareness. Useful for high school and university counselors and Native American studies. Good addition to any library.

The Native Tribes of North America: A Concise Encyclopedia. Michael Johnson. New York: Macmillan, 1994. 210 pp. ISBN 0–02–897189. LC 93–23429. High school and up.

Originally published in Great Britain, this book examines Native American tribes indigenous to north of the Rio Grande. Johnson divides these peoples into ten cultural and geographical groups, then by language family. The better-known tribes have longer entries, while the entries about the lesser-known tribes are very short. Johnson provides maps outlining the distribution of the tribes by linguistic family before 1900. Volume contains a full-color section on culture, habitation, tribal rites, transportation, and costume along with a section of black-and-white photographs from the 1800s to the present. The book also features illustrations, maps, charts, a bibliography, glossary, and index. Useful for studies on Native Americans.

Reference Encyclopedia of the American Indian, 1995, sixth edition. Volume 1. Barry T. Klein, ed. West Nyack, NY: Klein Publications, 1995. 1000 pp. ISBN 0–685–59688–5. LC N/A. High school and up; professional use.

Organized by category and arranged alphabetically or alpha-geographically. Essential quick reference tool for any aspect of Native American affairs.

Who Was Who in Native American History: Indians and Non–Indians from First Contacts through 1900. ed. Carl Waldman. New York: Facts on File, 1989. 416 pp. ISBN 0–8160–1797–2. High school and up.

Clear, concise dictionary-style listing of Native Americans and non-Native American individuals in the United States and Canada with short discussions of each person's role in history. Includes an appendix with Native Americans listed by tribe and non-Native Americans listed by most relevant contributions to Native American history (i.e., explorer or photographer). Excellent for research and Native American studies. Good addition to school and public libraries. Illustrated.

Nonfiction

The Aggressions of Civilization: Federal Indian Policy Since the 1880's. Sandra L. Cadwalader and Vine Deloria, Jr., eds. Philadelphia: Temple University Press, 1984. 258 pp. ISBN 0–87722–349–1. LC 84–94. High school and up. Out of print.

An interesting monograph dealing with the legal issues that white men have assumed would disappear if only ignored long enough. Chapters on the Indian Rights Association, reformers, policies, tribal claims, litigation, and Native American land rights. Includes an index and bibliography. Primarily of interest for research.

America's Ancient Treasures: A Guide to Archeological Sites and Museums in the United States and Canada, third revised edition. Franklin Folsom and Mary Etting Folsom. 4th edition revised. Albuquerque, NM: University of New Mexico Press, 1993. 485 pp. ISBN 0–8263–1424–4. LC 92–032120. High school and up.

Gives voice to a few of the millions of people who once were a part of the life on this land. Divided into geographical subareas. Includes photographs and line drawings by Rachel Folsom. Includes a list of visitable archeological sites, glossary, suggested readings, and an index. Primarily useful for research.

American Heritage Book of Indians. William Brandon. Alvin M. Josephy, Jr., ed. New York: Random House, 1988. 424 pp. ISBN 0–8281–0301–1. LC 61–14871. Junior high and up.

Contains broad-based information on the culture and history of Native Americans for general readers; with an introduction by John F. Kennedy. Contains maps and an index. Useful for reports and units on Native American studies.

American Indian Language and Literature. Compiled by Jack W. Marken. Wheeling, WV: Harlan Davidson, Inc., 1978. Goldentree Bibliographics Series in

Language and Literature. 205 pp. ISBN 0–88295–553–5. LC 76–4624. High school and up.

Bibliography intended for anyone interested in material in the areas of languages and literature of Native Americans. Organized geographically. Includes an excellent index.

American Indian Voices. Karen Harvey, ed. Brookfield, CT: Millbrook Press, Inc., 1995. Writers of America Series. 144 pp. ISBN 1–56294–382–0. LC 94–21418. Junior high and high school.

The author describes the cultures and experiences of Native Americans and provides an introduction giving the cultural and literary traditons and dominant themes of the cultures. The collection contains poetry, prose, chants, speeches, and stories of Native American authors. Contains source notes and a bibliography. Valuable addition to library or classroom collections.

The American Indians. New York: Time-Life Books, 1992–. Nineteen volumes. 176 pp. each. High school and up.

This set covers Native Americans from their arrival on this continent to the present. Each volume addresses a different geographical area, customs, lifestyle, and culture of the numerous tribes that have and still do populate the North American continent. Free teacher's guide with each volume. Write publisher for additional information on each volume.

American Indians of the Southwest. Bertha P. Dutton. Albuquerque, NM: University of New Mexico Press, 1983. 317 pp. ISBN 0–8263–0704–3. LC 80–052274. Junior high and up.

A readable book on life in various Native American tribes of the southwest. The author shows how each tribe adapted to its unique environment and has a unique lifestyle. Includes an index, appendixes, and an extensive bibliography. Useful for units about Native Americans and for reports.

The Anasazi. Eleanor H. Ayer. New York: Walker and Company, 1993. 162 pp. ISBN 0–8027–8184–5. LC 92–14701. Junior high.

Ayer covers what is known of the Anasazi from their earliest days as basket makers to their time in the pueblos. What she cannot substantiate, she surmises. She includes a roster of Anasazi sites and a scattering of black-and-white photographs. Useful for whole language units.

Archaeology of the Lower Ohio River Valley. Jon Muller. Orlando, FL: Academic Press, 1986. New World Archaeological Record Series. 307 pp. ISBN 0–12–510331–X. LC 85–015050. High school and up.

Excellent source for information on the Mound Builders. Describes the archaeology of the region. Chapters each treat different periods of development beginning with the first human settlement before 10,000 B.C. and continuing up to the time of early European intrusions into the region. Includes an index, bibliography, tables, graphs, and illustrations. Good addition to high school or public libraries.

Bury My Heart at Wounded Knee: An Indian History of the American West. Dee Alexander Brown. New York: Henry Holt and Company, 1991. 512 pp. ISBN 0–8050–1730–5. LC 70–121633. High school and up.

A history of the European Americans' interaction with and exploitation of Native Americans in their colonization of the United States. The story is told from the perspective of Native Americans and culminates in their final defeat at Wounded Knee. Useful for American history units and Native American studies.

Creation's Journey: Native American Identity and Belief. Tom Hill and Richard W. Hill, Sr., eds. Washington, DC: Smithsonian Institute, 1994. 256 pp. ISBN 1–56098–453–8. LC 94–004757. Junior high and up.

The editors show the importance of Native American art in the everyday lives of its creators. Spiritual belief and ritual are important to each object. Mistakes, gaps, and misconceptions perpetuated by white ethnographers are addressed and corrected. Contains an index and illustrations. Of interest to art students and Native American studies.

Cycles of Life. New York: Time-Life Incorporated, 1994. American Indian Series. 184 pp. ISBN 0–8094–9583–X. LC 93–27327. Junior high and up.

Best of the American Indian Series to date. Well researched and thorough. This volume addresses the "cycles of life," or rites and rituals, of various tribes, especially those west of the Mississippi River. Some of the tribes addressed are the Apache, Hopi, Blackfeet, InNuit, Navajo, Sioux, Cheyenne, Tlingit, Cherokee, and Pueblo. Includes numerous black-and-white photos with good captions, several photo essays, a fine bibliography, and a thorough index. Excellent addition for a unit or collection on Native Americans.

The First Americans. Juan Schobinger. Grand Rapids, MI: William B. Eardman's Publishing Company, 1994. 190 pp. ISBN 0–8028–3766–2. LC 94–22543. High school and up.

Schobinger does an excellent job of describing the peoples native to South America and to the North American southwest. In describing each area's geography, geology, and climate, he makes the reader understand the importance of environment to culture and its influence on daily life, religion, art, and customs. Useful for units on Native Americans.

The First Americans: Photographs from the Library of Congress. Text by William H. Goetzman. Washington, DC: Golden, Fulcrum Publishing, Inc., 1991. 144 pp. ISBN 0–912–347–96–1. LC 91–12662. Junior high and up.

This beautiful photograph collection is divided into seven sections: Prologue: They Called Them Indians, Ceremonies, At Home, Crafts, Warriors, Portraits, and Epilogue. The volume contains a few color prints and many black-and-white photographs dating from the late 1800s to the present. There is no table of contents, making finding a desired area difficult, but the volume does contain a list of sources and an index as well as a list of LC numbers for the photographs. Consider for school and public libraries if more material on Native Americans is needed.

The First Americans: Then and Now. William H. Hodge. Fort Worth, TX: Harcourt, Brace Jovanovich College Publishers, 1981. 551 pp. ISBN 0–03–056721–1. LC 80–022310. High school and up.

Describes the life of 13 Native American groups as they were before and after white domination. Gives a New World prehistory which traces the development of Native Americans in the western hemisphere. The basic approach is a "then and now" description of these groups, ranging from the Eskimo of the north to the Navajos of the southwest. Contains references, black-and-white photographs, and maps. Useful for units on Native Americans.

First Houses: Native American Homes and Sacred Structures. Jean Ray A. Williamson and Guard Monroe. New York: Houghton Mifflin Company, 1993. 160 pp. ISBN 0–395–51081–3. LC 92–34900. Junior high.

The author blends fact with myth to describe the design and construction of traditional Native American dwellings. Some of the well-documented descriptions include the Navajo hogan, the Plains tipi, the Pueblo kiva, the Iroquois long house, and the Pawnee earth lodge. Particular attention is given to the sweat lodge and its religious and spiritual importance. Not suitable for reading from cover to cover. This book is best used for research or material for reports. Contains an excellent bibliography, glossary, further reading list and detailed descriptions. Good for social studies units. Illustrations.

Five Hundred Nations: An Illustrated History of North American Indians. Alvin M. Josephy. New York: Knopf, 1994. 468 pp. ISBN 0–679–42930–1. LC 94–29695. Junior high and up.

Companion to the television documentary by the same title. Josephy traces the history of North American Indians from the times of the earliest records through European expansion in the New World to the present. He does not dwell on particular tribes, but presents a panoramic view of Native Americans in general. Useful as an introduction to a unit about Native Americans.

Fourteen Families in Pueblo Pottery. Rick Dillingham. Albuquerque, NM: University of New Mexico Press, 1994. 308 pp. ISBN 0–8263–1498–8. (Paper: ISBN 0–8263–1499–6.) LC 93–028021. High school and up.

Follow-up to *Seven Families in Pueblo Pottery*, published in 1974. The author traces the genealogy of 14 families from seven pueblos. Each family's pottery is unique and eloquently expresses differences in style and perspective among the same generations. Illustrated. Of interest to art and pottery students. Useful for Native American studies. Foreword by J.J. Brody.

The Gift of Changing Woman. Tryntje Van Ness Seymour. New York: Henry Holt and Company, 1993. 40 pp. ISBN 0–8050–2577–4. LC 92–31833. Junior high and up.

When Apache girls reach puberty, they undergo a four-day ceremony called the "Changing Woman Ceremony." The first two days are private, but the public is allowed to witness the last two days. Seymour describes these two public days in a way that gives the reader a fuller understanding of this important event in a young woman's life. Source notes are included, along with full-color reproductions of paintings by ten Apache artists depicting the event. Good for Native American studies and women's studies.

The Girl Who Married the Moon: Stories from Native North American Culture. Joseph Bruchac and Gayle Rose. Mahwah, NJ: Bridgewater Books, 1994. 128 pp. ISBN 0–8167–3480–1. LC 93–043824. Junior high.

Companion volume to Bruchac's *Flying with the Eagle; Racing with the Great Bear*. Anthology of sixteen stories representing all areas of North America, focusing on the role of Native American women, rites of passage, pourquoi stories, and caution-ary tales. Striking black-and-white drawings. Background information. Acknowl-edgments for some of the stories as a source list. Useful for folk tales units, Native American units.

Great North American Indians: Profiles in Life and Leadership.
Frederick J. Dockstader. New York: Reinhold, 1977. 386 pp. ISBN 0–442–02148–8. LC 77–23733. High school and up. Out of print.

Biographical sketches of Native American individuals and major Native American figures. Historical summaries, personal accounts, and biographical notes. Portraits where available. Index. Bibliography for further reading. Useful for studies on notable Native Americans of the past.

Handbook of Indian Foods and Fibers of Arid America. Walter Ebeling. Berkeley, CA: University of California Press, 1986. 971 pp. ISBN 0–520–05436–9. LC 85–9262. High school and up. Out of print.

Old scholarly work detailing plants used by Native Americans in the arid parts of the West. Organized by region, each chapter offers a comprehensive description with illustrations of the diverse methods for harvesting and utilizing each food and/or fiber plant. In addition, cultural information is provided on the people who lived in each region as well as information on other food sources (insects, fishing, hunting), agricultural practices, and basketry. An appendix organized by plant—listing where it's found and how it was used—and an index by both Latin and common names are most helpful. Useful for Native American studies and for herbalists.

A History of Women in America. Carol Hymowitz and Michaele Weismann. New York: Bantam Books, Inc., 1984. 400 pp. ISBN 0–553–26914–3. LC 79–104456. High school and up.

A work detailing women's contributions to American history. Contains a section called "The Maverick West," which graphically details the role and treatment of Native Americans in the West in the 1800s. Includes index. Useful as supplementary material. More up-to-date material is available.

Indian Baskets of North America. Frank W. Lamb. Riverside, CA: Rubidoux, 1972. 155 pp. ISBN N/A. LC 72–189529. High school and up. Out of print.

A reference book dealing with information concerning basketry and art in Native American culture. A guide to collecting and studying Native American basketry. Organized following a geographic pattern of Native Americans in North America. Maps of the area, illustrations, and photographs are included. An alphabetical list of basket-making tribes is included, as well as a bibliography. Of interest to art students and those interested in basketry.

Indian Clothing Before Cortes: Mesoamerican Costumes from the Cadices. Patricia Rieff Anawalt. Norman, OK: University of Oklahoma Press, 1990. Civilization of the American Indian Series vol. 156. 256 pp. ISBN 0–8061–1650–1. LC 80–5942. High school and up.

A comprehensive description and analysis of costumes and clothing of six major groups of Native Americans in Mexico, such as the Aztecs and the Mayas. Includes a broad cultural survey and a discussion of how these clothing styles were reconstructed historically. Includes detailed drawings, figures, color plates, charts, and examples of the various costumes of these groups by Jean C. Sells. Useful for costuming information for dramas and Native American studies. Introduction by H. B. Nicholson.

The Indian Frontier of the American West, 1846–1890. Robert M. Utley. Albuquerque, NM: University of New Mexico Press, 1983. 347 pp. ISBN 0–8263–0716–7. LC 83–12516. Junior high and up.

Focuses on the dramatic, wide-ranging, multifaceted interaction among the 360,000 Native Americans west of the Mississippi River and American soldiers, government bureaucrats, religious reformers, and an overwhelming number of white settlers. Good historical accounting of events. Many photographs, a bibliography, an index, and maps are included. Useful for American history units and Native American studies.

Indian Givers: How the Indians of the Americas Transformed the World. Jack M. Weatherford. New York: Fawcett Book Group (Columbine), 1989. 288 pp. ISBN 0–449–90496–2. High school and up.

The title takes back the perjorative term "Indian giver" and uses it with pride. Traces the contributions made by Native Americans to our federal system of government, our democratic institutions, modern medicine, agriculture, architecture, and ecology. Useful for Native American studies.

Indian Wars. Robery M. Utley and Wilcomb E. Washburn. The American Heritage Library. Boston: Houghton Mifflin Company, 1985. 326 pp. ISBN 0–685–10831–7. LC 85–13474. High school and up.

Covers the history of over 300 years of warfare between the Native Americans and Europeans. Concentrates on the North American continent. Useful for social studies, American history, and Native American studies. Illustrated.

Indians of Texas: From Prehistoric to Modern Times. W. W. Newcomb, Jr. Austin: The University of Texas Press, 1961. Texas History Paperbacks Series, no.

Native American Nonfiction

4. 422 pp. ISBN 0–292–73271–6. LC 60–14312. High school and up; professional use; research.

Comprehensive, scholarly, and authoritative account covering all the Native Americans of Texas. Includes bibliography and index. Good resource for reports and units on Native Americans. Interesting to compare to later works for tone and treatment.

Killing Custer. James Welch and Paul Stekler. New York: W. W. Norton & Company, Inc., 1995. 288 pp. ISBN 0–393–03657–X. LC 94–5617. High school and up.

Interesting and well-written account of the Battle of the Little Big Horn. The authors offer an interesting perspective on a well-known historical event. While mainly sympathetic to the Native Americans, they point out that the Lakota were an aggressive tribe who had taken the land they were defending from other Native Americans. Includes index and illustrations. Useful for Native American studies.

The Long, Bitter Trail: Andrew Jackson and the Indians. Anthony F. Wallace. New York: Hill and Wang, 1993. A Critical Issue Series. 143 pp. ISBN 0–8090–6631–9. (Paper: ISBN 0–8090–1552–8.) LC 92–32609. Young adults.

Scholarly but sensitive account of the Indian Removal Act of 1830, which precipitated the "Trail of Tears," the harsh trek on which many Native Americans died while moving from east of the Mississippi River to the Oklahoma plains. Wallace describes the influences that spawned the policy which disenfranchised the Native American peoples within the boundaries of the United States and traces the movement and activities of the Cherokees, Chickasaws, Choctaws, Creeks, and Seminoles as they moved on to their new homes. Long, but easily read. Good addition to any collection on Native Americans. Edited by Eric Foner.

Mohawk Blood: A Native American Quest. Michael Baughman. New York: Lyons and Burford Publishers, Inc., 1995. 144 pp. ISBN 1–55821–376–7. LC 94–37289. High school and up.

Baughman blends the present and past Native American traditions of his Mohawk grandfather. He writes of his efforts to understand his ancestors and to incorporate their reverence for nature into his life. Useful for Native American studies.

Native America: Arts, Traditions, and Celebrations. Christine Mather. New York: Crown Publishing Group, 1990. 240 pp. ISBN 0–517–57436–5. LC 90–7059. High school and up.

Mather describes the history and tradition of Native American art and the influence of nature in all its areas. The photographs by Jack Parsons show how landscapes, baskets, pottery, moccasins, and blankets all reflect Native Americans' great respect for their environment and how it shapes their culture. Includes photographs and an index. Useful for art students and Native American studies.

Native American Dance: Ceremonies and Social Traditions. Charlotte Heth. Golden, CO: Fulcrum Publishing, 1993. 208 pp. ISBN 1–56373–020–0. LC 92–034969. Junior high and up.

The author covers the dance traditions of Native Americans from seven different areas in seven sections: Inside the Longhouse; The Fiesta; The White Mountain Apache Dance; Beauty, Humor and Power of Tewa Pueblo Dance; Southern Plains Dance; Northern Plains Dance; Contemporary Alaskan Native Dance; and Modern Native Dance. Includes foreword, introduction, select bibliography, discography, videography, list of contributors, index, and photos. Of interest to dance students. Useful for Native American units.

Native American Religions: An Introduction. Denis L. Carmody and John T. Carmody. Mahwah, NJ: Paulist Press, 1993. 288 pp. ISBN 0–8091–3404–7. LC 93–15547. High school and up.

The author states, "There is no Native American group that has not been traditionally religious." He addresses Native American religions by region: Eastern Woodlands, Far North, Plains, Southwest, Far West, MesoAmerica, and South America. He notes the backgrounds, attitudes, spiritual life, relationship to nature, the group, the self, and spirituality. Includes index, notes, study questions, bibliography, maps of regions discussed, illustrations. Useful for comparative religion classes and Native American studies.

North American Indians: A Comprehensive Account, Second edition. Alice Beck Kehoe. Englewood Cliffs, NJ: Prentice Hall, 1992. 625 pp. ISBN 0–13–624362–2. LC 91–20226. High school and up.

An all-inclusive account of the histories of Native Americans from Alaska and Canada to Mexico. The book is written from the perspective of Native Americans, and those policies or trends that affected them most strongly are covered. It is divided by geographic area. Each area is chronologized and covered from archaic times to the present day. A detailed bibliography is included at the end of each chapter, and an index is provided. Useful for Native American units.

The Plains Indians of the Twentieth Century. Peter Iverson. Norman, OK: University of Oklahoma Press, 1985. 267 pp. ISBN 0–8061–1866–0. LC 85–40475. High school and up.

This anthology of recent writings on Plains Indians attempts to enhance understanding of Native American history as a continuing story. Footnotes to original writings are included, as well as illustrations, maps, and an index. Useful as a reference tool. Introduction by Peter Iversin.

Spirit of the New England Tribes: Indian History and Folklore, 1620–1984. William S. Simmons. Hanover, NH: University Press of New England, 1986. 343 pp. ISBN 0–87451–372–3. LC 85–040936 Junior high and up.

Presents examples of southern New England Native American folklore, from the earliest European contact to the present day. Chapters such as Witches, Ghosts, Giants, and Treasures are presented in chronological order from the seventeenth century to the present. Includes bibliography, index, and index of folklore motifs. Useful for folklore studies and Native American studies.

Stolen Continents: The Americas Through Indian Eyes Since 1492. Ronald Wright. Boston: Houghton Mifflin Company, 1993. 448 pp. ISBN 0–395–65975–2. LC 91–36202. High school and up.

Wright addresses five distinct Native American groups—the Aztec, the Maya, the Inca, the Cherokee, and the Iroquois. He addresses history from the time of the first Europeans landing in the "new world" both from European and from Native American points of view. Some of his material is taken from recently recovered and translated material and the differences in points of view make fascinating reading. Includes photographs and a bibliography. Useful for Native American studies. Good addition to any library.

Studies in Play and Games. Brian Sutton-Smith. New York: Ayer Company Publishers, Inc., 1976. 108 pp. ISBN 0–405–07912–5. LC N/A. High school and up.

A 21-volume collection of studies on games, sports, and play activities of tribes and peoples divided into two parts: Part I—Central and South America; and Part II—North America. Includes history, descriptions of games, and some illustrations. Twenty-one volumes. Useful for research, units on Native Americans.

The Way of the Earth: Native America and the Environment. John Bierhorst. New York: Morrow Junior Books, 1994. 336 pp. ISBN 0–688–11560–8. LC 93–028971. Junior high and up.

Native Americans have long been known for their great regard for nature and the environment. Bierhorst has assembled a collection of stories, proverbs, myths, and parables which illustrate this great respect for the world we live in. Good for folklore and Native American studies.

The World of the American Indian. Jules B. Billard, ed. Washington DC: National Geographic Society, 1979 (revised 1993). 400 pp. ISBN 0–8704–972–9. LC 93–023294. High school and up.

An authoritative history of Native American culture and history geared for the general public with 448 illustrations. Useful for public libraries.

Videos

Videos: Fiction, not reviewed

Fish Hawk. Batavia, OH: Video Treasures 1991. 95 min.

Fish Hawk has lost his family, his pride, and his way. He seeks refuge in a bottle until a young boy leads him back to the path of self-respect. Filmed in Canada. 1 videocassette.

The Sign of the Beaver. Hightstown, NJ: American School Publishers. 1988. 35 min. Junior high.

A young boy is left alone in the wilderness to take care of himself while his family goes into town. When they do not come back, he must survive with the help of a Native American family. Will he want to go home when his family does return? Part of the Newberry video collection.

Sing Down the Moon. Hightstown, NJ: American School Publishers. 1986. 36 min. Junior high.

Spanish slavers attack a Navajo village and march the Native Americans to Ft. Sumter. Many do not survive. Newberry award series. Three volumes.

Videos: Nonfiction, reviewed

The Dakota Conflict. Produced by KTCA-TV, 1992. Bethesda, MD. Distributed by Atlas Video, 1993. 58 min. Color. High school and up.

While most Americans have heard of the battle at Wounded Knee, many do not realize that it was a part of the Dakota Conflict, or Great Sioux Uprising, in Minnesota and coincided with the Civil War. This video describes how the Sioux, exploited by whites and deprived of food and land, rebelled and killed the white settlers in their area. Thirty-eight Dakota Sioux were hanged in reprisal. Visuals are provided by documentary photos, and audio contains spoken lines from diaries, journals, and other primary sources. Narrated by radio personality Garrison Keillor and Native American actor Floyd Red Crow Westerman who played Ten Bears in the movie *Dances with Wolves*. Useful for units on the Civil War and Native Americans. Good addition to any library. Originally produced for television broadcast.

Dancing in Moccasins: Keeping Native American Traditions Alive. Princeton, NJ: Distributed by Films for the Humanities and Sciences, 1993. Rereleased 1994. 49 min. Color. Junior high and up.

This video was originally a television documentary. Interviews are taped with Native Americans who still live on the United States' 278 reservations; those who have left the reservations but returned there to live; those who left but attempt to maintain their culture; and those who left and have attempted to bury their culture. All speak of their frustration with trying to keep their culture alive, broken promises and treaties, racism and bigotry, and major differences between Native American and mainstream American mores. Shot mostly on reservations in the midwest. Good for sociology and history classes in junior high through community college.

First Texans: American Indian People in North America. Falls Church, VA: Landmark Media. 1991. 29 min. color. Preview available.

Eye-catching and thought-provoking opening with what appears to be traditional Native American dancing and music, but the dancers are dressed in both traditional and contemporary styles, expressing the importance of assimilation into today's culture as well as retaining the old customs, traditions, and culture. The video is divided into four sections. The first shows current professions. The second shows an historical survey comprised of vintage photos and footage of museum displays and archaeological sites. The third shows modern, urban Native Americans at social events, participating in sports, at school, and at worship. Male and female narrators contribute to show how Native Americans in the North Texas area have fitted themselves into modern American culture while continuing to remember, preserve, and revere their own ancient culture. Concentrates on Native Americans of Texas, but the message can be carried over to apply to any Native American group. Good addition to any video collection. Junior high and up.

The Indians of North America Video Collection II. Ten videocassettes. Produced by Schlessinger Video Productions, 1994. Distributed by Library Video Company, 1995. 30 min. each. Color. Junior high and high school.

Titles included are *Chinook, Creek, Crow, Huron, Lenape, Menominee, Naragansett, Potawatomi,* and *A History of Native Americans.* Companion set to *The Indians of North America Video Collection I.* Each video on a specific tribe tells the history of the tribe, describes its culture, and relates the tribe's efforts to preserve its heritage and customs in modern society. *A History of Native Americans* relates the common histories, government, relationships with the United States government, role of nature and use of natural resources, role of women in their societies, and could serve as an introduction to the series. Each video contains interviews with tribal members and is illustrated with maps, photographs, and paintings. Good for reports, units on Native Americans, American history and multicultural units.

Indians of the Northwest. Irwindale, CA: Produced by Turtle on the Move Productions, 1993. Distributed by Barr Films. Native American Series. 20 min. Color. Preview available. Junior high.

This easy-to-follow, entertaining, and informative video covers the Native American tribes of the northwest and their crafts, foods, ceremonies, and totems. Storytellers tell some Native American myths. The making of canoes from cedar and the making of clothes is demonstrated. Of value for a unit on Native Americans and social studies.

Native Americans: The History of a People. Madison, WI: Distributed by Knowledge Unlimited, 1992. 25 min. Color. Junior high and high school.

The story of the Native Americans—the first people to live on the North American continent. Two parts. This first part covers how Native Americans lived, concentrating on hunters who followed the herds that provided food, clothing, and shelter; mound builders whose culture vanished 600 years ago; and the Anasazi—builders of large stone buildings in Colorado, Arizona, New Mexico, and Utah. The second part covers how the lives of the Native Americans were changed forever by the arrival of European settlers. Philosophical and cultural differences, as well as the Europeans' opinion that the Native Americans were child-like savages, caused many a famous battle. The video goes on to show how Native Americans live today, the contributions they make to the United States, loss of their land, and how they are regaining control over their own lives and renewing their cultural ties. Good supplementary addition to any collection on Native Americans. Teacher's guide, 16 pp., available.

Native Americans: People of the Northwest Coast. Distributed by Rainbow Educational Video, 1994. 23 min. Color. Includes teacher's guide and catalog kit. Preview available. Junior high.

Fourth in a series that covers peoples of the desert, plains, and forest. Filmed in British Columbia. The story of life before the seventeenth century before the arrival of the Europeans is told by a 15-year-old girl, Golden Sparrow. She tells how the people of the northwest lived, hunted, cooked, fished, and made tools, weapons, and clothing. She tells of the religious belief that everything in nature has a spirit life and speculates on how life will be different since the Europeans have arrived. Good learning tool for junior high history and social studies classes.

Native Americans: People of the Plains. New York: Produced by Peter Matulavich Productions, 1993. Distributed by Rainbow Educational Video. 23 min. Color. Preview available. Junior high.

The importance of the buffalo to the Plains Indians is the theme of this educational, informative, and entertaining video. The story is told through the eyes of a young Native American boy as he and his father hunt for buffalo. Dramatizations show how every part of the buffalo was used. Hides provided clothing, blankets, and shelter. Meat was used for food. Hooves and horns were used for weapons and utensils. Sinews provided thread, string, and rope. Good for units on Native Americans.

The Right to Be. Distributed by Filmmakers Library, 1994. 27 min. Color. Preview available. High school and up.

Harriet Skye, a Lakota Sioux from the Standing Rock, North Dakota, Reservation, made this video when she graduated from the film school at New York University. She wanted to produce a realistic film about her tribe, presenting Lakota life and traditions as they really are rather than as they are viewed by other cultures. The film takes viewers to the United Tribes Community College and its Spirit Program, a Sweat Ceremony, and to a dam on the Missouri River whose construction caused the flooding of reservation land. Skye's work reveals the growing problems of unemployment, alcoholism, and poor economic conditions among Native Americans. Valuable tool for units on Native Americans.

Secrets of Little Bighorn. Princeton, NJ: Distributed by Films for the Humanities and Sciences, 1993. 25 min. color. Preview available. Junior high and up.

Archaeologists using metal detectors reconstruct the Battle of the Little Bighorn and dispel countless myths about the famous battle. When a fire swept the site of the battle, archaeologists using metal detectors found over 4,000 artifacts and ascertained that while the cavalry had only single-loading weapons, the Sioux had over 41 different types of guns. They further determined that, far from fighting a battle, the cavalry was trying desperately to retreat and the battle was quickly over. Contains black-and-white photos detailing the history of the battle and the events leading up to it. Drawings, photographs, and film clips support the archaeologists' finds. Valuable for American History units, units on Native Americans.

Strangers in Their Own Land. Oklahoma City, OK: Strangers in Their Own Land, Inc.1993. Approximately 50 min. Color. High school and up.

A valuable tool for understanding Native American culture, this documentary looks at the world of the Native American today, discusses the traditions of the past, the realities of the present, and the promise of the future. It also tells the history of people whose lands were stolen from them, who have faced discrimination, unemployment, alcoholism, and drug abuse, yet retain the will to preserve their traditions and culture. This video features rituals that have never been filmed before, such as the Kiowa black legging ceremony and a traditional wedding ceremony. Several Native Americans, including a medicine man; an elderly Kickapoo woman who speaks no English and retains the old customs, a physician; a Persian War Gulf veteran; and the Chief of the Cherokee Nation, Wilma Mankiller. Extremely valuable for units on Native America culture.

The Sunrise Dance. New York: Distributed by Filmmakers Library, 1994. 28 min. Color. Preview available. Junior high and up.

A 13-year-old Apache girl's actual rite of passage to adulthood ceremony is filmed. Some parts, such as the gift of a television set and off-the-rack clothing are modern rather than traditional, but the viewer is treated to the preparation activities, the purification rites, the "sweat lodge," the "Crown Dancers," and the more important highlights of the three-day ceremony. Parallels between the Hispanic Quinceanera, the Jewish Bar/Bat Mitzvah, and Roman Catholic First Communion can be drawn and discussed. Recommended for use in United States History classes and in Native American studies.

Surviving Columbus. Albuquerque, NM: Native American Public Broadcasting Consortium. Produced by PBS, 1992. 120 min. Color. Preview available. High school and up.

This video covers Pueblo history from the period before Columbus came to the New World, the conquest by the Spanish, a period of relative peace, the era of colonialization, and up to the present. All footage was shot in the American southwest. The strongest feature is the fact that it focuses on the connection between history and oral tradition. Good as an additional acquisition for libraries.

Totem Poles: The Stories They Tell. Cos Cob: Distributed by Double Diamond Corp., 1993. 14 min. Color. Junior high.

Totem poles built along the Pacific Northwest by the Tlingit, Haida, and Kwakiutl are shown and explained. Each figure, color, and combination has meaning. Photos and drawings show the totems in their natural settings. Background sounds of indigenous animals and tribal music sets the mood. Totem pole making is included at the end of the video. Good for units on Native Americans of the Northwest, Scout troops, and folklore classes.

Videos: Nonfiction, not reviewed

America's Great Indian Leaders. Chicago, IL: Questar Video, Inc. 1994. 65 min. Junior high and up.

Stories of Geronimo, Quanah Parker, Crazy Horse, and Chief Joseph. Narrated by members of their respective tribes, the Apache, Comanche, Sioux, and Nez Perce. Archival photographs. Original footage.

American Indian Arts and Crafts. Cortez, CO: INTERpark. Distributed by Finley-Holiday Film Corp. 1987. High school and up.

The Art of Navajo Weaving/The Durango Collection of Southwestern Textiles. 56 min.

Maria: Indian Pottery of San Ildelfonso. 1980/1989. 27 min.

Sandpainting: A Najavo Tradition. 37 min.

American Indian Cultures. Cortez, CO: INTERpark. Distributed by Finley-Holiday Film Corp. Five videos. High school and up.

Anasazi: The Ancient Ones. 1980/1991. 23 min.

Ancient Indian Cultures of Northern Arizona. 1988. 30 min.

The Story of Canyon De Chelly & Hubbell Trading Post. 1989. 30 min.

Mesa Verde National Park. 1991/1980. 60 min.

Monument Valley: Navajo Homeland. 1991. 30 min.

Ancient America. Film Archives, 1994. Four videos. 240 min. Junior high and up.

Hosted by Wes Sutdi, a Native American Cherokee actor. A documentary about the world of the ancient Native Americans.

Ancient Indian Cultures of Northern Arizona. Film Archives. 30 min. Junior high and up.

Explores the remains of the Sinagua tribe who once lived near what is now Flagstaff, Arizona.

Brook Medicine Eagle: Dancing Awake the Drum. Film Archives, 1993. 60 min. Junior high and up.

Brook Medicine Eagle leads the viewer on a journey into the past, where we watch the ceremony of dancing and drumming. She shares her vision and insight into survival and hope for the next seven generations.

The Chaco Legacy. Alexandria, VA: PBS Video, 1988. 60 min. Junior high and up.

The Chaco Canyon civilization lived, thrived, and developed a sophisticated culture, roads, and water systems, then simply and completely vanished.

The Faith Keeper. Film Archives, 1991. 58 min. Junior high and up.

Oren Lyons, chief of the Turtle Clan, gives an interview with Bill Moyers about his role as faithkeeper for his people's values, history, and traditions.

Geronimo: The Last Renegade/Custer and the 7th Cavalry. A & E Home Video. 1993/1992. Two videos. 50 min. each. Junior high and up.

Kenny Rogers narrates myths, legends, and realities of the old west. Original footage, authentic diaries, photos, expert commentary.

Geronimo and the Apache Resistance. PBS Home Video, 1991/1990. The American Video Collection. 60 min. Junior high and up.

Geronimo and his band fought the U.S. government troops for 25 years before they were defeated. Originally broadcast on the PBS series The American Experience; then manufactured and distributed by Pacific Arts Video Publishing, Beverly Hills, CA.

The Hopi. Better Books Company. Junior high and up.

The history, culture, and customs of the Hopi over 1000 years.

How the West Was Lost. Bethesda, MD. Discovery Enterprises Group. 1993. Three videos. 300 min. Junior high and up.

> *A Clash of Cultures.*
>
> *Always the Enemy.*
>
> *A Good Day to Die.*

The story of the struggle for the American west. The Navajo, the Nez Perce, the Apache, the Cheyenne, and the Lakota fought valiantly for the lands of their ancestors, but were no match for the greed of the whites. Originally broadcast on the Discovery Channel.

I Will Fight No More Forever. Wolper Productions: EDDE Entertainment. 1995/1975. 106 min. High school and up.

This docudrama is a re-enactment of the tragic story of Chief Joseph and the Nez Perce Indians who fought valiantly, but vainly, for their homeland. Recommended by the National Education Agency. Originally issued as a motion picture.

The Incas. PBS Home Video, distributed by Pacific Arts. Los Angeles. 1993/ 1980. 58 min. Junior high and up.

History of the Incas of Peru, their civilization, Machu Picchu, their lives, religion, and culture.

Incas Remembered. Canoga Park, CA: Monterey Home Video. 1986. 60 min. High school and up.

Traces the history and culture of the Incas, one of the world's most important early civilizations, and their achievements in math, science, etc. Part of the Janis Collection.

The Indian and His Homeland American Images. Whittier, CA: Finley-Holiday Film Corp. 1990/1988. 31 min. High school and up.

Three-hundred-year survey of the impact of European civilization on the natives of the New World and their land. Uses paintings, illustrations of noted western artists. Covers peoples and wildlife of America from 1590 to 1876. Part of "Our National Heritage" series.

Indians of the Eastern Woodlands. Los Angeles: Wood Knapp Video. 1994. 60 min. Junior high and up.

The history, lives, religion, and culture of the Eastern Woodland Native Americans. Part of the Ancient America Series: The Legacy of the American Indians.

Indians of North America Video Collection. Schlessinger Video Productions. 1995. Ten videos. 30 min each. Junior high and up.

Each video covers a separate tribe. Videos available separately.

The Apache. Northeast, subarctic.

The Aztec. Middle America (Mexico).

The Cherokee. Southeast.

The Cheyenne. Great Plains.

The Comanche. Great Plains.

The Iroquois. Northeast U.S. and Canada.

The Maya. Middle America (Mexico).

The Navajo. Southwest.

The Seminole. Southeast.

The Yankton Sioux. Great Plains.

Indians of North America Video Collection II. Film Archives, 1994. Ten videos. 30 min each.

A History of Native Americans.

The Chinook. Pacific Northwest.

The Creek. (Muskogee) Southeast.

The Crow. (Absaroke) Great Plains.

The Huron. (Ouedat) Southeastern Canada.

The Lenape. Middle Atlantic Coast.

The Menominee. Western Great Lakes Region.

The Narragansett. (Enishkeektompauog) Northeast.

The Potawatomi. (Bode' wad mi) Central Great Lakes Region.

The Pueblo. Southwest.

Indians of the Northwest. Film Archives, 1994. 60 min. Junior high and up.

The history, lives, religion, and culture of the Indians of the northwest.

Indians, Outlaws, and Angie Debo. Alexandria, VA. PBS Video. 1990/1988. 58 min. Junior high and up.

Told through the eyes of early 20th century pioneer and scholar Angie Debo. Story of how the five tribes of Oklahoma were robbed of their oil-rich lands by greedy whites. Part of the American Experience series.

Indians of the Southwest. Film Archives, 1994. 160 min. Junior high and up.

The history, lives, religion, and culture of the Indians of the southwest.

Last Stand at Little Big Horn. Boston, MA. WGBH, 1993. 60 min. Junior high and up.

Journals, diaries, archives, oral histories, and drawings are used to explain the famous battle between the whites and the Lakota Sioux, Cheyenne, and Crow tribes from a Native American point of view. Part of the American Experience Series (PBS).

A Matter of Choice. Wisconsin Public Television. 1990. 58 min. Junior high and up. Included in the Winds of Change Series.

The Hopi are the oldest continuously inhabited community in the United States. This video takes the viewer on a visit to this tribe as they struggle to find a place for themselves in the modern world.

A Matter of Promises. Beverly Hills, CA: PBS Home Video. 1990. 60 min. High school and up.

Members of the Navajo, the Onondaga, and Lummi describe their struggle to maintain their cultural identities, customs, and political sovereignty. Part of the Winds of Change Series.

Maya Lords of the Jungle. Beverly Hills, CA: PBS Home Video. 1993/1981. 60 min. Junior high and up.

Archaeologists take us on a dig site to see the remains of temples and tombs and to explain the Maya civilization. Part of the Odyssey PBS TV series.

Mesa Verde. Film Archives. 60 min. Junior high and up.

An anthropologist and archaeologist explore the ruins left at Mesa Verde by the Anasazi who flourished for over 1000 years, then disappeared.

More than Bows and Arrows. Seattle, WA: Wood Knapp Video. 1995. 60 min. High school and up.

Documentary of contributions made by Native Americans to the development of the United States and Canada. Program is narrated by Pulitzer Prize–winning author N. Scott Momaday. Program has won several awards. Part of the Ancient America Series.

Myths and Mound Builders. Washington, DC: WETA Public Broadcasting Associates. 1981. 60 min. Junior high and up.

Early settlers found strange mounds containing Native American artifacts. Explore the work of Cyrus Thomas as he uncovers their meaning. Part of the Odyssey PBS TV series.

Native American Indians. Irwindale, CA, Newark, NJ: Barr Films. 1994. Two video cassettes, 60 min. each. Junior high and up.

Documentary account of the Indians of the plains, the southwest, and California.

1. Indians of the Southwest

2. Indians of California

The Navajo. Better Books Company. Junior high and up.

Explores the history, customs, and culture of the Navajo in the harsh and beautiful land of northern Arizona.

Nomadic Indians of the West. Los Angeles, 1994. 60 min. Junior high and up.

History, culture, and lives of the nomadic Native Americans of the west. Part of the Ancient America Series—The Legacy of the American Indians.

Sacred Ground: The Story of the North American Indian's Relationship to the Land. Aspen, CO: Freewheelin' Films. 1993/1990. 60 min. Junior high and up.

Cliff Robertson narrates this expedition into the myths and facts that governed the Native American's beliefs, origins, architecture, and society. Study guide available. Originally released as a motion picture in 1977.

The Sacred Ways Collection. Bethesda, MD: Atlas Video, Inc., 1993/1983. Three videos. Junior high and up.

The Sun Dagger. 1983. 60 min.

Discovery of the celestial calendar of the ancient Anasazi who lived in New Mexico over 1000 years ago.

The Spirit of the Mask. 1993/1992. 50 min.

Explores the world of the Native Americans of northwest Canada, reveals their myths and rituals and offers insight into the relationship between the spirit world and the natural world.

Dreamtales. 1993. 32 min.

Compilation of myths of several groups of Native Americans including Maya, Inuit, Pawnee, the Campa of Peru, the Tupi of Brazil, and the Yahgan of Chile.

The Search for Ancient Americans. Van Nuys, CA: Vestron Video. 1992. 58 min. Junior high and up.

Go with archaeologists as they re-enact the finding of five major discoveries of ancient civilizations in the Americas. Part of the Infinite Voyage Series.

Seasons of a Navajo. Beverly Hills, CA: PBS Home Video, 1990/1984. 60 min. Junior high and up.

Documentary on the life of a Navajo family featuring ancient Anasazi ruins and Monument Valley. Part of the American Indian Collection.

Seeking the First Americans. Alexandria, VA: PBS Video, 1988/1980. 59 min. Odyssey PBS TV Series. High school and up.

Archaeologists search for the "first Americans" and disagree over whether it was Clovis Man from 11,000 B.C. or much earlier.

The Silent Enemy. Sandy Hook, CT: Video Images: Video Yesteryear, 1991/ 1930. 120 min.

Made in 1930 with Chief Yellow Robe and several members of the Ojibway tribe. They tell of their people's way of life that will soon be no more. Sound and silent. Black and white.

Sioux Legends. Custer, SD: Nauman Films. 1990/1973. 20 min. Junior high and up.

Native Sioux act out traditional legends showing the philosophy and religion of the Sioux. Filmed in the Badlands of South Dakota.

The Spirit of Crazy Horse. Beverly Hills, CA: PBS Home Video. 1991/1990. 60 min. High school and up.

History of the Sioux tribe from the invasion of whites to the American Indian Movement. Part of the American Indian Collection. Originally broadcast on the PBS Series Frontline.

Surviving Columbus: Story of the Pueblo People. Beverly Hills, CA: PBS Home Video. 1992. 120 min. Junior high and up.

History of the southwest as told from the perspective of the Native Americans who had built great civilizations while Europe was still in the Dark Ages and before Columbus landed.

Tahonka. Film Archives. 1968. 30 min. Junior high and up.

Re-enactment of the history of the Plains Indians from the pre-horse era to the massacre at Wounded Knee.

Wallace Black Elk: Return to the Sacred Hoop. Valley Head, AL: Four Directions Production Company. 1993. Quest of the Earth Keepers Series. 44 min.

Wallace Black Elk was raised in the strictest Lakota tradition and has dedicated his life to Earth Healing. He leads the viewer through a sacred ceremony of the Stone Peoples Lodge and a healing Cannunpa.

❋ HISPANIC AMERICANS ❋

Biographies

Alicia Alonso: First Lady of the Ballet. Sandra M. Martin. New York: Walker and Company, 1993. 104 pp. ISBN 0–8027–8242–6. LC 93–18098. Grades 7 and up.

Biography of the Cuban dancer who was a principal ballerina during the early days of the American Ballet Theater. The author describes Alonso's childhood and young adulthood under the regimes of Batista and Castro, her training, and the difficulties she faces since young women were not encouraged to pursue careers in dancing. Martin mentions that Alonso was initially refused entrance to the United States because of her former association with Castro, but gives little attention to how the politics of the time influenced her life and career. Useful for units on notable Hispanic Americans, women's studies, and overcoming adversity.

Barrio Teacher. Arcadia Lopez. Houston: Arte Publico Press, 1992. 96 pp. ISBN 1–55885–051–1. LC 92–006876. Junior high and up.

Arcadia Lopez tells of her childhood. The daughter of immigrants, she is poor and unable to speak English. She overcomes these barriers and achieves her lifelong goal of becoming a teacher in the barrio. Useful for a unit on notable Hispanic Americans and on overcoming adversity.

Henry Cisneros: Mexican American Political Leader. Christopher C. Henry. New York: Chelsea House Publishers, 1994. Hispanics of Achievement Series. 112 pp. ISBN 0–7910–2019–3. LC 94–185. Junior high.

The author examines the life of Henry Cisneros, former mayor of San Antonio, Texas and current Secretary of Housing and Urban Development. Describes his upbringing, his family, and his career. Mentions his legal difficulties over his extramarital affair only briefly. Includes black-and-white photographs, illustrations, and index. Useful for units on notable Hispanic Americans.

Hispanic Writers: A Selection of Sketches from Contemporary Authors. Linda Metzger, ed. Detroit: Gale Research Inc., 1990. 475 pp. ISBN 0–8103–7688–1. LC N/A. High school and up.

Provides in-depth information on authors of twentieth century Hispanic literature and culture, with emphasis on Hispanic authors from the United States, Puerto Rico, Cuba, Mexico, those Spanish-speaking countries of Central and South America, and those from Spain who have influenced literature in the Americas. Contains a guide to authors, an author listing, and a nationality index. The guide to authors provides a very brief synopsis of the life and work of each author represented, while the author listing provides very detailed biographic and bibliographic information. Topics include personal and career information, awards and honors received, and memberships and offices held in professional and civic organizations. Bibliographic information includes a chronology of books written and edited by the author in each genre and lists of other notable publications and contributions. Many of the entries are updated from Gale's Contemporary Authors series and were written especially for Hispanic Writers. Most of the originally Spanish materials are available in English translations. Each entry is indexed alphabetically by country of birth or citizenship. This is the most recent and most comprehensive reference tool available on Hispanic writers. Good for high school, academic, and public libraries.

Malinche: Slave Princess of Cortez. Gloria Duran. North Haven, CT: Shoe String Press, Inc., 1992. 248 pp. ISBN 0–208–02343–7. LC 92–31776. Junior high and up.

Born Malinali, Malinche was the daughter of an Aztec ruler who was sold into slavery at the age of twelve. Later, older and proficient in languages, she met Cortez, who named her Marina and kept her with him as mistress and interpreter. Worth considering since Malinche is seldom mentioned in other novels, but some parts are overly detailed and ponderous. Teachers might read some excerpts aloud. Limited usefulness for world history classes and units on exploration.

Raul Julia: Puerto Rican Actor. Rebecca Stefoff. New York: Chelsea House Publishers, 1994. Hispanics of Achievement Series. 112 pp. ISBN 0–79100–1556–4. LC 93–42532. Junior high.

Biography of Puerto Rican actor Raul Julia. The author emphasizes Julia's work, his struggle against ethnic stereotyping, and typecasting and his devotion to the humanitarian Hunger Project. Includes black-and-white photographs, chronology, and bibliography. Useful for studies of notable Hispanic Americans.

Silent Dancing: A Partial Remembrance of a Puerto Rican Childhood. Second Edition. Judith Ortiz Cofer. Houston: Arte Publico Press, 1991. 120 pp. ISBN 1–55885–015–5. LC 89–077428. High school and up.

"Recipient of the New York Public Library's 1991 Best Book for the Teen Age, a PEN citation, Martha Albrand Award for nonfiction, and a Pushcart Prize. Silent Dancing is Cofer's recollection of her childhood in Puerto Rico and New Jersey."— Annotation from Pinata Press catalog. Useful for studies of notable Hispanic Americans.

Ybor City Chronicles: A Memoir. Ferdie Pacheco. Gainesville, FL: University Press of Florida, 1994. 320 pp. ISBN 0–8130–1296–1. LC 94–000822. High school and up.

Ybor City Chronicles is Ferdie Pacheco's account of growing up in Tampa, Florida, from 1935 to 1945 among mostly Spanish, Cuban, and Italian neighbors, most of whom were in the cigar and restaurant business. He talks of his extended family and special feelings for his grandmother. Pacheco's drawings, paintings, and photographs enhance his narrative. Useful for multicultural studies.

Folklore, Literature, Poetry

Aplauso! Hispanic Children's Theater. Joe Rosenberg, ed. Houston: Arte Publico Press, 1995. 120 pp. ISBN 1–55885–136–4. LC 94–036005. Junior high and up.

Hispanic plays for children and young adults collected by Hispanic Children's Theater director Joe Rosenberg. The selections contain fantasy as well as realism. The characters range from Hispanic clowns to intergalactic pirates to microbes and countless other characters from Hispanic cultures. Useful for drama classes, drama clubs, and literature classes.

Between Borders: Essays of Mexicana Chicana History. Adelaida R. De Castillo, ed. Encino, CA: Floricanto Press, 1990. La Mejor Latina Series. 560 pp. ISBN 0–915745–14–3. High school and up.

The 25 pieces in this volume are divided into two equal sections. The first deals with theory, research methods and sources. The second set contains historical essays. Primarily on twentieth-century history, these articles treat such issues as labor and labor unions, and feminism and women's positions in Chicano and Mexican culture. Pieces are in Spanish or English. A good introduction to the field, this volume could be used as a text for a college-level course. Suitable for academic and public libraries. Illustrated.

A Bicultural Heritage: Themes for the Exploration of Mexican and Mexican-American Culture in Books for Children and Adolescents.
Isabel Schon. Metuchen, NJ: Scarecrow Press, 1978. 164 pp. ISBN 0–8108–1128–6. LC 78–4332. Professional use.

A superior collection of literature for kindergarten through twelfth grade students designed to promote an understanding, appreciation, and respect for the Mexican American culture. The author emphasizes literature that promotes a bicultural heritage. The contents are arranged according to grade levels and include titles that deal with customs, lifestyles, heroes, folklore, and history of Mexican Americans. Expected outcomes, discussions, evaluations, and follow-up activities are also arranged according to grade levels. A pre- and post-attitude survey and three appendixes, which contain additional readings and references, are also included. Of the 265 titles listed, a majority are fiction; however, biographical, historical, and artistic works are listed. *A Bicultural Heritage* is an excellent source for public school teachers in both regular and bilingual/bicultural programs, for librarians, and junior high and high school students who are interested in broadening their knowledge of the Mexican American culture. Although it is nearly 30 years old, it has been deemed worth reprinting.

Cool Salsa. Lori M. Carlson, ed. New York: Henry Holt and Company, 1994.
123 pp. ISBN 0–8050–3135–9. LC 93–45798. Junior high and up.

A diverse collection of poems in a myriad of styles expressing the joy, sorrow, frustration, and prejudice of growing up Latino in the United States. Some poems have both English and Spanish translations; some combine the two languages. They express the importance of both languages in establishing one's identity and joining both cultures. Useful for literature, multicultural studies, Spanish language students, bilingual classes.

Hispanic, Female, and Young: An Anthology. Phyllis Tashlik, ed. Houston:
Arte Publico Press, 1994. 249 pp. ISBN 1–55885–072–4. LC 93–4104. Junior high and up.

The stories, essays, and poems in this anthology were written, collected, and selected by Las Mujeres Hispanas, an eighth grade elective class in Spanish Harlem designed to introduce them to Hispanic women authors. Divided into nine chapters, each with its own topic. The last chapter contains interviews conducted by the young writers. No bibliography. Useful for women's studies and Hispanic American/Hispanic Women's studies.

Latino Voices. Frances R. Aparicio, ed. Brookfield, CT: Millbrook Press, Inc., 1994. Writers of America Series. 144 pp. ISBN 1–56294–388–X. LC 93–42893. Junior high and up.

Collection of Latino poetry, fiction, and excerpts from diaries and actual accounts of Latino immigrants and settlers. Each chapter had an introduction to the author's life, history, background, writings, and countries. Glossary of Spanish terms with each piece. Sources and bibliography are included. Useful for studies on notable Hispanic Americans, multicultural studies, and Hispanic American studies. Illustrated.

Paper Dance: Fifty-Five Latin Poets. Victor Hernandez Cruz, et al., eds. New York: Persea Books, Inc., 1995. 256 pp. ISBN 0–89255–201–8. LC 94–15586. High school and up.

Anthology of the work of Latino and Latina poets living in the United States. The title derives from the tempo of the poetry: some fast, some slow, some dignified, and some fun-loving. Some of the poets included are Julia Alvarez, Judith Ortiz Cofer, Juan Felipe Herrera, Pat Mora, Alberto Alvaro Rios, Luis Rodriguez, Tono Villenueva, Sandra M. Castillo, Adrian Castro, Silvia Curbelo, Diana Rivera, and Gina Valdez. Useful for poetry classes, Hispanic literature classes, Hispanic American studies, and multicultural studies. Edited by Leroy V. Quintana and Virgil Suarez. Introduction by Victor H. Cruz.

Voices from the Fields: Children of Migrant Farmworkers Tell Their Stories. Beth S. Atkin. New York: Little, Brown and Company, 1993. 96 pp. ISBN 0–316–05633–2. LC 92–32248. Junior high and up.

Nineteen children of migrant workers tell their stories in short autobiographical narratives, prose, and poetry. The themes are those of frequent moving, poverty, racism, gangs, prejudice, abusive employers, out-of-wedlock and teen pregnancy, and immigration problems. The works are in both Spanish and English. The author provides a brief commentary at the beginning of each selection. Excellent black-and-white photographs taken by the author. Useful for multicultural studies.

Woman of Her Word: Hispanic Women Write. Second edition. Evangelina Vigil, ed. Houston: Arte Publico Press, 1987. 180 pp. ISBN 0–934770–27–1. LC 83–72571. High school and up.

A compilation of prose, poetry, criticism, and art by Hispanic women from the Americas. Twenty-nine writers and artists from eight countries are represented. Primarily English with a few Spanish selections. An excellent introduction to the literature giving voice to varied cultures and perspectives. Accessible to most readers. Useful for Spanish language classes, Hispanic studies, women's studies.

Wounded in the House of a Friend. Sonia Sanchez. Boston: Beacon Press, 1995. 128 pp. ISBN 0–8070–6826–8. LC 94–38907. High school and up.

Sanchez breaks an eight-year hiatus from publication with a volume of poetry dealing with the more sordid side of life. Her themes include infidelity, spousal abuse, rape, drug addiction, and child-selling. As grim as her themes are, and as much as she reminds us that there is still war in Nicaragua, Bosnia, and Rwanda, she reminds us that there is hope. For older YAs.

Fiction for Young Adults

Across the Great River. Irene Beltran Hernandez. Houston: Arte Publico Press, 1991. 120 pp. ISBN 0–934770–96–4. LC 89–000289. Junior high and up.

Told by Kata, a young Mexican girl who must take on a leadership role when her parents are separated while illegally crossing the Rio Grande into the United States. They encounter smugglers, a folk hero, and the immigration officials before they are finally united.

The Boy Without a Flag: Tales of the South Bronx. Abraham Rodriguez. Minneapolis, MN: J. Milkweed Editions, 1992. 115 pp. ISBN 0–915943–74–3. LC 91–45672. Young Adults.

Rodriguez presents seven stories of Hispanic youth in the Bronx. He reflects the problems of the inner city, the poverty, violence, teen-age pregnancy, drug addiction, and crime. But he also shows the positive side of humanity. Tough, gritty. Street language. For more mature YAs. Illustrated by R. W. Scholls.

The Dirty War. Charles H. Slaughter. New York: Walker and Company, 1994. 176 pp. ISBN 0–8027–8312–0. LC 94–4355. Junior high.

Arte thinks little of politics as he tries to earn a living on the streets of Buenos Aires, Argentina. But the times are difficult in the late 1970s, and Arte's father disappears. Arte's mother joins the "Mothers of the Plaza de Mayo," a vocal group who dares protest the disappearances. Arte learns that no one is immune from terror and no one can remain apart from all that is happening.

Gift of the Poinsettia/El Regalo de la Flor de Nochebuena. Pat Mora and Charles Ramirez Berg. Houston: Arte Publico Press, 1995. 32 pp. ISBN 1–55885–137–2. LC 94–37233. Grades PK–5.

Carlos, a young Mexican boy, cannot afford a gift for the baby Jesus on Christmas Eve. The authors describe Carlos' quest for a gift during the nine nights of Las Posadas, the festival during which the villagers reenact Mary and Joseph's search for shelter culminating in their stay at the inn. The book also illustrates other Mexican traditions such as papel picado, cascarones (confetti eggs), and pinatas. Translation.

The Girl From Playa Blanca. Ofelia Dumas Lachtman. Houston: Arte Publico Press, 1995. 230 pp. ISBN 1–55885–148–8. LC 95–9864. Junior high and up.

Elena and her little brother, Carlos, leave their small, seaside village in Mexico to find their father, who has moved to Los Angeles to make a living for his family. Elena speaks English and is able to find a job and take care of herself and Carlos while she looks for their father. She finds more than she was looking for: love, friendship, and confidence.

Grab Hands and Run. Frances Temple. New York: Orchard Books, 1993. 176 pp. ISBN 0–531–05480–2. LC 92–34063. Junior high.

Twelve-year-old Felipe and his younger sister and mother must "grab hands and run" when Felipe's father disappears. They face danger, hunger, lack of shelter, and peril to Felipe's attractive mother as they flee to Canada. Another problem: will anyone be there to greet them when they reach their destination? Temple's narrative describes the political struggles in El Salvador, the differences in language and culture, and the family's experiences in a North American detention center.

Imagining Isabel. Omar S. Castaneda. New York: Dutton Children's Books, 1994. 192 pp. ISBN 0–525–67431–4. LC 93–50593. Junior high and up.

Sequel to *Among the Volcanoes*. Isabel Pacay marries her boyfriend, Lucas, and expects to settle into the routine of married life when a letter arrives from the National Education Commission of Guatemala inviting her to train as a teacher. Isabel enrolls in school and absorbs the opinions, thoughts, and cultures of her classmates. One day, she finds the body of a murdered political victim. She is questioned and threatened, but Isabel continues her education. She later finds out that finding the body and the subsequent questioning was a test—one she has passed—and she is invited to join the underground "network of trust" fighting political injustice in her country.

Jesse. Gary Soto. Orlando: Harcourt, Brace & Company, 1994. 144 pp. ISBN 0–15–240239–X. LC 94–11256. High school and up.

Jesse is coming of age in the late 1960s. He is 17 with all the insecurities of that age, including worrying about the draft. He and his brother are farm workers during the day to pay for their college classes at night. Jesse is torn between feeling that he should enlist in the military and feeling that he should join Cesar Chavez's protests. His first date is a disaster that ends with his being beaten by another student. His personal experiences with violence reflect the violence in the world around him. Jesse finally finds his place in the world, and it is not a rose garden.

Juanita Fights the School Board. Gloria Velasquez. Houston: Arte Publico Press, 1994. Roosevelt High School Series. 152 pp. ISBN 1–55885–119–4. (Paper: ISBN 1–55885–119–4.) LC 94–4914. Junior high and up.

First book in the Roosevelt High School Series by Gloria Velasquez. Juanita is expelled for getting into a fight with another student. Her self-image suffers badly and her family is very disappointed because Juanita was to have been the first in her family to graduate from high school. With the help of a school psychologist and a former civil rights attorney, Juanita, more determined than ever to succeed and fulfill her dream, decides to fight the discrimination against minorities at Roosevelt High and is reinstated.

Maya's Divided World. Gloria Velasquez. Houston: Arte Publico Press, 1995. Roosevelt High School Series. 125 pp. ISBN 1–55885–126–7. (Paper: ISBN 1–55885–126–7). LC 94–33573. Junior high and up.

Second book in a projected series about Roosevelt High School. Maya has a good life. Her parents are affluent, they have a nice house, and she lacks for nothing. Then her father moves out and her parents announce that they are getting a divorce. Maya blames her mother for not making a proper home for her father and putting him first. She reacts to this disruption in her life by running with a tough crowd until a friend persuades her to see a counselor. Multiple first-person narratives. Not as good as the first book in the series.

Mexican Ghost Tales of the Southwest. Alfred Avila. Edited by Kat Avila. Houston: Arte Publico Press, 1994. 176 pp. ISBN 1–55885–107–0. LC 94–6919. Junior high and up.

Twenty-one short, extremely creepy stories retold from oral and written sources. Good for book talks, reading and telling aloud.

A Place Where the Sea Remembers. Sandra Benitez. Minneapolis: Coffee House Press, 1993. 176 pp. ISBN 1–56689–011–X. LC 93–25176. Junior high and up.

Set in the small town of Santiago, Mexico. Chayo and her husband have been unable to have children, so they agree to adopt the unborn baby of Chayo's sister,

Marta. Then Chayo becomes pregnant and she and her husband change their minds. Marta is furious and puts a curse on Chayo's unborn child which results in divine retribution after a series of tragic events.

Pyramids of Class: Short Fiction from Modern Mexico. David Bowen and Juan A. Ascencio, eds. San Antonio, TX: Corona Publishing Company, 1994. 250 pp. ISBN 0–931722–99–3. (Paper: ISBN 0–931722–83–7). LC 94–071404. High school and up.

The editors have compiled a collection of 27 short, colorful stories, full of uniquely Mexican symbolism and superstition, truly revealing the feelings, the flavor, and the tempo of modern Mexico. Originally in Spanish. Translated by E. Grossman, M. S. Poden, C. Steele, and A. Zatz. Introduction by Ilan Stavans.

The Secret of Two Brothers. Irene Beltran Hernandez. Houston: Arte Publico Press, 1995. 182 pp. ISBN 1–55885–142–9. LC 95–9844. Junior high and up.

Newly released from prison, Beaver tries to make a new life for himself and his teenaged brother, Cande. Neighbors try to help, but the old pitfalls, including their father, who abused Cande while Beaver was in prison, are still there. Beaver learns about honor, starting over, and taking care of his responsibilities as he does his best to overcome the negative influences in his environment.

Sisters/Hermanas. Gary Paulsen. San Diego, CA: Harcourt, Brace & Company, 1993. 130 pp. ISBN 0–15–275323–0. Junior high.

Paulsen's story compares the lives of two 14-year-old girls. One is an illegal immigrant who has to sell herself on the streets to survive. The other is a "suburban princess" whose main concern is whether or not she will make the cheerleading squad. The book is published in two parts, English and Spanish. Mature subject matter—use with caution.

Soaring Eagle. Mary Pearce Finley. New York: Simon and Schuster, 1993. 176 pp. ISBN 0–671–75598–6. LC 92–38263. Junior high and up.

Julio's father has been away for three years, working in Taos. Julio is delighted when he comes home because he wants to get to know his father and his family history. The two set out the next day because of rumors that the United States will soon be at war with Mexico. His father is killed on the second day of the journey, and Julio is left alone to survive in the wilderness and to come to terms with the hatred he feels for those of different races.

Sparrow Hawk Red. Ben Mikaelsen. New York: Hyperion, 1993. 224 pp. ISBN 1–56282–387–6. LC 92–53458. Junior high.

Ricky Diaz's mother, an innocent bystander in an international drug war, has been killed. When Ricky overhears his father, an ex-drug enforcement agent, refuse a secret mission against the drug cartel, he decides to go himself. His fluent Spanish helps him to get along among the homeless children across the border and to penetrate the cartel's high-security compound. Fast-paced.

Sweet Fifteen. Diane Gonzales Bertrand. Houston: Arte Publico Press, 1995. 224 pp. ISBN 1–55885–122–4. (Paper: ISBN 1–55885–133–X). LC 94–32656. Junior high and up.

Rita Navarro, the seamstress helping Stephanie Bonillo get ready for her quinceanera, her coming-out party on her fifteenth birthday, wants to help her young client who is grieving over the loss of her father. She offers Stephanie a job in her seamstress shop. Stephanie's Uncle Brian visits and becomes interested in Rita. The reader is treated to a number of admirable virtues such as compassion, family traditions, respect for one's elders, love, and friendship. Somewhat longer than most stories for YAs.

Tommy Stands Alone. Gloria Velasquez. Houston: Arte Publico Press, 1995. Roosevelt High School Series. 135 pp. ISBN 1–55885–146–1. (Paper: ISBN 1–55885–147–X). LC 95–13551. Junior high and up.

Third book in the series. Tommy is uncomfortable dealing with his sexual orientation. In order to avoid being labeled as gay, he begins cutting classes, drinking, and avoiding the friends who are becoming aware of his sexual preferences. After a failed suicide attempt, he goes to the hospital where he develops a relationship with a counselor, Ms. Martinez, whose brother committed suicide when he found out that he was HIV positive. Some of Tommy's family and friends stand by him, but Tommy also learns the true meaning of bigotry. For older, more mature readers.

Walking Stars. Victor Villaseñor. Houston: Arte Publico Press, 1994. 202 pp. ISBN 1–55885–118–6. LC 94–7404. Junior high and up.

The author has collected a number of unusual short stories told to him as a child of the lives of his parents and grandparents and interpreted each with personal notes revealing the effect it had on his life. Some of the stories include a family dog going crazy at the death of his beloved master, a woman giving birth to twins, the rescue of the author from the guards of the American mines by his grandmother, and his father at age 11 racing over 100 miles to catch the train carrying his family to the United States.

Reference and Scholarly Works

An Annotated Bibliography of Chicano Folklore from the Southwestern United States. Compiled by Michael Heisley. Los Angeles, CA: Center for the Study of Comparative Folklore and Mythology, University of California at Los Angeles, 1977. 188 pp. ISBN N/A. LC 77–150553. Professional use. Out of print.

Probably the only recent bibliography on the subject. It is well organized into broad sections. Its excellent subject index makes it easy to use. It includes citations for interesting works on "refranes" (proverbs), "curanderos" (healers), "cuentos" (tales), and other interesting aspects of Chicano folklore. It should be in all Chicano studies collections. Useful for school and public librarians.

Arte Chicano: A Comprehensive Annotated Bibliography of Chicano Art, 1965–1981. Shifara M. Goldman and Thomas Ybarra-Frausto, eds. Berkeley, CA: Chicano Studies Library Publications Unit, University of California, 1985. Chicano Studies Library Publications No. 11. 778 pp. ISBN 0–685–08355–1. LC 85–29156. High school and up; professional use.

Annotated subject entries. Specific topics, issues, forms of art, individuals. Citations contain bibliographic information. Author\artist and title entries. Notes language of article. Source for locating materials on Chicano art. An overview of the development of Chicano art. Gives dates and places of exhibits. Discusses artists' techniques. Useful for art students, units of Hispanic studies, and professional use. Illustrated.

Beyond Stereotypes: The Critical Analysis of Chicana Literature. Maria Herrera-Sobek, ed. Tempe, AZ: Bilingual Press, 1985. 152 pp. ISBN 0–916950–54–9. LC 84–73316. High school and up.

This collection of six essays was taken from the symposium, "New Perspectives in Literature: Chicana Novelists and Poets." Presented in two sections dealing separately with prose and poetry, these articles explore the work of women in Chicano culture and in the writing of Chicanas. These critical pieces are academic in nature, making this collection of interest to students and teachers of literature.

Biblio-Politica: Chicano Perspectives on Library Services in the United States. Francisco Garcia–Ayvens and Richard F. Chabran, eds. Berkeley, CA: University of California Press, 1984. 283 pp. ISBN 0–918520–08–8. LC 84–70532. High school and up; professional use. Out of print.

This volume brings together 14 papers and essays on diverse themes by Chicano librarians and scholars. Public and academic librarianship are addressed along with methods of research in Chicano Studies and community characteristics. Included are technical papers on indexing, bibliographic databases, user surveys, and collection development. Also included are several more theoretical pieces on Chicano writing, students and library skills, and librarianship. Two bibliographies, *A Selective Survey of Chicano Manuscript Collections in U.S. Libraries* and *Library Service to the Spanish Speaking in the United States: A Selected Bibliography*, although outdated, are still useful, especially the former, which provides information about archival collections. Indexed. Recommended for librarians, college educators, and students.

Bibliography of Mexican American History. Compiled by Matt S. Mier. Westport, CT: Greenwood Publishing Group, 1984. 500 pp. ISBN 0–313–23776–X. LC 83–18585. High school and up.

This important source of Mexican American history provides access to information that is necessary to understand the Mexican American experience and its resulting contribution to America. Materials published between the 1848 Treaty of Guadalupe Hidalgo and the 1980s are emphasized; however, studies on earlier historic periods are included. The contents are both chronological and topical and include books—both primary and secondary works—monographs, thesis and dissertations, and periodicals (government documents, pamphlets, and chapters from books and journals). Topics covered include immigration, civil rights, discrimination, history and cultural development of the mestizo, and Hispanic social and political leadership. Most citations are in English although the works of Mexican scholars are in Spanish. Each entry is partially or briefly annotated. A valuable comprehensive research bibliography for today's universities and public libraries.

Books in Spanish for Children and Young Adults: An Annotated Guide/Libros Infantiles y Juveniles en Espanol: Una Guia Anotada. Compiled by Isabel Schon. Metuchen, NJ: Scarecrow Press, Inc., 1987. 313 pp. ISBN 0–8108–2004–8. LC 87–9785. High school and up, professional use.

Highlighted in this bibliography are the works in Spanish by Hispanic authors of Latin American countries and Spain. This work is particularly useful in selecting Spanish language materials for children. Entries are organized by broad subject categories such as fiction and history within each country. Useful for bilingual classes, Spanish language students.

Borderlands Sourcebook: A Guide to the Literature on Northern Mexico and the American Southwest. Ellwyn R. Stoddard, Richard I.

Nostrand, and Jonathan P. West, eds. Norman, OK: University of Oklahoma Press, 1983. 462 pp. ISBN 0–8061–7718–4. LC 82–40331. High school and up; academic and professional use. Out of print.

An excellent reference to reputable materials on border-area topics which have been written and evaluated by scholars knowledgeable on borderland topics. The emphasis is on social science literature available in Northern Mexico, California, Arizona, New Mexico, Colorado, and Texas. Literature on the humanities are excluded except for brief references to art, architecture, and religion. Topics covered include history and archaeology; geography and the environment; economy; politics, law, and demography; and society and culture. More than 50 tables and maps graphically illustrate the information. Bibliographic essays are available on each section, and a large bibliography completes the work. It is an excellent purchase for academic libraries to provide for graduate students and faculty who are interested in the region.

Chicano Literature: A Reference Guide. Julio A. Martinez and Francisco A. Lomeli, eds. Westport, CT: Greenwood Press, 1985. 576 pp. ISBN 0–2313–3691–7. LC 83–22583. Professional use.

Comprehensive information on authors chosen for inclusion. Articles on the historical aspect of the literature, including the novel, the theater and poetry. Miscellaneous topics demonstrating the diversity of this field of material, such as children's literature and Chicano philosophy. Representative cross-section of a subject matter. Original studies in all major areas and authors. Chronology of literature. Glossary. Bibliography, not inclusive, helps identify primary and second-ary sources. Useful as a selection tool for high school, academic, and public librarians.

Chicano Organization Directory. Compiled by Cesar Caballero. New York: Neal-Schuman Publishers, 1985. 221 pp. ISBN 0–918212–65–0. LC 83–8333. High school and up; professional use.

Contains lists of active organizations that responded to questionnaire. Does not claim to be complete. Nonprofit agencies which provide services primarily to Mexican Americans included. Chicano Studies programs in colleges and universi-ties. Social, business, educational and professional organizations in the United States. Lists names, addresses, type of organization, purposes and goals, officers, and publications (if any). Useful to high school, and academic counsellors, public libraries.

Chicano Periodical Index: A Cumulative Index to Selected Chicano Periodicals Between 1967 and 1978. Compiled by the Committee for the

Development of Subject Access to Chicano Literatures. New York: G. K. Hall, 1981. 972 pp. ISBN 0–8161–0363–1. LC 81–2831.

Chicano Periodical Index: A Cumulative Index to Selected Chicano Periodicals Between 1979 and 1981. Compiled by the Committee for the Development of Subject Access to Chicano Literatures. New York: G.K. Hall, 1983. 648 pp. ISBN 0–8161–0393–3. LC 83–8453.

This is the most important reference tool that has been published recently with a Chicano theme. It is the only index that exists for literature written by Chicanos. Entries are organized alphabetically by subject. It contains an author/title index, as well as a thesaurus that is useful in indexing Chicano Studies materials. This title is mandatory for all types of libraries serving the Chicano public.

Chicano Perspectives in Literature: A Critical and Annotated Bibliography. Francisco Lomeli and Donaldo W. Urioste. Albuquerque, NM: Pajarito Publications, 1976. 120 pp. Out of print. Academic and professional use. ISBN N/A. LC N/A.

Although this volume is out of print, it continues to be an excellent bibliography on Chicano literature. Entries are organized in broad categories by genre. No subject or title indexes are included. Useful for addition to and comparison with more recent works. Useful for Hispanic literature studies and as a selection tool for academic and public libraries.

Chicano Scholars and Writers: A Bio–Bibliographical Directory. Edited and compiled by Julio A. Martinez. Metuchen, NJ: Scarecrow Press, 1979. 589 pp. ISBN 0–8108–1205–3. LC 78–32076. Academic and professional use.

Documented in this work is information on 500 scholars and writers. It includes entries for Chicanos and Anglo-Americans who have had an interest in Chicano themes. The entries contain personal data, education attainment, professional and/or community affiliations, honors, and publications. A subject index is a handy part of this publication. Although this work needs to be updated, it is still the only one of its kind and should be obtained by most public and academic libraries.

El Diccionario del Espanol/Chicano. Roberto A. Galvan and Richard V. Teschner. Lincolnwood, IL: Passport Books, 1993. 152 pp. ISBN 0–8325–9634–5. LC N/A. Junior high and up.

This is a revised edition of *El Diccionario del Espanol de Tejas* (1975). It was expanded to a total of 8,000 entries, and its scope broadened to include the lexicon of other southwestern states. A dictionary such as this one is very useful for people who wish to "periquear" (talk/communicate) with Chicanos. Good for school and public libraries.

Dictionary of Mexican American History. Matt S. Meier and Feliciana Rivera, eds. Westport, CT: Greenwood Press, 1981. 472 pp. ISBN 0–313–21203–1. LC 80–24750. Junior high and up.

Dictionary of Chicano Studies could have been the title of this work. Although written from a historical perspective, it contains entries which relate to the areas of Chicano culture and literature. It was written with a wide audience in mind and contains short articles, cross-references, and some suggested readings. A complete text of the Treaty of Guadalupe/Hidalgo (the treaty that officially ended the war between the U.S. and Mexico in 1848) is included, as well as a short glossary of Chicano terms, some historical maps, and statistical tables. Its index is excellent. Wide usage; good for a starting point for reports. Good for school, academic, and public libraries as well as professional use.

A Dictionary of Mexican American Proverbs. Compiled by Mark Glazer. Westport, CT: Greenwood Press, 1987. 376 pp. ISBN 0–313–25385–4. LC 87–23721. Junior high and up.

Alphabetical arrangement (Spanish language). Includes the phrase and variants. English translation. Key word underlined. Indexed. Spanish/English. Gives source of proverb and how many times included in survey. Useful for multicultural, Hispanic American studies, and comparison with European American proverbs.

Handbook of Hispanic Cultures in the United States. Four volumes. Nicolas Kanellos and Claudio Esteva–Fabregat, eds. Houston: Arte Publico Press, 1994. ISBN 1–55885–103–8. LC 93–13348. High school and up.

Comprehensive collection covering Hispanic cultures in the United States. Each volume contains a general introduction, summaries and conclusions, bibliography, index. *Volume 1: Anthropology.* 374 pp. ISBN 1–55885–102–X. *Volume 2: History.* 339 pp. ISBN 1–55885–074–0. *Volume 3: Literature and Art.* 413 pp. ISBN 1–55885–074–0. *Volume 4: Sociology.* 364 pp. ISBN 1–55885–101–1. Useful for Hispanic studies, American history classes.

The Hispanic Almanac, second edition. Washington, DC: Hispanic Policy Development Project, Inc., 1990. 203 pp. ISBN 0–918911–00–1. LC N/A. High school and up.

A one-volume comprehensive collection. Contains socioeconomic profiles of Hispanics. The five largest binational markets along the U.S./Mexico Border are profiled, along with the island market of Puerto Rico and 27 domestic Hispanic markets. Population growth projection charts. Current objective data about Hispanics. Useful for school, academic, and public libraries. Useful for serious research.

Hispanic American Almanac. Kannellos. Detroit: Gale Research, Inc., 1992. ISBN 0–8103–7944–9. LC N/A. High school and up.

Contains a chronology from 50,000 B.C. to March 1991. Includes historical overview, chapters on explorers and colonizers, significant documents, and prominent Hispanics. Covers history, art, culture, traditions, music, etc. Each of 25 chapters contains an introduction, references, notes, black-and-white photographs. Also includes illustrations, glossary, general bibliography, and index. Useful for Hispanic American studies and reports.

Hispanic-American Material Culture: A Directory of Collections, Sites, Archives, and Festivals in the United States. Compiled by Joe S. Grahm. Westport, CT: Greenwood Press, 1989. 281 pp. ISBN 0–313–24789–7. LC 89–1922. High school and up.

Indexed. Lists festivals, according to state, with addresses, activities, and dates. Details extent of collections. Arranged alphabetically by state and includes addresses and hours of operation. Useful for school, academic, and public libraries.

Hispanic Americans Information Directory 1990–1991. Darren L. Smith, ed. Detroit: Gale Research, Inc., 1993. 486 pp. ISBN 0–8103–7840–X. LC N/A. High school and up, professional use. Out of print.

This unique book is designed to provide information on agencies, programs, publications, and services concerned with Hispanic Americans. The emphasis is on information for and about Hispanics. More than 4,700 entries. The topics include approximately 250 nonprofit organizations directly concerned with Hispanic Americans and their regional, state, and local associations. Hispanic library and museum collections are identified, as well as approximately fifty awards, honors, and prizes which are bestowed upon those who serve the Hispanic community. The entries also include colleges and universities that offer Hispanic study programs, government agencies and programs, and university related and nonprofit organization research centers. Information on the top 500 Hispanic owned businesses, bilingual and migrant education, Hispanic radio and television stations, publishers and videos is available in the *Hispanic American Information Directory*. Each entry is indexed by name and by keyword. Useful for Hispanic American studies, high school and university counselors, libraries serving Hispanic populations.

A Hispanic Heritage: A Guide to Juvenile Books about Hispanic People and Cultures: Series III. Isabel Schon. Metuchen, NJ: Scarecrow Press, Inc., 1988. 158 pp. ISBN 0–8108–2133–8. LC 88–18094. Professional use.

Excellent selection of literature for students from kindergarten through high school. The emphasis is on books published in the United States from 1960 to the early

1970s that relate to ten Spanish-speaking countries. The contents are arranged by countries and include Argentina, Chile, Colombia, Cuba, Mexico, Panama, Peru, Puerto Rico, Spain, Venezuela, and the Hispanic-heritage people in the United States. The entries include a short analysis which summarizes specific ideas explored, provides critical reviews, and indicates recommended titles. The selection of recommended titles is based on current information, high potential for involving and entertaining the reader, and for the ability to provide insight into the Hispanic culture. Author, subject, and title indexes are included for the user's convenience. Good selection tool for school, academic, and public libraries.

Hispanic Resource Directory 1992–1994: A Comprehensive Guide to Over 6,000 National, State, and Local Organizations, Agencies, Programs, and Media Concerned with Hispanic Americans. Alan Edward Schorr. Juneau, AK: Denali Press, 1992. 384 pp. ISBN 0–938737–26–0. LC 88–70503. High school and up; professional use.

Designed to provide easy access to information on the Hispanic community. The emphasis is on organizations and agencies which serve Hispanics, information and data on the Hispanic community, and organizations whose membership is primarily Hispanic. The contents, which are arranged by state and city, include contact information on 951 local, regional, and national organizations and a coded list of services. When information is available, the entries contain the name of the key contact person, staff size, number of members, and number of chapters or affiliates. Many listings also contain annual budgets, ongoing publications, and a brief overview of the organization's purpose. Excludes information on organizations and agencies which focus on service to Hispanic refugee and immigrant populations. Nine appendixes list approximately 1,300 additional organizations. The appendixes include such topics as postsecondary educational institutions that have a 20 percent Mexican American enrollment, statistical information (social, political, and economic) on the Hispanic population, Federal Hispanic Employment Program managers, and Hispanic book publishers and distributors. The appendixes also identify agencies that are involved in human rights and equal opportunity, bilingual education, and migrant health and educational matters. Indexed by organization name, contact person name, and service. Useful for Hispanic studies, high school and university counselors and public libraries serving a Hispanic population. Foreword by Solomon Ortiz and Roger Mahoney.

Hispanics and the Humanities in the Southwest: A Directory of Resources. F. Arturo Rosales and David William Foster, eds. Tempe, AZ: Center for Latin American Studies, Arizona State University, 1983. 256 pp. ISBN 0–87918–055–2. LC 83–20993. High school and up.

Stated purpose of directory is to acquaint people with the possibilities regarding humanities projects in the states of California, Arizona, Texas, and New Mexico. Includes essays on the history of Hispanics in these areas. These are useful also in classrooms. Annotated listings of scholars, media outlets, libraries and museums. Lists groups that are willing to cooperate in Hispanic-oriented projects. Media outlets who direct their programming to the Hispanic community included. Useful for multicultural, Hispanic American studies, high school and academic counselors and public libraries serving Hispanic populations.

Latino Materials: A Multimedia Guide for Children and Young Adults. Compiled by Daniel Flores Duran. New York: Neal Schuman Publishers, 1979. 264 pp. ISBN 0–87436–262–8. LC 78–18470. Professional use.

Dr. Duran's work is an annotated bibliography of books and 16mm films suitable for Chicano and Puerto Rican children and young adults. It also cites materials useful to librarians and educators serving Chicano youth. The entries are both critical and descriptive and contain valuable information such as recommended grade level. Useful for school and public librarians.

Latinos in the United States: A Historical Bibliography. Albert Camarillo, ed. Santa Barbara, CA: ABC-Clio, 1986. ABC-Clio Research Guides Series No. 18. 332 pp. ISBN 0–87436–458–2. LC 86–26448. High school and up.

This excellent source contains journal literature on all the Hispanic-origin populations in the United States. The emphasis is on materials published in America: History and Life between 1973 and 1985. The contents are arranged according to national origin, except the first chapter, which deals with general materials (bibliographies, historiography, archives, and collections) and the second chapter, which concentrates on Latinos in the borderlands prior to 1848. The 1,382 citations are primarily drawn from the humanities and social sciences and include such topics as Spanish exploration and settlement, cultural and social adaptation, immigration, current employment and population studies, language, education, and health. Both contemporary and historical studies are included. This interdisciplinary work is highly useful for college and university students, scholars, reference librarians, and readers who are interested in research.

The Mexican American: A Critical Guide to Research Aids. Compiled by Barbara J. Robinson and J. Cordell Robinson. Greenwood, CT: Jai Press, Inc., 1980. 287 pp. ISBN 0–89232–006–0. LC 76–5643. High school and up.

This is the best bibliography, currently in print, of reference sources on the Chicano. Its entries, organized into broad categories by types of material and subject, contain excellent annotations. A monograph entitled *Quien Sabe? A Preliminary List of Chicano Reference Materials* updates this bibliography to a large extent. Robinson's work is useful for college/university students and researchers. All librarians should become very familiar with the contents of this work. Edited by Robert D. Stueart. Foundations in Library and Information Science, Vol. 1.

Mexican-American Bibliographies. Carlos E. Cortes, ed. New York: Arno Press, 1974. 493 pp. ISBN 0–405–05682–6. LC 73–14421. Professional use.

An anthology bringing together five early bibliographies of materials about Mexican Americans dating from 1929 to 1960. The five works have been reprinted in their original form, not joined into one coherent resource. Hence, each section of the volume must be used as an independent resource, each with its own form of organization and categories such as history, economic conditions, and education. Several contain brief annotations. Useful to high school, academic, and public librarians.

Mexican American Biographies: A Historical Dictionary, 1836–1987. Matt S. Mier. Westport, CT: Greenwood Publishing Group, 1988. 279 pp. ISBN 0–313–24521–5. LC 87–12025. High school and up.

Alphabetically lists and gives a biographical sketch of prominent Mexican Americans from 1836 to 1987. Persons are also indexed by professional activity and state. Useful as a starting point for reports on notable Hispanic Americans.

The Mexican-American People. Leo Grebler, Joan W. Moore, and Ralph C. Guzman. Compiled by the Mexican-American Study Project at the University of California, Los Angeles. New York: The Free Press, 1970. 777 pp. ISBN N/A. LC 73–81931. High school and up. Out of print.

A comprehensive study of the socioeconomic position of Mexican Americans in selected urban areas of the five southwestern states. Tables and text cover statistics of jobs/occupations, census-derived demographic information, assimilation, political interaction, and social mobility. Useful for historical research and for comparison to more up-to-date statistics.

Mexican and Mexican-American Agricultural Labor in the United States: An International Bibliography. Martin H. Sable. New York: Haworth Press, 1987. 429 pp. ISBN 0–86656–542–6. LC 85–27346. High school and up; professional use.

This book contains a bibliography that identifies both popular and scholarly literature and a directory of Mexican American organizations, labor unions, government agencies, and research centers. The work emphasizes materials published from the eighteenth century to 1984. Some entries in Spanish and other languages. The contents are divided into two sections, popular and scholarly. Topics covered in both categories of the bibliography are general agricultural labor, immigration of Mexican agricultural labor, Mexican-American farm labor, migrant agriculture labor, agricultural labor unions, and farm labor strikes. Several appendixes and indexes. Appendix A lists audio-visual materials, and assesses their audience, Appendix B identifies available archival and manuscript materials, Appendix C lists names and addresses of periodicals, and Appendix D (the directory section) lists names and addresses of public and private organizations. Concludes with a title index giving addresses for the A-V materials in Appendix A and an author index which identifies and describes manuscripts from appendix B. Useful for research, high school, and academic librarians.

A Selected and Annotated Bibliography of Chicano Studies, second edition. Compiled by Charles M. Tatum. Boulder, CO: Society of Spanish Speaking and Spanish American Studies, Department of Modern Languages and Literature, University of Colorado, 1979. 121 pp. ISBN 0–89295–011–0. LC 79–64044. Professional use.

Dr. Tatum's bibliography was the most up-to-date annotated source of bibliographic citations of work on the Chicano. It is a good source for materials in the following categories: art, the Chicana, folklore, journals, language, literature, and music. The section on literature is subdivided by genre and accounts for its strongest point. Thus, it is useful as an update to Lomeli's bibliography of Chicano literature. Unfortunately, it lacks a subject index. This bibliography should be used in conjunction with Trejo's comprehensive, better organized, but not as up-to-date *Bibliographia Chicana*. Use as additional source, but seek more up-to-date information.

Spanish Surnames in the Southwestern United States: A Dictionary. Compiled by Richard Woods and Grace Alvarez-Altman. New York: G. K. Hall, 1978. 154 pp. ISBN 0–8161–8145–4. LC 78–4127. High school and up. Out of print.

The etymology, meaning, and location in Spain where the surname is used the most is given for each entry. This is the only publication that provides this information in English. Useful for genealogical research, Hispanic American studies, and Spanish language classes.

Nonfiction

The Cuban Americans. Renee Gernand. New York: Chelsea House Publishers, 1995. Immigrant Experiences Series. 107 pp. ISBN 0–7910–3376–7. LC 94–42011. Junior high and up.

Revised version of the older Peoples of North America series by Chelsea House. Little has been changed. Bibliography has been expanded and updated. Well organized, carefully written, accurate, readable. Traces the origins of the Cuban Americans, their reasons for coming to the United States, their problems and successes in their new homes. Useful for multicultural studies.

Everything You Need to Know About Latino History. Himilce Novas. New York: NAL/Dutton, 1994. 272 pp. ISBN 0–452–27100–2. LC 94–18225. High school and up.

In spite of the fact that, if present demographic trends continue, Latinos will be the largest ethnic minority in the United States within a decade, most people, including Latinos, know very little about Latino history, the contributions made to the United States by Latinos, ties to Spanish-speaking countries, and the cultural roots of Latinos. Novas remedies this in a snappy, easy-to-read, enjoyable style. Excellent for multicultural studies.

A Guide to the History of Texas. Light Townsend Cummins and Alvin R. Bailey, Jr., eds. Westport, CT: Greenwood Publishing Group, 1988. Reference Guides to State History and Research Series. 308 pp. ISBN 0–313–24563–0. LC 87–15021. Junior high and up.

Divided into two parts, this guide records historical essays and major archival repositories of Texas. Due to the space limitations, this guide does not contain comprehensive information. It is intended to be used by students and beginners in research. Also, it is a useful tool for doing research on Texas.

The Hispanic Struggle for Social Justice. James D. Cockcroft. Danbury, CT: Franklin Watts, 1994. The Hispanic Experience in the Americas Series. 176 pp. ISBN 0–531–11185–7. LC 94–23968. High School and up.

Cockcroft examines the history of Hispanics in the United States from the western frontier days to the present. He describes Mexican Americans, Puerto Ricans, and other Latinos; their ethnic history, national issues, labor, immigration, feminism, civil rights; and the farm workers' struggle to form a union. Dispels the myth of macho men dominating submissive women. Overlaps considerably with *Latinas:*

Hispanic Women in the United States. Useful for multicultural and Hispanic American studies. Illustrations.

Latinas: Hispanic Women in the United States. Hedda Garza. New York: Watts, Inc., 1994. The Hispanic Experience in the United States Series. 224 pp. ISBN 0–531–11186–5. LC 94–30598. Junior high and up.

The author details the lives and roles of Hispanic women in the United States from the frontier days to the present. She dispels the old stereotype of the macho husband and the submissive, downtrodden wife. Garza celebrates the strength of these women and shares details of their daily lives and culture. Overlaps considerably with *The Hispanic Struggle for Social Justice: The Hispanic Experience in the Americas.* Useful for multicultural units, Hispanic American studies, and women's studies.

Mexico's Ancient City of Teotihuacan: The First Metropolis in the Americas. Caroline Arnold. New York: Houghton Mifflin Company, 1994. 48 pp. ISBN 0–395–66584–1. LC 93–40811. Junior high.

Teotihuacan was Mexico's largest and most important city for over 800 years. Arnold explores the ruins and pieces together a picture of what the people and their lives were like when the city was in its glory. Full-color photographs by Richard Hewitt reveal the ruins, statues of deities, paintings in stone, masks, and ceremonial centers such as the Pyramid of the Sun and Pyramid of the Moon. Brief discussion of the Aztecs, Toltecs, and other civilizations that came later. Good for social studies and world history units.

The Mystery of the Ancient Maya. Carolyn Meyer and Charles Gallenkamp. NY: Margaret K. McElderry Books for Young Readers, 1995. 178 pp. ISBN 0–689–50619–8. LC 84–024209. Junior high.

Revised edition of the 1985 work. Traces the culture, art, daily lives, social structure, written language of the Maya from early explorations to modern archaeologists. Looks at advances in studies of the language and mathematics. Well written. Includes black-and-white photos, reproductions, maps, charts, and diagrams. Useful for world history units.

Perspectives in Mexican-American Studies, Volume 3: Community, Identity, and Education. Thomas Gelsinon, ed. Tucson, AZ: University of Arizona, Mexican American Studies and Research Center, 1992. 210 pp. ISBN 0–939363–03–8. LC N/A. Academic libraries.

Including articles and essays, this is one of an excellent annual series which discusses

Mexican Americans from the pre–Columbian Era to the present. Easy to read and suitable for use in the university. Introduction by Juan R. Garcia.

Puerto Rico: America's Fifty-First State. David J. Abodaher. Danbury, CT: Franklin Watts, Inc., 1993. 112 pp. ISBN 0–531–13024–X. LC 92–39474. Junior high and up.

Abodaher believes that the only three possible courses for Puerto Rico are to remain as they are, to become the United States' 51st state, or to become completely independent. While he addresses Puerto Rican politics, Abodaher primarily relates the history of Puerto Rico and its people. Maps, index, photographs, reproductions, suggestions for further reading. Useful for American history, Hispanic American history units.

Spanish American Authors: The Twentieth Century. Angel Flores. Bronx, NY: H.W. Wilson, 1992. 915 pp. ISBN 0–8242–0806–4. LC 92–7591. High school and up.

Extensive and valuable information on 330 authors considered by Flores to be the epitome of Spanish American writers of this century. Includes biographical and autobiographical information as well as covering the themes and styles of each author. DRAWBACKS: No topical index, no title index, no means of access by country, and no cross-references for surnames make accessing this information difficult. Useful for studies of Spanish American writers and multicultural literature studies.

Tales of a Shaman's Apprentice: An Ethnobotanist Searches for New Medicines in the Amazonian Rain Forest. Mark J. Plotkin. New York: Viking Penguin, 1993. 320 pp. ISBN 0–670–83137–9. LC 92–50768. Junior high and up.

Mark Plotkin spent ten years in the rain forests of Guyana and Suriname learning local lore and herbs from the shamans. Modern society has taken its toll on this ancient culture. Young people no longer value the old ways, and the shamans have no one to whom to pass on their knowledge. Plotkin discusses organizations that are working to return some drug profits to the Indians and establish shaman apprentice programs so that the old knowledge does not die out. Useful to those with an interest in alternative medicine and multicultural studies. Also available in trade cloth, ISBN 0–014–012991–X.

Videos

Videos: Fiction, not reviewed

Maricela. Chicago, IL. Public Media Video. 1992/1985. 58 min. Junior high and up.

A young El Salvadoran girl and her mother, a teacher, move from their country to the United States and into an upper-middle-class home. Includes a teacher's guide. Wonderworks Family movie originally broadcast on PBS.

Sweet 15. Chicago, IL. Public Media Video. 1990. 120 min. Junior high and up.

The quinceanera is an important event in a young Mexican American girl's life. The celebration of her fifteenth birthday announces her graduation into womanhood. Marta Delacruz has been looking forward to hers and is very upset when her father cancels it. Then she finds out that he is not a U.S. citizen and her outlook changes. Wonderworks Family movie originally broadcast on PBS.

Videos, Nonfiction, reviewed

Adelante Mujeres. Windsor, CA: National Women's History Project, 1995. 30 min. Color. Includes teacher's guide. 20pp. Preview available. Junior high and high school.

This video presents a chronological overview of Mexican American history, including the coming of the Spanish to the New World; Mexican acquisition and loss of land; and the Mexican American influence on United States culture, emphasizing the lives, roles, contributions, and efforts of Mexican American women. Visuals include period artwork, photos, illustrations, and modern film footage. The audio track has appropriate volume and good selections of music. Good for studies on minority cultures or women's studies.

One World, Many Worlds: Hispanic Diversity in the United States. Bohemia, NY: Rainbow Educational Video, 1993. 22 min. Color. Preview and guide (22pp.) available. Junior high.

The video provides a survey of Spanish exploration and colonization and its effects on native populations, the languages and religions imposed by colonization, and the results of mixing the races. Describes the struggles for independence in Central and South America, the Mexican American War, Hispanic emigration to the United States, the Latinos' struggle against discrimination and racism, and their influence on American culture. Helps middle school students gain an appreciation for the history and contributions of Hispanic Americans. Useful in social studies and units on cultural diversity.

Videos: Nonfiction, not reviewed

Folkloric Dances of Mexico. Bellaire, TX: Inside Mexico, 1990. 115 min. Junior high and up.

The thirtieth anniversary of the Ballet Folklorico is celebrated with songs and dances from Mexico, past and present.

Guide to Hispanic Excellence. Film Archives, 1994. Three videos. 35 min. each.

Volume One, Hispanic Excellence: Sports.

Focuses on Chi Chi Rodriguez, golf star; Tab Ramos, soccer star; and Pablo Morales, Olymic gold medalist.

Volume Two, Hispanic Excellence: Leaders.

Focuses on Dr. Antonia C. Novello, first Hispanic woman U.S. Surgeon General; Joseph Unanue, owner of U.S.'s largest Hispanic food company; and Raul Yzaguirre, advocate of justice and equity for Hispanics in Washington, D.C.

Volume Three, Hispanic Excellence: Arts and Entertainment.

Featuring Little Joe Hernandez, leader of the country's most popular Tex-Mex band; John Leguizamo, comedian; and Jackie Nespral, television news anchor.

Hispanic Culture. Eight volumes. Media Basics Video. 25 min. each.

Puerto Rico: History and Culture

Spanish Conquest of America

People of the Caribbean

Mexican People and Culture

Bilingual America

The Glory of Spain

The Spanish Language

Modern Puerto Rico

Hispanics of Achievement Video Collection. Film Archives, 1994. Ten volume set. 30 min. each. Also available in Spanish—special order.

Joan Baez. (1941–). Folk Singer.

Simon Bolivar. (1783–1830). Latin American Revolutionary.

Cesar Chavez. (1927–1993). Mexican American labor leader.

Roberto Clemente.(1934–1972). Puerto Rican baseball player.

Hernan Cortez. (1485–1547). Spanish explorer.

Ferdinand and Isabelle. (1452–1516) (1451–1504). Spanish Monarchs.

Pablo Neruda. (1904–1973). Chilean poet and diplomat.

Juan and Evita Peron. (1895–1974) (1919–1952). President and First Lady of Argentina.

George Santayana. (1863–1952). Spanish philosopher and poet.

Pancho Villa. (1878–1923). Mexican revolutionary.

Mexico: Lost Civilizations of an Ancient Land. Media Basics Video. AI100. 18 min. Junior high and up.

Academy Award–winning film tribute to seven of Mexico's important sites including Teotihuacan, Uxmal, and Chichen Itza.

Mexico, Our Neighbor to the South. Mill, IL: United Learning 1993. 20 min each. Junior high and up.

Mexico: The People and Their Land shows Mexico's geography, natural resources, government, expanding population, industries, employment opportunities, and plans for the future.

Mexico: The People and Their Customs shows the heritage and cultural diversity of the Mexican people.

Sounds of Mexico. NY: Gessler Publishing Company, 1993/1990. 45 min. Teacher's guide available.

This video covers the different parts of Mexico, the music of each region, and its instruments. Language and Lifestyles Series.

The Yucatan: Past and Present. Media Basics Video. 60 min.

History of the peninsula shared by Mexico and Guatemala. A visit to archaeological sites of the Maya and other peoples of this ancient land.

 ASIAN AMERICANS

Biographies

American in Disguise. By Daniel I. Okimoto. New York: Walker/Weatherhill, 1971. 206 pp. ISBN 0–8027–2438–8. LC 70–121065. High School and up. Out of print.

Harvard-educated Nisei tells of his experiences in America, including the author's family's internment during World War II, the continuing racism against Japanese Americans, and the author's feelings about his own interracial marriage. Useful in that it gives a first-person account of the experience of Japanese Americans.

Bruce Lee: Fighting Spirit. Bruce Thomas. Berkeley, CA: Frog, Ltd. 1994. 329 pp. ISBN 1–883319–11–0. LC 94–025723. High school and up.

Biography of martial arts expert and actor Bruce Lee. Traces his training in martial arts, his start in show business, his roles on television, and his movie career. Lee worked hard to bring the martial arts into public awareness as an ethnic art form as well as entertainment and combat. Useful for units on notable Asian Americans and martial arts fans.

A Dream of Water. Kyoko Mori. New York: Fawcett, 1995. 256 pp. ISBN 0–449–91043–1. LC 94–1438. Young adults.

Young adult readers who have read *Shizuko's Daughter* by the same author will recognize many of the details of Mori's life. While *Shizuko's Daughter* is fictionalized, it is clearly based on the author's life in which her mother commits suicide, leaving Mori and her younger brother to live with a cold, indifferent father and a cruel, manipulative stepmother. Mori left Japan, returning only once after earning a Ph.D. and launching her career as an author. She tells of having rejected her Japanese culture only to rediscover its value in her life. Useful for units on Japanese American authors and in writing classes.

Extraordinary Asian Pacific Americans. Susan Sinnot. Danbury, CT: Children's Press, 1993. Extraordinary People Series. 270 pp. ISBN 0–516–03152– X. LC 93–12678. Grade 4 and up.

Beautiful photographs; fine page design, and rich, detailed Asian motifs enhance the appeal of this collection of nearly 100 stories of Asian Pacific Americans from Yung Wing, the first Asian American to write an autobiography, to Greg Louganis, Olympic diver, who came from Samoa. Also covers the Japanese internment camps, Chinatowns, and Chinese laundries. A valuable addition to any collection on Asian Pacific Americans.

Kristi Yamaguchi: Pure Gold. Jeff Savage. Morristown, PA: Silver Burdett Press, 1993. Taking Part Series. 64 pp. ISBN 0–87518–583–3. LC 92–42190. Grades 3 and up.

Attractive, full-color photographs enhance the inspiring story of Olympic skater Kristi Yamaguchi, who overcame a babyhood in foot casts to become a gold medal winner in the 1992 Olympics. Recommended for junior high and public libraries. Useful for units on notable Japanese Americans, women athletes, and ice skating.

No Tears for Mao: Growing Up In the Cultural Revolution. Niu-Niu. Chicago: Academy Chicago, 1994. 286 pp. ISBN 0–89733–410–8. LC 94–40601. Young Adults.

Niu-niu grew up during Mao's Cultural Revolution. She went from a secure childhood to scrabbling for her very existence after seeing her parents arrested for "crimes against the state" and her grandfather beaten to death before her eyes. Niu-niu, now an actress and film maker living in France, tells the story from the point of view of the child she was when these events were taking place. Useful for Asian history units and Chinese history studies.

Stubborn Twig: Three Generations in the Life of a Japanese American Family. Lauren Kessler. New York: Random House, 1993. 334 pp. ISBN 0–679– 41426–6. LC 93–3593. Young adults.

The author traces a Japanese American family living in the Pacific Northwest over three generations, beginning in 1903 when Masuo Yasui arrives in Hood River, Oregon. His story is typical of immigrants of his time. He works hard, suffers the pangs of loneliness, struggles with customs and a new language, then faces anti-Japanese sentiment. The family continued to face discrimination for many years, but built a successful business and prospered until Yasui was arrested and imprisoned as a spy. His relatives were scattered and some were interned. This book makes racism and discrimination come alive for the reader. Good for social studies or American history units.

When Heaven and Earth Changed Places: A Vietnamese Woman's Journey from War to Peace. Le Ly Hayslip. New York: NAL/Dutton, 1993. 368 pp. ISBN 0–452–26417–0. High school and up.

Le Ly Hayslip is a Vietnamese American, a refugee with three "American" sons. Her story portrays the horrors of a people caught in war who have to be willing to do anything to survive, even though they are reluctant to betray traditional values. It is a story of lives destroyed and of people who grow up in terror. The author's story is autobiographical, but it reveals the truth about what all Vietnamese refugees left behind, why they fled, and how they survived. She does not say much about her life in the United States: the refugee experience becomes individualized once the refugees reach America. Instead, by focusing on Vietnam and a Vietnamese perspective of the war, the author provides some understanding of what caused so many people to flee. This Vietnamese perspective is important in understanding the Vietnamese American culture. Useful for multicultural units, units on Vietnamese Americans.

The Winged Seed. Li-Young Lee. New York: Simon and Schuster, 1995. 224 pp. ISBN 0–671–70708–6. LC 94–37072. High school and up.

Chinese poet Li-Young Lee tells the story of his life in a lyric manner very close to the style of his poetry. Lee's father was a doctor who turned to religion and became a preacher while in prison. His mother was raised in a traditional Chinese home. Lee shares his memories of his harsh childhood in Indonesia, exile, punishment, hardship, divine intervention, and endurance in a gripping manner. Gives excellent insight into the man and the life that gave birth to his poetry. Useful for Chinese literature units and units on notable Chinese authors.

Folklore, Literature, Poetry

American Dragons: Twenty-Five Asian American Voices. Laurence Yep, ed. New York: HarperCollins Publishers, Inc., 1993. 256 pp. ISBN 0–06–021494–5. LC 92–28489. Junior high and up.

Laurence Yep has written a number of excellent books for children and young adults. He has assembled here the stories, poems, essays, and one dramatic monologue of several Asian American authors. Not all of the stories are uniformly excellent, but it is an interesting collection of old and new voices from several Asian countries. Good for Asian literature units.

American Eyes: New Asian-American Short Stories for Young Adults.
Lori M. Carlson, ed. New York: Henry Holt and Co., Inc., 1994. 160 pp. ISBN 0–
8050–3544–3. LC 94–22391. Young adults.

This collection of short stories gives an unsentimental picture of Asian life and
feelings of what constitutes "home." It does not romanticize, nor does it offer
heroes. It is a "slice of life" as only Asians can know it and describe it. This work
clearly illustrates the commonality of our needs, desires, and dreams. Uniformly
excellent.

Beyond Spring: T'zu Poems of the Sung Dynasty. Translated by Julie
Landau. New York: Columbia University Press, 1994. 275 pp. ISBN 0–231–
09678–X. LC 93–46479. Young Adults.

These poems echo throughout the years and evoke the same emotions now as they
must have then. They are not dated, but show clearly that people, love, heartbreak,
disappointment, and hope have not changed over the centuries. Not light verse. A
useful addition to a curriculum on worldwide poetry. Translations from the Asian
Classics Series.

Cambodian Folk Stories From The Gatiloke. Muriel Paskin Carrison.
Translated by the Venerable Kong Chhean. Boston: Charles E. Tuttle Company,
Inc., 1993. 140 pp. ISBN 0–8048–1905–X. LC 86–51325. Junior high and up.

Folktales from Cambodia covering topics such as scoundrels and rascals, kings and
lords, and foolishness and fun are told in this book, followed by a background and
explanation of each story. The stories follow an introduction to the Gatiloke, which
explains where the stories originated, from whom they originate, and the ideas
behind them. The book includes an appendix about Cambodia's land, people,
history, village life, and celebrations. There is also a glossary, a recommended
reading list, and a map of Cambodia. This would be a great addition to any
children's library and a very useful source for those interested in the Cambodian
culture.

Cambodian Literary Reader and Glossary. Im Proum, ed. Ithaca, NY:
Cornell University, Southeast Asian Program Publications, 1988. 596 pp. ISBN 0–
300–02069–4. LC 76–050538. High school and up.

Third and final volume in series beginning with the *Cambodian System of Writing
Reader* and the *Intermediate Cambodian Reader*. It may be used independently as a
survey of Cambodian literature since it includes a cumulative glossary of the
vocabulary introduced in all three volumes.

Part One consists of 32 readings selected from the important and best known works of Cambodian literature. Examples of the types of readings include: historical prose, modern novel, short poems and songs, and romantic and religious epics. Part Two consists of a Cambodian-English glossary containing 4,000 items from this volume and 6,000 items from the other two volumes. This constitutes a combined dictionary of 10,000 entries. Useful for world literature units and foreign language studies.

Dragons, Gods, and Spirits from Chinese Mythology. Tao Tao Liu
Sanders. New York: Peter Bedrick Books, 1995. The World Mythology Series. 132 pp. ISBN 0–87226–922–1. LC 94–8354. Junior high and high school.

Poorly designed volume detailing stories from Chinese sources relating tales of dragons, spirits, gods, myths of origins, and Buddhist and Taoist tales. Might have some value for comparing literatures of different cultures. Illustrated by Johnny Pau.

The Hawk's Well: A Collection of Japanese American Art and Literature, Volume I. Ed Hiura. San Jose, CA: Asian American Art Projects, 1986. 209 pp. ISBN N/A. LC N/A. High school and up. Out of print.

This is a beautiful 200-page book containing a mixture of poems, short narratives, drawings, artwork, and black-and-white photos of Japanese Americans taken in the early part of this century. An introduction describes some of the artists and discusses the nature of Japanese American art and how it is distinct from either Japanese or "white" American art. Many of the poems deal with the internment experience, but the collection is primarily an artistic rather than historical collection. Gives the reader a sense of the Japanese American experience. Useful for art students and students of Japanese American culture.

The Heritage of Vietnamese Poetry. Edited and translated by Huynh Sanh
Thong. Ann Arbor, MI: Books On Demand, 1988. 349 pp. ISBN 0–685–23691–9. LC 78–17092. High school and up.

An anthology of 475 traditional Vietnamese poems, divided into 13 broad categories, provides a comprehensive view of poetry spanning the end of the tenth century to the beginning of the twentieth century. Historical development of Vietnamese literature from a cultural, political and historical basis is covered in the introduction. Diagrams and textual explanations of the type of verse used and individual themes of particular relevance provided. The note section clarifies parts of every poem, and biographical sketches of the authors follow. Good for units on world literature.

An Introduction to Vietnamese Literature. Maurice M. Durand and Nguyen T. Huan. Translated by D. M. Hawke. New York: Columbia University Press, 1985. 232 pp. ISBN 0–231–05852–7. LC 84–12754. High school and up.

A general overview of the literature in relation to Vietnamese history from 257 B.C. to 1975 A.D. Folk literature, poetry, and the contemporary novels are discussed. Some poems and excerpts are included. Indexed. Useful for units on world literature.

Join In: Multiethnic Short Stories by Outstanding Writers for Young Adults. Donald Gallo, ed. New York: Delacorte Press, 1993. 272 pp. ISBN 0–385–31080–3. LC 92–43169. Junior high and up.

This collection relates the experiences of multiethnic teens adjusting to Caucasian society. They have the same hopes, dreams, and worries as their white schoolmates, yet they must adhere to their families' cultures as well. Not uniformly well written, but worth adding to a multiethnic collection.

Myths and Legends of the Polynesians. Johannes C. Anderson. New York: AMS Press, Inc., Charles E. Tuttle, 1986. 513 pp. ISBN 0–404–14200–1. LC 75–035170. High school and up.

A scholarly account of the history, arts, and mythology of the Polynesian races. Useful for units on comparative mythology, legends, and Hawaiian culture. Illustrated by Richard Wallwork.

The Open Boat: Poems from Asian America. Garret Hongo, ed. New York: Doubleday and Company, Inc., 1993. 352 pp. ISBN 0–385–42338–1. LC 92–11089. Junior high and up.

Lyric collection of poems by writers from every imaginable Asian country. Some were born abroad, but all live in the United States now. The selections are modern and contemporary and many deal with the experience of immigration and learning to live in another country and cope with another culture. A welcome addition to any library. Illustrations by Garrett Hongo.

The Poetry of Vietnam. Nguyen Ngoc Bich, ed. Translated by Burton Raffel and William S. Nerwin. New York: The Asian Literature Program, 1969. 23 pp. High school and up. ISBN N/A. LC N/A. Out of print.

A wonderful collection of traditional Vietnamese poetry with over 50 authors and 150 poems enclosed. A must for the collector of Vietnamese literature and art.

Rama: A Legend. Jamake Highwater. New York: Henry Holt and Co., Inc., 1994. 185 pp. ISBN 0–8050–3052–2. LC 94–11586. Junior high.

Based on the Ramayana, this book relates the story of Rama, a young man who is wrongfully banished from his father's kingdom and then from Earth. His wife, Sita, is kidnapped, and Rama faces demons, a jealous queen, magical creatures, monsters, and untold danger before he can rescue Sita and regain his proper place.

Fiction for Young Adults

American Visa. Ping Wang. Minneapolis: Coffee House Press, 1994. 179 pp. ISBN 1–56689–025–X. LC 94–12599. Young Adults.

Told in the first person, *American Visa* is the story of a Chinese girl, Seaweed, who is snatched from her college studies to be retrained as a peasant during Mao's Cultural Revolution. She works hard, learns English, and has a chance to go to America, where she continues to work hard and send money home to her family. Sometimes inspiring, sometimes gloomy, always engaging.

Boat People: A Novel. Mary Gardner. New York: W.W. Norton & Co., Inc., 1993. 288 pp. ISBN 0–393–03738–X. LC 94–27505. Young Adults.

Winner of the 1993 Associated Writing Programs Award. The author brings together a group of Vietnamese fishermen and a Vietnamese doctor living in Galveston, Texas. The fishermen are doing what they have always done. The doctor is trying to blend in. They and an African American woman who is working with Vietnamese children come together in a predictable, but heartwarming finale. The clear message is that we are *all* boat people in one way or another.

Bittersweet. Leslie Li. Boston: Charles E. Tuttle Company, Inc., 1994. 512 pp. ISBN 0–8048–3036–3. LC 92–15385. Young Adults.

Good companion piece to Pearl S. Buck's *The Good Earth*. Bittersweet's life as a woman under China's patriarchical system spans the Boxer Rebellion, the War of Revolution between the Kuomintang and the Communists, monarchy, anarchy, western imperialism, Japanese imperialism, Sun Yat-sen's fledgling democracy, Chiang Kai-shek's dictatorship, British Colonialism in Hong Kong, and capitalism in the United States.

A Bridge Between Us. Julie Shigekuni. New York: Doubleday and Co., Inc., 1995. 253 pp. ISBN 0–385–47678–7. LC 94–003668. Mature young adults.

Nomi, a fourth-generation Japanese American, is not handling adolescence well. Her promiscuity causes problems with her very traditional mother, her suicidal grandmother, and her acid-tongued great-grandmother. The personal histories of all four women are revealed as Nomi finds her way through the swamp of adolescence and finds herself reenacting their lives.

Child of the Owl. By Laurence Yep. New York: HarperCollins, 1977. 224 pp. ISBN 0–06–026743–7. LC 76–24314. Junior high.

Twelve-year-old Casey is sent to live with her maternal grandmother (Paw-Paw) in San Francisco's Chinatown after her gambler father, Barney, is beaten up. She knows little about her Chinese heritage, and hasn't even experienced a normal childhood, with Barney always trying to stay just one step ahead of the bill collectors. Casey learns what it means to be Chinese by observing Paw-Paw's way of life. It is a wonderfully written story and won the Boston Globe–Horn Book Fiction Award for 1977.

China Trade. S. J. Rozan. New York: St. Martin's Press, Inc., 1994. 256 pp. ISBN 0–312–11254–8. Young Adults.

Lydia Chin, a Chinese American private eye, becomes involved in a case of rare porcelains being stolen from a museum. Since she is intimately familiar with Chinatown, she is able to investigate the connection between the Tongs and a black market in stolen art. First novel of a series yet to come.

The Examination. Malcom Bosse. New York: Farrar, Straus & Giroux, 1994. 296 pp. ISBN 0–374–32234–1. LC 94–050955. Junior high and high school.

Set in the Ming Dynasty, late sixteenth to early seventeenth century C.E. Applicants must take several examinations to qualify for public office. Lao Chen, having passed the local exams, travels to Beijing to take the nationals. He is accompanied by his more practical and less learned brother, Hong. One brother obtains public office; the other becomes a revolutionary.

The Girl-Son. Anne. E. Neuberger. Minneapolis: The Learner Group, 1994. Adventures in Time Series. 132 pp. ISBN 0–87614–846–1. LC 94–6725. Junior High.

Fictionalized biography of Korean educator Induk Pahk (1886–1980). When Induk was young, girls were not considered worth educating or capable of reading or writing. She was disguised as a boy so she could go to school. As she grew older, ideas about educating girls changed and she was able to go to high school and college and later founded a school. Directions for determining one's birth sign according to the Chinese zodiac are included.

Hiroshima. Laurence Yep. New York: Scholastic, Inc., 1995. 64 pp. ISBN 0–590–20832–2. LC 94–18195. Junior high.

Laurence Yep has created a composite of several real children who were in Hiroshima at the time the atom bomb was dropped in 1945 to tell the story of one little girl who later comes to the United States for treatment. He describes the attack, the mushroom cloud, the destruction of the city, the aftermath, and the continuing controversy over whether or not the bomb should have been dropped. His descriptions are clear, simple, and graphic. Written for younger YAs, but will be enjoyable for older YAs who are interested in the subject.

Love and Infamy. Frank Deford. New York: Viking Penguin, 1993. 576 pp. ISBN 0–670–82995–1. LC 93–4131. Young adults.

An American boy, Cotton Drake, and a Japanese boy, Kiyoshi Serikawa, meet in grade school and become best friends. They are separated briefly when each goes to a different college, but come back together to start a business in Japan in 1936. The story continues through the building tension between Japan and the United States, and the differences in perception and beliefs between the Americans and Japanese are portrayed accurately and movingly. Fast pace. Highly readable.

Ming: A Novel of Seventeenth Century China. Robert B. Oxnam. New York: St. Martin's Press, Inc., 1994. 288 pp. ISBN 0–312–11315–3. LC 94–36361. High school and up.

The end of the Ming Dynasty when the Manchu barbarians from the north conquer China is the setting of this story of star-crossed lovers. Longyan, son of the family by a concubine, cannot learn to read and write. Meihua, his sister-in-law, has broken with tradition by secretly learning to read and write. They come together through a Jesuit who would like access to prominent Chinese families just as war breaks out. Gives insight into the world of the Chinese social customs and tells a good story at the same time.

Native Speaker. Chang-Rae Lee. New York: Riverhead Books, 1995. 336 pp. ISBN 1–57322–001–9. LC 94–32241. High school and up.

Second generation Korean Henry Park is a spy assigned to get close to an up-and-coming Korean American politician. But Park finds himself forced to face the reality of what he is, where he comes from, what he believes in, and evaluating his loyalties.

Paradise of the Blind. Duong Thu Huong. Translated by Phan Huy Duong and Nina McPherson. New York: William Morrow and Company, Inc., 1993. 272 pp. ISBN 0–688–11445–8. LC 92–18599. Young adults.

Huong's book about a young girl in Vietnam in the 1970s under Communist rule was banned in her own country. After the Communist takeover, life changes for nearly everyone. The old values are derided and new ones take their place. But Hang's mother is suspended between two worlds. She must make her place in the new order, yet she is bound by tradition to serve her Uncle Chinh and expects Hang to do likewise until she is sent to Russia to work. The descriptions are a combination of beauty and desolation.

Peach Blossom Spring. Adapted by Fergus M. Bordewich. NY: Simon and Schuster Children's (Green Tiger Press), 1994. 203 pp. ISBN 0–671–78710–1. LC 92–19676. Junior high.

Based on a story by early Chinese poet Tao Yuanming (365–427 C.E.). Navigating an unfamiliar stream, an old fisherman finds a utopian valley where no one has had any contact with the outside world for several hundred years. The man decides to forsake the outside world for the tranquility he has found, but wants to go home to get some of his belongings. He is permitted to go, but warned not to tell anyone about the valley. He does tell, of course, and never again finds his way back to the valley. For younger YAs. Illustrated by Yang Ming-Yi.

The Revenge of the Forty-seven Samurai. Erik Christian Haugaard. Boston: Houghton Mifflin Company, 1995. 226 pp. ISBN 0–395–70809–5. LC 94–007691. Grade 3 and up.

When Lord Asano, a feudal lord, meets an unjust and dishonorable death, 47 of his 200 samurai determine to avenge him. The story, based on a historical event still commemorated in Japan, is told through the eyes of a young servant named Jiro. Details of ancient Japanese life and ideals of loyalty and honor make the book a fascinating read.

Saying Goodbye. Marie G. Lee. Boston: Houghton Mifflin Company, 1994. 219 pp. ISBN 0–395–67066–7. LC 93–26092. Junior high and high school.

Finding one's cultural identity, racism, coming of age, and making choices are the themes of this story of Harvard freshman Ellen Sung, age 20, who puts aside her personal desire to be a writer to follow in her sister's footsteps into medical school.

She falls in love with Korean American Jae, but runs into political and personal problems which force her to decide between her African American roommate and her Korean culture.

Shadow of the Dragon. Sherry Garland. Orlando, FL: Harcourt, Brace, and Company, 1993. 314 pp. ISBN 0–15–273530–5. LC 93–17258. Junior high and high school.

Danny Vo, a Vietnamese American, is a typical teenager who concerns himself with getting a job, a driver's license, and a beautiful blonde girl named Tiffany. But at home, Danny must revert to the old ways and be a dutiful son. His cousin, Sang Le, recently released from a Vietnamese re-education camp, comes to live with them. His bad grades and inability to get a job influence him to join a gang. Before Danny can get him away, Sang Le is beaten to death by a gang of skinheads, one of whom is Tiffany's brother. A strong coming of age novel.

Shin's Tricycle. Tatsuharu Kodama. New York: Walker and Co., 1995. 32 pp. ISBN 0–8027–8375–9. LC 95–007326. Junior high.

Kodama's book illustrates the horror of atomic war in graphic fashion. The story is told by a teacher who saw his child die. Shin had always wanted a tricycle and was riding it with pride the day the atomic bomb was dropped. He did not die instantly, but was horribly burned. His tricycle was buried with him, but later exhumed and placed on exhibit in the Peace Museum in Hiroshima. Not for younger readers. Translated by Kazuko Hokumen Jones; Illustrated by Noriyuki Ando.

Shizuko's Daughter. Kyoko Mori. New York: Henry Holt and Co., Inc., 1993. 240 pp. ISBN 9–8050–2557–X. LC 92–26956. Junior high and up.

Unable to tolerate a shattered marriage, Shizuko commits suicide, leaving her husband to marry his mistress of eight years and to rear their 12-year-old daughter, Yuki. The new stepmother does her best to erase any trace of the first wife and makes Yuki's life miserable. The father is uncaring and refuses to get involved. As Yuki matures, she makes her own decisions about her life in this touchingly presented coming of age story set in modern Japan. Somewhat fictionalized version of the author's life.

Stella: On the Edge of Popularity. Lauren Lee. Chicago: Polychrome Publishing Corporation, 1994. 178 pp. ISBN 1–879965–08–9. LC 93–43917. Junior high.

Korean American Stella Sung Ok wants very much to be popular and to fit in with American girls. She gradually learns that friendship is more important than popularity, that she must take responsibility for her own actions, and that respect cannot be demanded—it must be earned. A readable, fun story with the underlying message that it is wrong to stereotype people and to make fun of those who are different.

The Sunita Experiment. Mitali Perkins. New York: Little, Brown and Company 1993. 144 pp. ISBN 0–316–69943–8. LC 92–37267. Junior high.

Sunita Sen finds her westernized world turned upside down when her East Indian grandparents come to stay for a year. Her parents discourage boys from coming over; her mother reverts to traditional Indian attire and takes a year's leave of absence from her college teaching job; and their household becomes typically East Indian. Confused and embarrassed, Sunita shuns her friends to keep them from seeing how her family is living, but they stand by her. Cultural differences are portrayed by positive solutions and strong role models.

Thief of Hearts. Laurence Yep. New York: HarperCollins Publishers, Inc., 1995. 208 pp. ISBN 0–06–025342–8. LC 94–18703. Junior high.

Stacy has never considered herself to be anything but an American and has had no interest in her Chinese culture until a classmate calls her a "half-breed." She, her mother, and her grandmother go on a trip to San Francisco's Chinatown, where Stacy learns about her Chinese heritage and to be at peace with being part of two worlds.

Tree of Heaven. R.C. Binstock. New York: Soho Press, Inc., 1995. 224 pp. ISBN 1–56947–038–3. LC 94–41552. Young adults.

Listed as an adult book for young adults, *Tree of Heaven* is the poignant story of Kuroda, a Japanese scholar who is shamed by his father into becoming a soldier, and Li, a young Chinese girl. Kuroda is dismayed to find that he enjoys fighting, but he is appalled by the brutality shown by his fellow soldiers toward the Chinese. He prevents them from raping Li and begins the emotional bonding of two enemies. Set during Japan's invasion of China in the 1930s. For more mature readers.

Under the Blood-Red Sun. Graham Salisbury. New York: Delacorte Press, 1994. 256 pp. ISBN 0–385–32099–X. LC 94–000444. Junior High and up.

Born in Hawaii to Japanese parents who fled poverty in Japan, Tomi is bewildered by the responses of the people around him after the Japanese bomb Pearl Harbor. He is forced to try to tone down his grandfather's fierce pride in Japan. His father is sent to an internment camp and his mother loses her job. The story offers no easy answers, but shows empathy for both cultures.

Reference and Scholarly Works
Cambodian Americans

Intermediate Cambodian Reader. Franklin E. Huffman and Im Proum, eds., Ithaca, NY: Cornell University, Southeast Asian Program Publications, 1982. 499 pp. ISBN 0–300–01552–6. LC 72–179474. High school and up.

Sequel to *Cambodian System of Writing and Beginning Reader With Drills and Glossary*. Serves as an intermediate reader to develop student's ability to the point of reading unedited Cambodian with the aid of a dictionary. Part One contains 37 readings, graded in difficulty. Part Two consists of an alphabetical Cambodian-English glossary containing 4,000 vocabulary items from this reader and 2,000 items from the *Cambodian System of Writing* reader.

Modern Spoken Cambodian. Franklin E. Huffman. Ithaca, NY: Cornell University, Southeast Asian Program Publications, 1987. 451 pp. ISBN 0–300–01316–7. LC 71–104615. High school and up.

A guide to the basic structures of standard spoken Cambodian. Includes pronunciation drills, useful words and phrases in 28 different situations, and a Cambodian-English/English-Cambodian glossary (both transliterated). Explanations of why certain words or phrases are used can provide useful information on Cambodia, past and present. Index. Recommended to come before *Cambodian System of Writing and Beginning Reader*. Useful for foreign language students.

Chinese Americans

China and America: A Bibliography of Interactions, Foreign and Domestic. Compiled by James M. McCutcheon. Ann Arbor, MI: Books On Demand, 1972. 85 pp. ISBN 0–8357–8678–1. LC 74–190449. High school and up.

This book covers a wide range of subjects, each with its own bibliography. Many different kinds of print material are given, some of it unpublished. Some of the subjects covered are the Chinese communities in the United States (with separate sections on Hawaii and California), Chinese and American foreign policy, and public opinion. It is indexed by the personal names of the authors and by the titles of their works. Useful for world history and government units.

Japanese Americans

A Buried Past: An Annotated Bibliography of the Japanese American Research Project Collection. Compiled by Yuj Ichioka, Yasuo Sakata, Nobuya Tsuchida, and Eri Yasuhara. University of California Press, 1974. 227 pp. ISBN 0–520–024541–5. LC 73–83063. High school and up. Out of print.

Extensive annotated Bibliography of information on or related to Japanese Americans. Bibliography includes: books, government documents, church records, literature, poetry, newspapers, magazines, directories, who's who, biographies, autobiographies, personal papers, dissertations, and theses. Would be especially helpful for college-level research.

Cambridge Encyclopedia of Japan. Richard J. Bowning and Peter Kornidel, eds. New York: Cambridge University Press, 1993. 352 pp. ISBN 0–521–40352–9. High school and up.

This encyclopedia is divided into eight sections: geography, history, society, arts and crafts, language and literature, thought, economy, and politics. Articles are all signed by university professors. Comprehensive coverage. Good index, photographs, maps, and chapter of further reading. Excellent addition to any high school or university library.

Japan Statistical Yearbook, 1995. Bristol, CT: Taylor & Francis, Inc., 1995. 840 pp. ISBN 4–8223–1720–X. High school and up.

A comprehensive and systematic summary on all fields, including national land, population, economy, society, and culture of Japan. Supersedes the *Statistical Yearbook of the Empire of Japan*, published from 1882 through 1940. Useful and readily available to a wide range of individual and institutional users. A bilingual source whose major drawback is an index and guide to sources in Japanese only. Useful for research.

Japanese American History: An A to Z Reference from 1868 to the Present. Japanese-American National Museum Staff. New York: Facts on File, 1993. 400 pp. ISBN 0–8160–2680–7. LC 92–35753. Young adults.

Provides the history of Japanese immigration to the United States, a chronology of major events of interest affecting Japanese such as the internment during World War II, and encyclopedia-type entries on a variety of subjects such as people, places, historical events, and vocabulary. Black-and-white photos. Valuable for high school and university collections. Preface by Daniel K. Inouye.

Kenkyusha's New English-Japanese Dictionary. Yoshio Koine, ed. New York: French & European Publications, Inc., 1980. 2,477 pp. ISBN 0–7859–7127–0. LC 81–101348. High school and up.

This dictionary is patterned after the Webster's and Oxford dictionaries and is considered one of the most widely used standard dictionaries. After the English entry and pronunciation guide, Japanese characters follow to indicate the subject matter and definition. Included is a listing of widely used phrases entitled Foreign Phrases and Quotations, mainly in Latin, French, and German. There is also a companion Japanese-English edition. Useful for libraries serving a Japanese or Japanese American population.

Kodansha Encyclopedia of Japan. Itsaka, Edwin Reischauer, and Shigeto Tsuru, eds. New York: Kodansha America, Inc., 1983. 207 pp. ISBN 0–87011–620–7. LC 83–080778. High school and up.

This nine volume set, including index, broadly defines its scope as Japan's past and present, its interactions with the West, and aims "to provide an up-to-date and sophisticated compilation of knowledge about Japan to the English-speaking world; to introduce the topic at a level appropriate to a high-school student and proceed far enough to provide a good starting point for more advanced students with some knowledge of Japan." The set includes broad, lengthy survey articles, introducing most of the major areas into which Japanese culture can be divided. Cross-references from the general article lead the reader to articles of medium length on subtopics mentioned in them and to thousands of shorter articles that make up most of the set. Some of the topics covered in the general articles include agriculture, animals, art, clothing, cooking, education, film, flower arrangements, Japanese language, literature, medicine, religion, society, traditional theater, and the history of women. Cross-references are indicated in the text or entry-heading in boldface. Besides nearly 1,000 illustrations (photos, maps, graphs, tables), the set offers a brief but useful guide to the Romanization and transliteration of Japanese, as well as to the conversion of money, weights and measures, and the calendar. Recommended for libraries serving a Japanese American population, multicultural units, and world history units.

Pictorial Encyclopedia of Japanese Life and Events. Translated by Gaynor Sakimori. New York: Japan Publications, 1994. Pictorian Encyclopedia of Japan Series. 112 pp. ISBN 0–685–67819–9. LC N/A. Junior high and up.

Full-color photographs. A description of daily life in Japan based on the calendar year and emphasizing major holidays. Coverage is strictly of native Japanese. Other minority groups are barely mentioned and not shown in photographs. Wonderful for browsing. Some topics include the role of women, positive and negative aspects of Japanese life, and national responsibility for World War II. Useful for multicultural and world history units.

The Shogakukan Japanese-English Dictionary of Current Terms.
Iwatsu Keisuke. Matsumoto Michihiro, ed. Tokyo: Shogakukan, 1984. 951 pp. ISBN 4–095–05061–6. LC 84–177872. High school and up. Out of print.

Words and phrases are grouped together as they would be used in discussing various concepts. Includes a listing of Japanese companies, the Constitution of Japan in English and Japanese, a diagram of the levels of Japanese government, and an alphabetical index of where English words and phrases are located in the text. Very current in content. Primarily useful for research.

Korean Americans

A Handbook of Korea, ninth Edition. Seoul, Korea: Korean Overseas Information Staff. New York: Irvington Publishers, 1992. 824 pp. ISBN 0–8290–2631–2. LC N/A. High school and up.

Slick but comprehensive treatise of Korea. Informative sections on almost every aspect of Korean life and culture plus a bibliography, index, color plates, and map. Since this is a publication of the South Korean Government, librarians should be aware of potential bias in the presentation of some sections. Useful for multicultural studies.

Korea Annual: A Comprehensive Handbook on Korea. Yonhap News Agency Staff. San Francisco: Western Publications Service, Annual. 836 pp. ISBN changes annually. LC N/A. High school and up.

Yearly almanac of Korea. Includes chronological highlights of the year, review of the government and economy, social affairs, education, culture, sports, laws, and documents. Who's Who section describes important Koreans. Useful as a source for reports and research.

Pacific Islanders

Books About Hawaii: Fifty Basic Authors. Arthur Grove Day. Ann Arbor, MI: Books on Demand. 1977. 131 pp. ISBN 0–7837–1309–6. LC 77–007997. High school and up.

Annotated bibliography of 50 basic works which would form the start of a good collection on Hawaii. Includes works by and about native authors as well as such people as Robert Louis Stevenson and James Michener. Fiction and nonfiction. Reprint.

Hawaiian Word Book. Robin Burningham, illustrator. Honolulu: The Bess Press, 1990. 104 pp. ISBN 0–9358–4812–6. LC 82–73895. Junior high and up.

Designed to teach over 200 basic Hawaiian words and to introduce the Hawaiian language and culture to everyone, the book offers an easy, accurate, and fun way to learn basic Hawaiian vocabulary. Beautifully illustrated words deal with various aspects of Hawaiian culture, nature, lifestyle, food, and clothing. Useful for multicultural studies and units on Hawaii.

Vietnamese Americans

Read Vietnamese: A Graded Course in Written Vietnamese. Nguyen-Dinh-Hoa. Rutland, VT: C. K. Tuttle, 1966. 189 pp. ISBN N/A. LC 66–18965. High school and up. Out of print.

Designed to teach the written language of Vietnam to the student who already has an understanding of the spoken language. Includes word lists, antonyms, and translation exercises. Key to exercises and glossary also included.

Standard Pronouncing Vietnamese–English Dictionary. Revised edition. Le-Ba-Khanh and Le-Ba-Kong. Hong Kong: Hong Kong Youth Press, 1988. 498 pp. ISBN N/A. LC 82–209214. High school and up. Out of print.

Alphabetically arranged dictionary divided into Vietnamese-English and English-Vietnamese. Pronunciation guides for stressed vowels is not provided. Illustrative phrases for word usage are given. Of use to libraries serving Vietnamese Americans and for bilingual classes.

Asian Americans—Multiethnic

Asian American: A Study Guide and Sourcebook. Lynn P. Dunn. San Francisco: R & E Publishers, Inc., 1975. Ethnic Studies Series. 111 pp. ISBN 0–88247–304–2. LC 74–31620. High school and up.

This book is one of a four-volume series on American minorities. In each volume three themes are treated: identity, conflict, and integration/nationalism. This volume serves as a text or guide for students (includes high school level) in the study of Asian Americans as well as a beginning reference text. It provides sufficiently broad and adequate reference. Within a given thematic section, the "study outline" is historical and chronological in development. The "notes and sources" column provides reference to sources and parallels the "study outline." Also provides glossary and who's who features. Valuable for comparison's sake. Today's students will want a more up-to-date sourcebook.

Asian Pacific Americans: A Handbook On How to Cover and Portray Our Nation's Fastest Growing Minority Group. Bill Sing, ed. Los Angeles, CA: National Conference of Christians and Jews, 1989. 80 pp. ISBN N/A. LC 89–197169. High school and up. Out of print.

This short, inexpensive book is intended for those involved in providing media coverage of Asian Pacific Americans, but it is a good resource for anyone wanting to raise his or her consciousness. It concisely describes issues of concern to Asian Pacific Americans, tips on sensitivity, and ideas for improved and appropriate media coverage. It also contains a guide to name usage, demographic statistics, a glossary of important terms and events, and a resource directory of organizations.

Dictionary of Asian American History. Hyung-Chan Kim, ed. Westport, CT: Greenwood Publishing Group, Inc., 1986. 642 pp. ISBN 0–313–23760–3. LC 85–030188. High school and up.

This fine reference work is divided into two major sections: (1) essays treating historical development of different ethnic groups from Asian countries and the Pacific Islands and (2) treatises on the place of Asian and Pacific Americans in the American social order by scholars in the field of Asian and Pacific American studies. Includes chronology, 1980 census report, and general subject index. Useful for research on Asian Americans.

Original Martial Arts Encyclopedia: Tradition, History, Pioneers. John Corcoran and Emil Farkas. Los Angeles, CA: Pro-Action, 1993. 450 pp. ISBN 0–9615126–3–6. LC 92–81677. Young adults.

A comprehensive work on the history and traditions of the martial arts as well as people who have worked to teach and make them famous. Movements are explained step by step, but lack sequential pictures. Emphasis is on karate rather than tae kwon do. Useful to those interested in the martial arts, high school, academic, and public libraries. Edited by Stuart Sobel. Reprint.

Roots: An Asian American Reader. Amy Tachiki, et. al., eds. Los Angeles: UCLA Asian American Studies Center, 1971. 345 pp. ISBN 0–934052–06–9. High school.

Assembled for the Asian American as well as the general reader, this collection contains a variety of materials from many perspectives. Included are sociological and historical pictures of Asian Americans as well as a section on communities. Not only a handy repository of secondary writings on the subject, but a documentary collection from our time. Interesting reading, but the lack of an index hinders academic use.

Nonfiction

Cambodian Americans

Cambodia. Claudia Canesso. New York: Chelsea House Publishers, 1989. Places and Peoples of the World Series. 96 pp. ISBN 1–55546–798–9. LC 88–30435. Junior high and up.

This young adult book presents the history of Cambodia, a brief chronology, and a study of the current situation in that country. It contains information about the geography, history, government, economy, people, and culture of Cambodia. It has a quick facts section, glossary, and index. It is an excellent source for anyone who wants information about Cambodia and Cambodians but does not have the time or inclination to read college-level books. It would also serve very well as an introduction to the Cambodian culture or as a broad overview of Cambodians and their country.

Cambodia: 1975–1982. Michael Vickery. Boston: South End Press, 1994. 361 pp. ISBN 0–896980–190–7. LC 83–061478. University, professional level.

This discusses what led up to the fall of Cambodia, the rise of the Kampuchea, and what brought on the Cambodian Revolution. Information is readily accessible, but this work is better for university students or researchers.

Cambodia 1975–1978: Rendezvous With Death. Karl D. Jackson, ed. Princeton, NJ: Princeton University Press, 1992. 344 pp. ISBN 0–691–07807–6. LC 88–26764. High school and up.

This book covers the explanation of the Cambodian Revolution by a variety of authors in essay form touching on the history, economy, social changes, and political changes. There are pictures and an extensive bibliography. Good for units on Asian American history and world history.

Cambodia: A Country Study. Third Edition. Russell R. Ross. Washington, DC: United States Government Printing Office, 1990. Area Handbook Series. 398 pp. ISBN 0–16–020–838–6. LC 89–600150. High school and up.

This government document covers comprehensive information about the history, economy, government, and politics of Cambodia. It includes a glossary, bibliography, statistical tables, maps, and pictures. Useful for Asian studies, multicultural studies, and world history.

Cambodia—Its People, Its Society, Its Culture. David J. Steinberg and Herbert H. Vreeland. Ann Arbor, MI: Books On Demand, 1959. Survey of World Cultures Series. 365 pp. ISBN 0–8357–7978–5. LC 59–013226. High school and up.

An overview of Cambodia that includes history, culture, and society is given in this book. Geography and languages along with religion, are also discussed. Useful for Asian studies, multicultural studies, and world history. Reprint.

Cambodian Writing System and Reader. Franklin E. Huffman. Ithaca, NY: Spoken Language Services, Inc., 1982. Spoken Language Series. 365 pp. ISBN 0–87950–470–6. LC 78–104614. High school and up.

Prepares students to read and write Cambodian. Designed in conjunction with the author's *Modern Spoken Cambodian*. Has three parts. Part One presents formal analysis of the relationship between the phonology of modern Cambodian and the symbols used to represent them. Part Two provides the student with a systematic, step-by-step approach to reading and writing Cambodian syllables. Consists of 225 cumulative exercises, providing a symbol-to-sound operation. Part Three consists of 50 reading selections graded in difficulty, ranging from short simple narratives to essays on various aspects of Cambodian culture. Designed to be used following parts One and Two. A glossary includes not only some 2,000 vocabulary items introduced in the reader but also examples used throughout the other sections of the book. The glossary should be helpful in reading other Cambodian materials. This book is an outgrowth of three years of study of Cambodian at the School of

Oriental & African Studies of the University of London in Southeast Asia and at Cornell University. Useful for foreign language studies.

Haing Ngor: A Cambodian Odyssey. Haing Ngor with Roger Warner. New York: Warner Books, Inc., 1987. 352 pp. ISBN 0446–38990–0. LC 87–027355. High school and up.

Haing Ngor, best known to most Americans for his Oscar-winning portrayal of Dith Pran in the film *The Killing Fields*, has given us a stunning record of his experiences under the Khmer Rouge regime and as a refugee. Though it is best read from start to finish as a chronicle and human drama, the work is well indexed, and could be used as a reference for information on aspects of Cambodian culture before the Khmer Rouge as well as on the events and atrocities that took place during their rule. The writing is vivid, and the story compelling. Throughout the book, Ngor's search for an adequate explanation for the horrors that happened to him and his country provides significant insight into the culture. This is an extremely valuable resource for understanding what happened in the Cambodian holocaust and what refugees have had to live through. It would be appropriate for any high school, public, or university library.

A History of Cambodia. Second Edition. David P. Chandler. Boulder, CO: Westview Press, 1992. 287 pp. ISBN 0–8133–0926–3. LC 91–41680. Gifted high school students and up.

This is the first book to chronicle Cambodian history from its beginnings to the twentieth century and the first scholarly history of Cambodia to appear in English. It draws on 19th and 20th century Khmer archives and documents. Illustrations, a bibliographic essay and an index are included. The ten chapters are divided chronologically. It is important as a reference tool because of its uniqueness. Good addition to any library.

Kampuchea Between China and Vietnam. Chang Pao-Min. Singapore: Singapore University Press, 1985. 20 pp. ISBN 9971–69–089–6. LC 85–940889. High school and up. Out of print.

This book discusses what led up to the conflicts in Cambodia and the diplomacy needed and used. This also has five appendixes that include treaties. Useful for Asian history units and world history units. It would be interesting to contrast with more recent works to see how views and attitudes have changed.

The Khmers of Cambodia: The Story of A Mysterious People. Indianapolis: Bobbs-Merrill Company, 1970. 160 pp. ISBN N/A. LC 76–103863. High school and up. Out of print.

Written before the destruction and devastation of the Pol Pot regime, this work about the Khmers focuses on the people of Cambodia, their way of life, and their rich history rather than the terrible struggles they were to face in the coming years. Topics covered are the geography of Cambodia; the great kings and empires of Cambodia; life under the Sihanouk leadership; the Cambodian way of life; village life; the bonze (young men studying to become monks); the isolated hill people; and Cambodia's relationship with the modern world up to 1970, with a discussion of the foreshadowing of things to come. It is an important work because it provides an account of pre-Pol Pot Cambodia as seen firsthand by the author that can never be seen again.

Places and Peoples of the World—Cambodia. Claudia Canesso. New York: Chelsea House, 1989. 92 pp. ISBN 1–55546–166–2(set). LC 88–30435. Junior high and up.

This young adult book presents the history of Cambodia, a brief chronology, and a study of the current situation in that country. It contains information about the geography, history, government, economy, people, and culture of Cambodia. It has a quick facts section, glossary, and index. Although it was written for upper elementary and junior high school students, it is an excellent source for anyone who wants information about Cambodia and Cambodians but does not have the time or inclination to read college-level books. It would also serve very well as an introduction to the Cambodian culture or as a broad overview of Cambodians and their country. Illustrations. Part of a 211 volume set.

The Quality of Mercy. William Shawcross. New York: Simon and Schuster, 1984. 464 pp. ISBN 0–671–44022–5. LC 84–1353. High school and up. Out of print.

Shawcross, who traveled through Cambodia, has written a study of Cambodia, its history, and the terrible struggles of its people. The work of countries and governments involved in helping Cambodian refugees is explained and evaluated. This book is a good source for those interested in an in-depth account and history of the plight of the Cambodian people and the refugees from Cambodia.

Teenage Refugees from Cambodia Speak Out. Valerie Tekavec. New York: Rosen Publishing Group, Inc., 1994. In Their Own Voices Series. 64 pp. ISBN 0–8239–1848–3. LC 94–41411. Junior high and high school.

These teenagers fled the "killing fields" of Pol Pot and his murderous cronies. This short volume—with its first-person accounts of the horrors of war, the difficulties of fleeing the country, and adjustment to a new life—is gripping and powerful. The author gives a description of Cambodia, its culture, and the problems facing the country. A bibliography, glossary, and black-and-white photos add to the usefulness of the volume. Useful for units on immigrants and their reasons for leaving their countries of origin and for world history units.

When the War Was Over. Elizabeth Becker. New York: Simon and Schuster, 1986. 502 pp. ISBN 0–317–53639–7 High school and up.

Elizabeth Becker, through interviews and personal experience, describes what happened in Cambodia after the Americans left and traces the history of the Khmer Rouge. By sharing personal experiences, the author has made the book more readable and easy to understand. Useful for Asian history units.

Chinese Americans

"Behave like your actions reflect on all Chinese." Donald Dale Jackson. Smithsonian 21 (February 1991): 115–125. High school and up.

In a very personal account, Chinese Americans remember their people who had the perseverance to climb the "Gold Mountain." In just a few pages the whole history of the Chinese in America is told by the author and the individuals he interviewed. This article is an excellent beginning before engaging in a more extensive study.

Bitter Melon: Inside America's Last Rural Chinese Town. Jeff Motlow. Jeff Gillenkirk, editor. Berkeley, CA: Heyday Books, 1993. 144 pp. ISBN 0–930588–58–4 LC 87–010418. High school and up.

A history of Locke, California, as told by individuals who were associated with the town. Although Lockeport (later Locke) had been established by the Chinese Americans themselves, it was a segregated community. Though it is an oral history, this book would have been enhanced by an index. High school students should like the personal viewpoints and the many pictures. Bibliography and illustrations. This short book is an excellent source of the Chinese American viewpoint on life in the United States.

Bitter Strength: A History of the Chinese in the United States, 1850–1870. Gunther P. Barth. Ann Arbor, MI: Books on Demand, 1964. 319 pp. ISBN 0–7837–1669–9. LC 64–21785. High school and up.

An analysis of the forces that led to the hostility expressed toward the Chinese immigrants in the United States and to their eventual exclusion. Attitudes toward

Chinese Americans today were formed during this important period in their history. Included is a short glossary of Chinese characters with the Romanized spelling that approximates the Cantonese pronunciation. Index. An excellent tool for understanding the Chinese immigrant and for social studies units. Reprint.

China Images in the Life and Times of Henry Luce. Patricia Neils. Lanham, MD: Rowman and Littlefield, 1990. 384 pp. ISBN 0–8476–7634–X. LC 90–8087. High school and up.

Henry Luce, founder, editor and publisher of *Time* and *Life* magazines highly influenced the attitudes of the American public and foreign policy towards China from 1923 to 1967, with his God-fearing, anti-Communist opinions. Neils has two objectives: she looks at the effect of popular images on public opinion and she supports the validity of Luce's opinions by comparing them with historical fact, as well as with what was reported in other papers and magazines. Luce withstood the forties, was reviled in the sixties, and was resuscitated in the nineties by Neils. Extensive notes are provided with each chapter, as well as a lengthy bibliography and detailed index. Useful for world history units.

China: Under Communism. Michael G. Kort. Brookfield, CT: Millbrook Press, Inc., 1995. 176 pp. ISBN 1–56294–450–9. LC 94–8312. Junior high and up.

Kort begins with chapters devoted to the Chinese Empire and to the Republican Era, then goes into the convoluted history of China under the leadership of Chairman Mao and the problems created by his growing megalomania which were repeatedly covered up and corrected by his more pragmatic party members. Lively style. Balanced. Up-to-date. Impeccable scholarship. Black-and-white photos. Minimal flaws. Useful for Asian history units.

Chinese American Portraits: Personal Histories, 1828–1988. Ruthanne Lum McCunn. San Francisco: Chronicle Books, 1988. 174 pp. ISBN 0–87701–491–4. LC 87–30773. High school and up. Out of print.

Chinese Americans relate their personal histories in separate chapters focused on individual families. Customs, hopes, fears, and achievements are chronicled and accompanied by a large number of historic and contemporary photographs, some very personal. The final chapter lists some major United States legislation that has affected Chinese Americans. It is indexed, illustrated, and has a bibliography following each chapter. Useful for units on the history and contributions of the Chinese in this country.

Chinese Americans. Alexandra Bandon. Morristown, PA: Silver Burdett Press, 1994. Footsteps to America Series. 112 pp. ISBN 0–02–768149–1. LC 93–32711. Junior high and up.

Bandon describes conditions in China which motivated early Chinese settlers to migrate to the United States, their journeys here, conditions they found and were required to endure, the prejudices they encountered, and their new lifestyles. She then goes on to describe the current status of Chinese Americans with short personal essays and photographs. Mistakes include typographical errors. Useful as a supplementary source for Chinese studies, Asian studies, and the history of the Chinese in this country.

Chinese Gold: The Chinese in the Monterey Bay Region. Sandy Lydon. Capitola, CA: Capitola Book Company, 1985. 550 pp. ISBN 0–932319–00–9. LC 84–72699. High school and up.

The author states that Chinese contributions were fundamental to the Monterey Bay region's economic development, but that very little has been written about them until this book. It covers the history of the Chinese in the area starting with the first immigrants before the Spaniards. The author discusses the various economic enterprises of the Chinese in the area, the various Chinatowns, as well as the anti-Chinese movement. The book has many excellent historical photographs and maps. It is a very thorough book, as indicated by the extensive bibliography, and it is sensitively written. There is a lengthy index. Highly recommended for high school, academic, and public libraries.

Chinese in American Life: Some Aspects of Their History, Status, Problems, and Contributions. Seattle, WA: University of Washington Press, 1963. 352 pp. ISBN N/A. LC 62–9273. High school and up. Out of print.

A well-researched record of the Chinese abroad, both as immigrants to the United States and as Chinese American citizens. The author intends for this positive history to inspire in Chinese Americans pride in their accomplishments. Written before the 1965 laws gave Chinese Americans equal status with European immigrants, the book is also aimed toward helping other Americans understand them. It covers both political and social aspects of Chinese American life. It is indexed, has statistical tables, a bibliography, and extensive end notes. Useful for units on contributions of other cultures to this nation.

The Chinese in San Francisco: A Pictorial History. Laverne Mau Dicker. New York: Dover Publications, Inc., 1980. 134 pp. ISBN 0–486–23868–7. LC 79–050669. High school and up.

Presents Chinese American history in San Francisco from 1847 to 1979 in a series of short articles and 168 black-and-white photographs. Articles list historical dates of significance. Plates are from both public and private collections. Includes bibliography. Interesting as an additional acquisition. Preface by Thomas W. Chin.

The Chinese in the United States of America. Rose Hum Lee. Hong Kong: Hong Kong University Press, 1960. 465 pp. ISBN N/A. LC 60–003959. High school and up. Out of print.

An excellent picture of the Chinese immigrants' family life, their view of themselves, and other American's views of them. Covers all aspects of Chinese American life from the beginning. The glossary includes Chinese characters and the anglicized spelling for many terms. It is indexed, has a bibliography, a glossary and a list of Chinese institutions and associations. Useful as an additional acquisition and for research.

Chinese of America. Jack Chen. New York: Harper and Row, 1981. 275 pp. ISBN 0–06–250139–9. LC 80–7749. High school and up. Out of print.

History of the Chinese in America from 1785 to 1981. This solidly documented, comprehensive, yet highly readable history brings alive the Chinese American experience, from the arrival of the first Chinese to the issues and achievements of the present. Includes tables, graphs, maps, appendix, and index. Useful for history units and studies on the contributions and experiences of Chinese immigrants.

Chinese Women of America: A Pictorial History. Judy Yung. Seattle, WA: University of Washington Press, 1986. 128 pp. ISBN 0–295–96358–1. LC 85–040974. High school and up.

This wonderful work provides a history of Chinese women in America between 1834 and 1985. Over 130 excellent photographs document this time period of pioneers, struggle, and eventual development of contemporary women. Tables and maps of female population, education, labor force, and major occupations are also included. Useful for women's studies and Asian American studies units.

Empires Beyond the Great Wall: The Heritage of Genghis Khan. Adam T. Kessler. Los Angeles: Natural History Museum of Los Angeles County, 1995. 176 pp. ISBN 0–938644–34–3. (Paper: ISBN 0–938644–34–5). LC 93–87480. High school and up.

Kessler's book addresses a treasury of artifacts never before seen in this country. He describes various tribes of Mongol nomads from the region of China known as the Northern Steppes. A worthy addition to any collection in need of material dealing with ancient Chinese history. Translated by Bettne Birge. Photographed by Marc Carter. Introduction by Zhao Fangzhi.

Ethnic Islands: The Emergence of Urban Chinese Americans. Ronald Takaki. New York: Chelsea House Publishers, 1994. Asian American Experience Series. 125 pp. ISBN 0–7910–2180–7. LC 93–37513. Junior high and high school.

Adapted from the author's adult work *Strangers from a Different Shore*. The story of Chinese immigration during the 20th century is told from letters, writings, and oral histories, conversations, speeches, and songs. The book opens with a description of Chinese immigration patterns, the formations of the various Chinatowns, and the living patterns in the United States during the latter part of the 19th century and early 20th century, covers the lives of children, and concludes by covering immigration after 1965. Black-and-white photos, mostly fuzzy. Many first-person accounts of Chinese American life. Useful for units on the history of the Chinese in this country and for comparisons of the early immigrations to the flux after 1965 and to the present.

From Canton to California: The Epic of Chinese Immigration. Corinne K. Hoexter. Miami, FL: Brown Book Company, 1976. 304 pp. ISBN 0–590–07344–3. LC 76–14504. High school and up.

This is a history of the Chinese in the United States beginning in their early days in California. Information includes why the Chinese came to America, where they came from, how they lived in this country, and how they tried to adapt to the difficult and dangerous conditions that surrounded them in the old west. It is also a lengthy biography of Dr. Ng Poon Chew, who, as editor of the first Chinese language newspaper in the United States, became a leader for all Chinese Americans. It is very thorough. Throughout the book are excellent old photographs and illustrations from several archives. There is quite a lengthy bibliography and an index. The book is intended to show how deeply involved the Chinese were in building the American west.

From the Earth: Chinese Vegetarian Cooking. Yin–Fei Lo. New York: Macmillan Publishing Co., Inc., 1995. 336 pp. ISBN 0–02–632985–9. LC 94–022664. High school and up.

Includes 200 mainly vegetable recipes. Includes recipes for mussels, clams, and oysters—the only three types of seafood that Buddhists may eat—and turnip cakes for the lunar new year. Includes instructions for gathering the correct ingredients and cookware. Many traditional, some original recipes. Some exotic ingredients may be hard to find. Useful for social studies units, multicultural units, and for anyone who likes to cook.

Fusang: The Chinese Who Built America. Stan Steiner. New York: Harper & Row, 1979. 259 pp. ISBN 0–06–014087–9. LC 78–2172. High school and up. Out of print.

In 499 A.D. a Chinese priest by the name of Hui told of the Kingdom of Fu Sang to the east of China which is possibly America. This is a book about the Chinese who discovered America, who built America, and who became America. Book One goes back into the past all the way to Fu Sang showing the daring of the Chinese explorers to navigate the unknown to America. Book Two portrays the epic feat of the Chinese in the building of the west. They built the whole or part of nearly every railroad line in the west and also worked as fishermen and farmers. Book Three tells of the anti-Chinese sentiments, but goes on to tell that, in the decades of civil rights legislation, Chinese Americans began to reclaim their American history and proclaim their American heritage. The bibliography is annotated and there is an index. Useful for units on Chinese Americans and their growth as American citizens.

Grass Soup. Second Edition. Zhang Zianliang. Lincoln, MA: David R. Godine Publishers, Inc., 1995. 256 pp. ISBN 1–56792–030–6. LC 95–15867. High school and up.

Poet Zhang Zianliang who was imprisoned for over 20 years because of his use of politically incorrect words and thoughts in his poetry and prose. During his incarceration, he kept a secret diary in which he recorded the inhumanities perpetrated upon the prisoners by the guards and the government. This diary is the basis for his book, *Grass Soup*, whose title comes from the thin soup, made from grass, which was a staple in the inadequate diet provided to prisoners. Useful for units on notable Asian Americans and Chinese authors. Translated by Martha Avery.

The New Chinatown. Peter Kwong. New York: Farrar, Straus & Giroux, 1988. 195 pp. ISBN 0–374–52121–2. LC 95–4773. High school and up.

The author presents his research work of modern study of New York City's Chinatown. He discovers a great deal many stories about internal conflicts and of the "tong." Useful for units on Chinese Americans and racial conflict.

New World and Pacific Civilizations: Culture of America, Asia, and the Pacific. Goran Burenhult and David H. Thomas, eds. San Francisco: HarperSan Francisco, 1994. History of Humankind series. 240 pp. ISBN 0–06–250269–7. LC 94–3916. High school and up.

The fourth volume in the series, this book describes the development and evolution of the cultures in Mesoamerica, the Andes, Japan, the Pacific Islands, and North

America. A noted group of scholars present their latest findings and discoveries. Easy to read. Covers many lesser-known indigenous peoples. Illustrations, photographs of major archaeological sites, maps, reproductions of art work, ritual objects, and amazing crafts add to the appeal. Contains a glossary of terms. Good for anthropological studies, human race studies, and multicultural studies.

A Search for Meaning: Essays of a Chinese American. Albert H. Yee. San Francisco, CA: Chinese Historical Society of America, 1984. 309 pp. ISBN N/A. LC 84–204691. High school and up. Out of print.

Yee's objectives in this book are (1) to enhance world peace by broadening Americans' appreciation of Chinese Americans and (2) to stimulate reflection about the blending of east and west as found in the experiences of Chinese Americans. These seven autobiographical essays reflect Yee's psychoanalytical background and span five decades, from the 1920s to the 1970s. He uses his experiences in medicine, in traveling back to China, in World War II and the Korean War to form his honest and sophisticated self-reflection. Possibly of use for research on Chinese Americans, multicultural units.

Two Years in the Melting Pot. Liu Zongren. San Francisco: China Books and Periodicals, Inc., 1988. 221 pp. ISBN 0–8351–2048–1. LC N/A. High school and up.

This book chronicles Zongren's 22-month visit to the United States from 1980 to 1982. He portrays honestly and poignantly his struggle to understand the United States through his mind and senses, shaped by completely different experiences. He addresses questions of class, gender, nationality, and race in a new context. Zongren shapes his impressions and thoughts into sculpted, spare, and eloquent English. Useful for multicultural studies.

The Unwelcome Immigrant: The American Image of the Chinese, 1785–1882. Stuart Creighton Miller. Ann Arbor, MI: Books On Demand, 1969. 271 pp. ISBN 0–685–23355–3. LC 76–081763. High school and up.

The author aims to present a reconstruction of the events and values that shaped the United States' views of the Chinese and led to the national fear of them as immigrants. The Chinese were the only immigrant group that was barred from entering the United States. He explores the development of the negative stereotypes that made assimilation difficult. There is an index, extensive end notes, and a bibliographic note offering some other suggestions for further study. Of use for comparing how immigration has changed since 1969.

Japanese Americans

America-Bound: The Japanese and the Opening of the American West. Hisashi Tsurutani. Tokyo: The Japan Times, 1989. 228 pp. ISBN 4–7890–0442–2. LC 89–158825. High school and up. Out of print.

It is an interesting and readable book that gives a detailed story of Japanese immigrants who first went to America. The uniqueness of this book is that it reveals the conditions in Japan which caused the emigration and their parallelism with those people's experience in America. Well researched from statistics, letters, newspaper articles. Of use for units on immigration and why people choose to leave their native lands. Includes index.

Americans from Japan. Bradford Smith. New York: J.B. Lippincott, 1948. 409 pp. University libraries. Out of print.

A history of the Japanese Americans with an emphasis on the Japanese settling in Hawaii and World War II internment. Tells its history mostly through the use of personal experiences of various Japanese Americans. Offers a viewpoint sympathetic to the Japanese American internees written soon after the World War II relocation.

Children of the Atomic Bomb: An American Physician's Memoir of Nagasaki, Hiroshima, and the Marshall Islands. James Yamazaki and Louis B. Fleming. Raleigh, NC: Duke University Press, 1995. Asia-Pacific Series: Culture, Politics, and Society. 200 pp. ISBN 0–8223–1658–7. LC 95–006683. Young adults.

Yamazaki, an army surgeon who was captured at the Battle of the Bulge, became a pediatrician after the war. He enlisted in the commission investigating the casualties caused by the atomic bomb. This book is his account of returning to Japan for the first time as a Nisei and hearing firsthand accounts of the bomb and its aftermath from victims and colleagues. Interesting in that it expresses the experience, thoughts, and feelings of a Japanese American on the dropping of the atomic bombs over Nagasaki and Hiroshima. Foreword by John Dower. Illustrated.

Citizen 13660. Mine Okubo. Seattle, WA: University of Washington Press, 1983. 226 pp. ISBN 0–295–95989–4. LC 82–020221. Junior high and up.

This book consists of drawings and narrative by a woman describing her experience of life in a Japanese internment camp (first at a racetrack near San Francisco, then at a permanent camp in Utah). The book gives a good sense for the day-to-day existence in the camps—how people coped with boredom, lack of privacy, and the need to do useful work. The tone is primarily descriptive with just a few glimpses of the frustration and injustice she felt. Easy to read. Recommended for junior high or print-challenged high school students studying World War II.

Executive Order 9066: The Internment of 110,000 Japanese Americans. Richard Conrat and Maisie Conrat. Los Angeles, CA: California Historical Society, 1972. 120 pp. ISBN 0–262–53023–6. LC 72–9024. High school and up. Out of print.

Relates in photographs the image of the results of Executive Order 9066. Includes a brief history of the Japanese American. Useful for American history units and units on World War II.

Exile Within: the Schooling of Japanese Americans 1942–1945. Cambridge, MA: Harvard University Press, 1987. 224 pp. ISBN 0–674–27526–8. LC 86–025792. High school and up.

Exile Within tells the story of the children in the evacuation camps during World War II and the educational institutions in the camps, which taught democracy while denying civil liberty. Focuses on educational practices and theory and the effects of the incarceration and government policies. Scholarly. Includes photographs and index. Useful for studies on World War II and Japanese American internment.

Farewell to Manzanar. Jeanne Wakatsuki Houston and James D. Houston. New York: Bantam Books, Inc., 1983. 160 pp. ISBN 0–553–27258–6. Junior high school and up.

True story of a Japanese American family's internment written by a woman who, as a child, was interned at Manzanar with her family. Useful for units on Japanese American studies and for personalizing the Japanese American experience.

A Fence Away from Freedom: Japanese Americans and World War II. Ellen Levine. New York: Putnam Publishing Group, 1995. 288 pp. ISBN 0–399–22638–9. LC 95–013357. High school and up.

Levine describes one of the most shameful chapters in the history of the United States—the internment of Japanese Americans in what could only be called concentration camps for the duration of World War II. The stories of these people are told in the voices of those who were young at the time, but old enough to remember and resent the degradation to which they were subjected. Some were families of men fighting on the side of the United States. Some resisted. Some of the chapters and individual stories could be books in and of themselves. It's long, but gives an accurate picture of the time. Recommended for high school, academic, and public libraries.

Hiroshima. Victoria Sherrow. Morristown, PA: Silver Burdett Press (New Discovery Books), 1994. 128 pp. ISBN 0–02–782467–5. LC 93–30428. Junior high and high school.

Short, easy to read, good source notes. Sherrow uses the city of Hiroshima as a basis to discuss the dawn of the atomic age and the race between rival countries to split the atom and become the first to harness atomic energy. She describes the bombing of Hiroshima and Nagasaki. She does not editorialize, but challenges the reader to contemplate future use of nuclear power and its implications. Useful as a tool to initiate discussion of war in general, World War II in particular, and the uses of atomic energy.

Hiroshima: Why America Dropped the Atomic Bomb. Ronald Takaki. New York: Little, Brown and Company, 1995. 208 pp. ISBN 0–316–83122–0. LC 95–013546. Young adults.

Takaki's book is flawed in historical detail. One example is that he calls General MacArthur the "supreme commander in the Pacific" when he was, in fact, chief only of the southwest area. Takaki theorizes that Truman dropped the bomb as a symbol of virility and that if MacArthur had been consulted, the atomic bomb would not have been dropped. Takaki is the only historian to espouse these views, and this book would be of use only to show his point of view. Illustrated.

I Am An American: A True Story of Japanese Internment. Jerry Stanley. New York: Crown Publishing Group, 1994. 112 pp. ISBN 0–517–57986–1. LC 93–41330. Junior high and high school.

The story of Japanese Americans interned during World War II is revealed through photo essays focusing on the experiences of one high school boy, Shi Nomura. The chronology of the bombing of Pearl Harbor, the rising hysteria, the internment of Japanese Americans, their return to what was left of their homes and lives, racism directed at them because they were of a different race, and the very late recent apology by the government. Includes black-and-white photos and bibliographic essay of sources used and people interviewed. Useful for studies on Japanese Americans. Recommended for junior high and high school libraries.

Issei, the World of the First Generation Japanese Immigrants 1885–1924. Yuji Ichioka. New York: The Free Press, 1988. 380 pp. ISBN 0–02–915370–0. LC 88–3693. High school and up.

A detailed history of the first generation of Japanese immigrants and the deep hostility they encountered in the United States. A history of a racial minority struggling to survive in a hostile land. Useful for multicultural studies and units or discussions on racism. Illustrated.

Issei and Nisei: The Settling of Japanese America. Ronald Takaki. New York: Chelsea House Publishers, 1994. Asian American Experience Series. 126 pp. ISBN 0–7910–2179–3. LC 93–27381. Junior high and high school.

Adapted from the author's adult work, *Strangers from a Different Shore*. Issei are first generation Japanese Americans; Nisei are second generation. Takaki's book describes the reasons for the Japanese immigration to the United States, prejudice they encountered here, the conditions, the jobs they found, and the second Japanese economy they developed. Useful for studies on immigration, Japanese Americans, and racism.

JACL: In Quest of Justice. Bill Hosokawa. Monterey Park, CA: Japanese American Citizens League, 1982. 383 pp. ISBN 0–318–18650–0. LC 81–22576. High school and up.

A history of the Japanese American Citizens' League: its origins, trials, accomplishments, failures, dreams, ideals, and individuals. Gives a new perspective on the inner workings of an active human rights group within a culture commonly perceived as submissive. Useful for discussions of stereotypes, Japanese Americans, and learning about other cultures.

The Japanese in America. Noel L. Leathers. Minneapolis: The Lerner Group, 1991. In America Series. 72 pp. ISBN 0–82250241–0. LC 67–015684. High school.

Short, easily read history of Japanese in America with pictures and charts. Indexed. Use as supplementary material or for print-challenged students.

Japanese in the United States. A Critical Study of the Problems of the Japanese Immigrants and Their Children. Ichihashi, Yamoto. No. 1. North Stratford, CT: Ayer Company Publishers, Inc., 1978. American Immigration Collection Series, 426 pp. ISBN 0–405–00528–8. LC 69–018780. Academic libraries.

An objective, critical study of the Japanese immigrants and their children. The main body of the book has four subdivisions: the coming of the Japanese, an analysis of the salient facts relating to alien Japanese residents, an historical examination of anti-Japanese agitations, and a survey of the so-called second generation problems.

The book is a comprehensive account until its date of publication (1932) and remains the standard source on the subject. It describes the character, causes, and geographical distribution of Japanese immigration. It includes a statistical table of occupational distribution from 1908 to 1928, various details bearing on the Gentlemen's Agreement (1903–1923), alien Japanese admitted to and departed from Hawaii (1909–1923), and age distribution of alien Japanese (1909–1928). Useful for research, but should be supplemented with more up-to-date material.

The Japanese Texans. Thomas K. Walls. San Antonio, TX: University of Texas Institute of Texan Cultures, 1987. 254 pp. ISBN 0–86701–021–5. LC 87–50131. High School. Out of print.

The history of the Japanese in Texas from 1885 to 1987. Many interesting stories of individuals. Includes photographs and a chronology. Indexed. Useful for multicultural studies and units on Japanese Americans.

Judgment at the Smithsonian. Philip Nobile, ed. New York: Marlowe and Company, 1995. 256 pp. ISBN 1–56924–841–9. LC 95–34445. Young adults.

The Smithsonian's proposed exhibit about the dropping of the atomic bombs on Hiroshima and Nagasaki had to be cancelled when its contents ignited a controversy between veterans' groups and those who hold the view that Japan would never have invaded the United States. Nobile, who supports the opinion that dropping the atomic bomb was a war crime on the scale of the Holocaust and that the leaders who made the decision should be tried for war crimes, published his script for the display anyway. Useful to represent an additional point of view on World War II for American history units.

Manzanar. John Armor and Peter Wright with photos by Ansel Adams. New York: Random House, 1988. 167 pp. ISBN 0–8129–1727–8. LC 88–40155. High school and up.

Ansel Adams' beautiful photographs eloquently chronicle a shameful event in the United States' past. The black-and-white photos with simple titles allow the pictures to speak for themselves. Useful for units on the history of Japanese Americans, World War II, and race relations. Commentaries by John Hersey.

Nisei: The Quiet Americans. Bill Hosokawa. Niwot, CO: University Press of Colorado, 1992. 550 pp. ISBN 0–87081–273–4. LC 92–38737. High school and up.

The history of the Issei and Nisei told in a personal and entertaining way. Includes many photographs, a guide to pronunciation of Japanese names, and an index. Useful for units on Japanese Americans and American history.

Prisoners Without Trial: Japanese-Americans in World War II. Roger Daniels. Hill and Wang, 1993. A Critical Issues Series. 146 pp. ISBN 0–8090–7897–X. LC 92–27144. Young adults.

This short book is a capsulization of Daniels' previous works on the incarceration of the Japanese Americans during World War II. He supports and reminds us of the old saying that those who do not learn from history are doomed to repeat it. Well written and ideal for students writing research papers or just reading for pleasure and/or information. Edited by Eric Foner.

Rain of Ruin: A Photographic History of Hiroshima and Nagasaki. Daniel M. Goldstein and Katherine V. Dillon. McLean, VA: Brassey's, Inc. 1995. World War II Commemorative Series. 256 pp. ISBN 1–57488–033–0. Young adults.

Over 400 black-and-white photos of the devastation wreaked by the dropping of the atomic bombs on Hiroshima and Nagasaki. The writers support the dropping the bombs and focus on the Air Force personnel and their missions. Some of the photos included are aerial and ground-level views of the devastation radiating from ground zero. The authors deplore the loss of lives while supporting the attack's intent of preventing an invasion and saving American lives. Useful for units on World War II.

Thirty-Five Years in the Frying Pan. Bill Hosokawa. NY: McGraw-Hill, 1978. 284 pp. ISBN 0–070–30435–1. LC 78–9534. Academic libraries. Out of print.

Collection of newspaper articles from Hosokawa's column "In the Frying Pan" from the *Pacific Citizen*, the publication of the Japanese American Citizens' League. His reminiscences cover internment, racism, and assimilation of the Japanese Americans into American society. Useful for sociological studies and research.

Voices from the Camps: Internment of Japanese Americans During World War II. Larry Dane Brimmer. Danbury, CT: Franklin Watts, 1994. 160 pp. ISBN 0–531–11179–2. LC 93–31956. Junior high and up.

Several personal accounts are woven into this description of the Japanese American internment during World War II. The author gives a background of the Asians on the west coast, the attack on Pearl Harbor and its aftermath, vivid descriptions of the Japanese relocation centers, and the contributions of Japanese Americans during the war. Glossy black-and-white photographs. Good companion volume to *Farewell to Manzanar* by Jeanne W. and James D. Houston and *The Journey* by Sheila Hamanaka. Some minor inaccuracies in detail, but well written and readable. Good addition to a unit on World War II.

Weapons for Victory: The Hiroshima Decision Fifty Years Later. Robert James Maddox. Columbia, MO: University of Missouri Press, 1995. 200 pp. ISBN 0–8262–1037–6. Young adults.

Maddox, a historian, defends the dropping of the atomic bomb on Hiroshima and Nagasaki and disputes the theories that Japan was on the verge of surrender, that several highly placed generals did not approve of dropping atomic bombs, or the meaning of Japan's negative response to the Potsdam Declaration. This book will appeal to readers who agree with Maddox's view. Useful for comparison to *Hiroshima: Why America Dropped the Atomic Bomb* by Ronald Takaki and *Judgment at the Smithsonian* by Philip Nobile and for units on World War II.

Korean Americans

From the Land of Morning Calm: The Koreans in America. Ronald Takaki. New York: Chelsea House Publishers, 1994. Asian American Experience series. 125 pp. ISBN 0–7910–2181–5. LC 93–43713. Junior high and high school.

Compelling personal narratives tell the story of Korean immigration to the United States, from the first wave of immigrants, their experiences on Hawaii and the mainland, the attack of Japan on their homeland, the effects of World War II and the Korean War on their communities, and relationships with Caucasian America. Examines immigration since 1965 and gives the reader a look at Koreatown in Los Angeles before and after the riots in 1992. Black-and-white photographs. Useful for units on Korean Americans and multicultural units.

Korea: Tradition and Transformation, A History of the Korean People. By Andrew C. Nahm. Elizabeth, NJ: Hollym International Corporation, 1988. 583 pp. ISBN 0–930878–56–6. LC 86–081681. High school and up.

This work attempts to meet the need for coverage of both North and South Korea in one comprehensive volume. The land, climate, and people are described and major historical processes in political, economic, cultural, and social aspects are highlighted. Chapters cover the Koryo and Yi dynasties, Korea under Japanese rule, liberation, and modern transformation. Includes chronology, appendixes, bibliography, maps, charts, and index. Useful as a source for reports.

The Korean Americans. Brian Lehrer. New York: Chelsea House Publishers, 1995. The Immigrant Experience Series. 108 pp. ISBN 0–7910–3352–0. LC 94–040428. High school and up.

The history, culture, and religion of the Korean people are discussed in this work. The factors which encouraged their emigration and their acceptance as an ethnic group are detailed. Daniel Patrick Moynihan discusses prejudice in the introduction. Many black-and-white photographs are included plus color plates of Korean art. Useful for multicultural units and discussions on racism and prejudice.

The Korean Immigrant in America. Byong-suh Kim and Sang Hyun Lee, eds. N.p.: The Association of Korean Christian Scholars in North America, 1980. 175 pp. ISBN 0–032014–0504. LC–80–66817. High school and up. Out of print.

The essays compiled in this book discuss various topics in the quest for Korean Americans to assimilate into American society. Essays are included on the topics of communities, social and economic adjustments, education, religion, and immigration. Also included is a bibliography of additional sources on Korean Americans. Possibly useful for research and comparisons of assimilation of immigrants in the early 1980s to the present.

The Korean War: America at War. Maurice Isserman. New York: Facts on File, 1992. America at War Series. 128 pp. ISBN 0–8160–2688–2. LC 92–10201. Junior high and up.

Well written and well researched. Isserman's book traces the beginnings of the Korean War, also called the Korean Conflict since it was the United States' first major undeclared war, its politics, the mistakes made, and what it was like for the participants. Thought-provoking. Useful for American history units. Edited by John Bowman.

Korea's Cultural Roots, third edition. Dr. Jon Carter Covell. Elizabeth, NJ: Hollym International Corporation, 1986. 132 pp. ISBN 0–930878–32–9. LC 83–081319. High school and up.

Some of the complex mutations, myths, religions, and symbolism of Korea are explained in this work. A description is also given of the ceremonies, art, symbols, and architecture of the Shaman, Buddhist, and neo-Confucian roots. This is a good source for illustrations of religious ceremonies, symbols, and art. It does not include the effect of Christianity on Korean history. An index is included. Useful for multicultural units and discussions of how vastly the cultures of the east and west differ.

Recent Archaeological Discoveries in the Republic of Korea. Kim Won Yong. Paris, France: UNESCO, 1983. 79 pp. ISBN 92–3–102001–3. LC 84–178506. Academic libraries.

In 1961, a Department of Archaeology and Anthropology was inaugurated at Seoul University. This was the beginning of a new era in Korean archaeology, and many of the discoveries described in this work are a result of the efforts of that university. UNESCO began a survey of archaeological sites in 1979 that were considered as having historical and cultural value. This book is a result of the survey carried out in the Republic of Korea. The format is chronological and numerous plates and illustrations are included. Useful for studies of archaeology and Korean history.

Six Korean Women: The Socialization of Shamans. Youngsook Kim Harvey. St. Paul, MN: West Publishing, 1979. 326 pp. ISBN 0–8299–0243–0. LC 78–27500. High school and up. Out of print.

This book presents definitions and examples of the long-practiced ritual of Shamanism in Korea. It includes biographical histories of six Korean female shamans. Also included in this book is an extensive bibliography of additional sources and a glossary of terms. Reviews of selected literature of Shamanism also help to make this a good starting point for research on this subject. Good for women's studies.

Pacific Islanders

Ambassadors in Arms. Thomas Murphy. Honolulu: The University of Hawaii Press, 1954. 339 pp. ISBN N/A. LC 54–7835. High school and up.

The story of the 100th Infantry Battalion during World War II. Made up of Americans of Japanese ancestry from Hawaii, they fought so valiantly that they were designated as the most decorated unit in US military history. Useful for World War II units.

The Filipinos in America. Alfredo Muñoz. Los Angeles, CA: Mountainview Publishers, 1971. 209 pp. ISBN N/A. LC 77–186813. Academic libraries.

A slightly outdated look at Filipinos in the United States, their status, and biographical data on outstanding Filipino professionals, athletes, and entertainers. Good for research. A more up-to-date source would be better for current information.

Historical Dictionary of Oceania. Frank King and Robert Craig, eds. Westport, CT: Greenwood Press, 1981. 416 pp. ISBN 0–313–21060–8. LC 80–024779. High school and up.

Extensive coverage of the history, people, and events of the Pacific. Includes maps, index, bibliographies, and an extensive chronology. Entries are cross-referenced. Possibly useful for research. Illustrations. Introduction by Hartey C. Grattan.

The Japanese Frontier in Hawaii 1868–1898. Hilary Conroy. New York: Ayers Company Publishers, Inc., 1979. Asian Experience in North America Series. 175 pp. ISBN 0–4051–1306–4. LC 78–054840. Academic libraries.

A well-documented political and economic account of the importation of Japanese laborers. Possibly useful for units on World War II, Hawaiian history.

Pacific Nations and Territories, third revised edition. Reilly Ridgell. Honolulu: The Bess Press, Inc, 1995. 184 pp. ISBN 0–57306–001–1. LC 88–070787. High school and up.

Ideal for anyone interested in the Pacific, this extensively revised second edition is also an excellent high school text. It includes chapters on all island groups of Micronesia, Melanesia, and Polynesia. Includes index, more than 100 photographs and 60 drawings, diagrams, maps, and charts. Useful for Polynesian studies and multicultural studies.

Vietnamese Americans

Blacks and Vietnam. Robert W. Mullen. Lanham, MD: University Press of America, 1981. 99 pp. ISBN 0–8191–1527–4. LC 80–8235. High school and up. Out of print.

Based on a dissertation by the author, this work attempts to identify both the identification with and relationship between African Americans and the Vietnamese people's struggle to gain freedom. It delves into the inconsistency of fighting for freedom in another country in the absence of civil rights in America. The lack of cohesiveness of the African American population necessary to deal with civil rights issues is addressed. Good for units on racism and the Vietnam war.

Culture Clash. Ellen Matthews. Chicago: Intercultural Press, 1982. 135 pp. ISBN 09–33662–48–3. LC 81–85714. High school and up. Out of print.

Differing in focus from the work listed above, this book discusses in detail the Vietnamese refugee experience from the point at which a refugee family reaches the United States. The author's family sponsored a refugee couple, and the book is her diary of the experience. It has to be remembered that the focus is narrow—one refugee family and the American family that sponsored them—but the author's insights and the things that she learned are probably applicable to many similar situations. The book details the struggle of the early Vietnamese Americans and the discrepancies between what they thought life in America would be like and what it was really like. The family's early experiences as refugees are still very much a part of Vietnamese American culture. Useful for multicultural units and Vietnamese American studies.

"A Divided Life: How My Amerasian Foster Daughter is Coming to Terms with the Past." By Joseph Cerquone. Washington Post (June 10, 1990): C1. High school and up.

This article presents the experience of a more recent group of Vietnamese refugees, the Amerasians, as well as provides a very recent view of the Vietnamese Americans. This article itself is a good resource for information on the Vietnamese Americans, but it was added to this bibliography as an example of the effectiveness of the media as a source of information on ethnic culture groups. Newspapers reflect local experience and attitudes and are therefore the best source of information with a local focus. This is important for anyone working with a culture group or anyone who wants to understand the cultural experience of his neighbors, since experience will differ with place. Using the local media to supplement other informational resources adds a new dimension to the understanding of the culture.

Escape to Freedom: The Story of the International Rescue Committee. Aaron Levenstein. Westport, CT: Greenwood Publishing Group, Inc., 1983. Studies in Freedom Series, No. 2. 350 pp. ISBN 0–313–23815–4. LC 82–21078. Academic libraries.

The scope of this book covers much more than Vietnamese refugees—neither the Vietnamese or any other refugee group are the focus. There is, however, a chapter on the Vietnamese that provides some detail about Vietnamese refugees, both internal and external. The discussions on the earlier (mostly internal) refugees provide good background information and a chronology of the situation. The end of the chapter does deal briefly with the refugees in the United States and touches on American attitudes. There is a short bibliography for each chapter. The book was not written to provide extensive information about the refugee groups discussed, but to tell of the work of the International Rescue Committee. It does fulfill this goal, and in the process touches on the Vietnamese experience, but is not a resource for much information on Vietnamese Americans.

From Vietnam to America: A Chronicle of the Vietnamese Immigration to the United States. Gail Paradise Kelly. Boulder, CO: Westview Press, 1977. 254 pp. ISBN 0–891–58326–2. LC 77–6383. High school and up. Out of print.

The first part of the book describes why the refugees left Vietnam, the conditions of their departure, and how American policy affected the composition of the population that came to the U.S. The second part of the book covers the refugee camps in the U.S. where refugees waited to be resettled. Useful for units on immigration and why various peoples leave their homes to come to the United States.

Hearts of Sorrow: Vietnamese American Lives. James F. Freeman. Stanford, CA: Stanford University Press, 1989. 446 pp. ISBN 0–8047–1585–8. LC 89–032115. High school and up.

In the introduction to this book, the author writes: "The narratives in this book provide a glimpse into the lives of Vietnamese-Americans, revealing some of their deepest hopes and fears and documenting what they consider to be their successes and failures." The book, however, goes beyond being a collection of biographical sketches and becomes a sociological study. The author interviewed a wide range of Vietnamese American refugees with vastly different backgrounds and, while each narrator's individual identity is preserved, the author also summarizes the refugee experience as a whole. An extensive bibliography is provided, and many of these other studies and works are referred to in the introductions that precede each section to provide a background for the personal narratives. The book does an excellent job of chronicling the Vietnamese American refugee experience, beginning many years before the war and ending recently, so the picture that is presented is quite complete. The personal points of view, combined with the author's own careful study, create a credible and human sociological study. Good addition for high school, academic, and public libraries.

Inside Hanoi's Secret Archives: Solving the MIA Mystery. Malcom McConnell. New York: Simon and Schuster, 1995. 464 pp. ISBN 0–671–87118–8. LC 94–38692. High school and up

McConnell dismisses the ideas that United States officers have withheld information and phony information spread by ill-informed groups and organizations in the United States and reveals that Hanoi did indeed withhold information about American MIAs, that many POWs were interned in southern Laos, and that American prisoners were tortured. His sources are documents obtained by former Defense Intelligence Agency employee Ted Schweitzer. The book discusses the long struggle to obtain definitive and final information about our missing troops. Useful for studies on the Vietnam war.

The Vietnamese in Oklahoma City: A Study in Ethnic Change. Charles C. Muzny. New York: AMS Press, Inc., 1989. Immigrant Communities: Ethnic Minorities in the U.S. and Canada Series No. 37. 200 pp. ISBN 0–404–19447–8. LC 88–035115. High school and up.

A statistical framework of the Vietnamese refugee population in Oklahoma City. Data was collected between 1979 and 1984. Includes information on employment patterns, education, and residence, as well as recreation and entertainment activities. Useful for historic perspective and comparison to modern statistics.

Vietnamese Tradition on Trial, 1920–1945. David Marr. Berkeley, CA: University of California Press, 1981. 450 pp. ISBN 0–520–05081–9. LC 80–15802. High school and up.

This work describes the lifestyles of the Vietnamese: the morality and ethics of the people, the role of women, and politics and language from 1920 to 1945. Useful for comparison to the same subjects today. Illustrations.

Asian Americans—Multiethnic

Aiiieeeee!: An Anthology of Asian-American Writers. Frank Chin, Jeffrey Paul Han, Lawson Fusao Inada, and Shawn Hsu Wong, eds. New York: NAL/ Dutton, 1991. 304 pp. ISBN 0–451–62836–5. LC N/A. High school and up.

An anthology of Chinese, Filipino, and Japanese American writings that the editors have chosen to express each group's feelings. Criticisms of the works of both Asian Americans and others who have written about them are included in the preface. This group of authors is the product of American culture and rebels against the suppression of being stereotyped. Not indexed. Useful for multicultural studies, Asian-American writers, racism, and stereotypes.

Asian American: Chinese and Japanese in the United States since 1850. Roger Daniels. Seattle, WA: University of Washington Press, 1990. 402 pp. ISBN 0–295–97018–9. LC 88–005643. High school and up.

Synthesizes the Asian American experience, examining and placing into perspective its essential role in American history. It is focused on individuals. Contains maps of original evacuation zones and WRA camps, photographs, and tables detailing population. Useful for multicultural studies and Asian American studies.

Asian American Experiences in the United States: Oral Histories of First to Fourth Generation Americans from China, the Philippines, Japan, India, the Pacific Islands, Vietnam, and Cambodia. Joann Faung Jean Lee. Jefferson, NC: McFarland and Company Publishers, 1991. 228 pp. ISBN 0–89950–585–6. LC 90–053504. High school and up.

Lee devotes one quarter of her book to the experiences of Chinese Americans, as depicted in interviews. Her working premise begins with the idea that important distinctions in traditions, rituals, and values define each ethnic group, but the dominant culture perceives Asians as a singular racial group. To retain a historical context for the interviews, Lee includes important judicial rulings and acts of congress which affected the immigration, citizenship, marriage, and employment opportunities of Asians. Individuals interviewed cross generations, gender, and nationality, though all lived in the metropolitan New York area. The interviews are short, yet insightful, but not grouped according to ethnic-national origin as the premise might suggest. Useful for multicultural units and Asian American studies. Illustrations.

Asian Americans: Emerging Minorities. Second Edition. Harry H. Kitano and Roger Daniels. Englewood Cliffs, NJ: Prentice Hall, 1994. 208 pp. ISBN 0–13–315185–9. LC 94–022745. High school and up.

This recent collaboration by the authors is an update of the victories and hardships of the Asian American. This book strives to show how the Asian Americans are no longer of peasant stock, but are largely well educated, contributing members of our society. The section on Koreans breaks their arrival into three different "waves." This book includes a bibliography, several pages of tables, and an index. Could be used at the high school level.

Asian Americans and Pacific Islanders: Is There Such an Ethnic Group? Lemuel Ignacio. San Jose, CA: Filipino Development Associates, 1976. 305 pp. ISBN N/A. LC 76–3005. Academic libraries.

A look at the work of the Pacific/Asian Coalition and its organization in the 1970s.

Deals mainly with Asian Americans and Filipinos; only lightly touches on Pacific Islanders. Newer, more comprehensive material would be better.

Becoming Americans: Asian Sojourners, Immigrants, and Refugees in the Western United States. Tricia Knoll. Manzanita, OR: Coast to Coast Books, 1982. 354 pp. ISBN 0–9602664–3–7. (Paper: ISBN 0–9602664–3–7). LC 82–004539. High school and up.

Tricia Knoll has provided brief accounts of the people from seven different countries, including Cambodia. In the chapters on each group of people she gives a brief recent history of the country, explains the reasons people left and their culture, and introduces some of those who came to the U.S. The end of each chapter includes a very brief chronology. Also included are several appendixes, an index, and maps. This book is a must for anyone interested in becoming more aware of the Cambodian or Asian American culture because it is written in a very personalized, warm way. Introduction by Edwin Reischauer.

Buddhism. Madhu Bazaz Wangu. New York: Facts on File, 1992. World Religion Series. 128 pp. ISBN 0–8160–2442–1. LC–92 33177. Junior high and up.

Wangu provides a detailed discussion of Buddhism and its influence on the cultures in which it flourishes. He describes the life and times of Buddha, how the religion spread from India to other Asian countries, its effects on daily life, government, worship, rites, festivals, religious observance, and Buddhism today in many countries. Provides maps, photos, reproductions, list for further reading, glossary, and index. Useful for classes, discussions on comparative religion, and cultural differences.

Confucianism. Thomas and Dorothy Hoobler. New York: Facts on File, 1992. World Religion Series. 128 pp. ISBN 0–8160–2445–6. LC 92–33178. High school and up.

The authors describe the beliefs and writings of Confucius, which were codified into specific rules and rituals that spread throughout China, then into other Asian countries such as Japan and Korea. In some areas, Confucius even became deified. They go on to describe how Mao attempted to eradicate the religion's influence and heritage. Includes maps, photos, reproductions, list for further reading, glossary, and an index. Useful for comparative religion, cultural differences units, or discussions.

Contemporary American Immigrants: Patterns of Filipino, Korean, and Chinese Settlement in the United States. By Luciano Mangiafico. Westport, CT: Greenwood Publishing Group, Inc., 1988. 229 pp. ISBN 0–275–92726–1. LC 87–017752. Academic libraries.

In this book, the author provides the statistics from the United States Bureau of Census on Chinese immigrants to the U.S. User will find the information of history, social and demographic characteristics, current emigration trends and problems, and prospects for the future of Chinese immigration.

East Asia: From Chinese Predominance to the Rise of the Pacific Rim. Arthur Cottrell. New York: Oxford University Press, 1994. 339 pp. ISBN 0–19– 508840–9. LC 93–26263. Young adults.

Three time periods are covered: the Chinese Predominance from B.C. to the fourteenth century, the New Balance of Power from the fourteenth to the twentieth century, and the Rise of the Pacific Rim. The author covers not only Japan, China, and Korea, but also thoroughly addresses Indonesia, Malaysia, Singapore, the Philippines, and the nations of Indochina. Illustrated by sketches. Good addition to a collection on East Asian history.

Indochinese Refugee Dilemma. Valerie O'Connor Sutter. Baton Rouge, LA: Louisiana State University Press, 1990. 256 pp. ISBN 0–8071–1556–8. LC 89– 34129. Academic libraries.

This book is a study of the problems, political and personal, faced by Indochinese refugees from many countries including Cambodia. The study is based on the perspective of political realism as expressed in the writings of Herbert Butterfield, Reinhold Niebuhr, Hans Morganthau, George Kenner, and Kenneth W. Thompson. Sutter provides in-depth studies of the national problems and the reasons for the exodus; the situations refugees face in first asylum countries; the U.S. resettlement situation; and other humanitarian concerns. Those working with refugees and/or interested in refugees will find this comprehensive and scholarly work helpful.

Strangers at the Gates Again: Asian American Immigration after 1965. Ronald Takaki. New York: Chelsea House Publishers, 1995. 124 pp. ISBN 0–7910–2190–4. LC 94–21105. Junior high and up.

Adaptation of Takaki's adult book, *Strangers from a Different Shore: A History of Asian Americans*. This book covers the last thirty years of Asian immigration. Takaki describes the differences between the difficulties experienced by the first immigrants and later ones. For example, many left their countries because they could not find jobs in their fields only to find the same problem here. Somewhat generalized. Black-and-white photographs. Has a sense of incompleteness that the longer, adult version does not have, but would be suitable for reports for junior high and high school.

Strangers from a Different Shore: A History of Asian Americans.
Ronald Takaki. New York: Viking Penguin, 1990. 570 pp. ISBN 0–14–013885–4.
LC 90–6816. High school and up.

A narrative history of Asian Americans that includes the views of Chinese Americans on their lives in a new land. It is a good reference material because of its large amount of statistical information.

Videos

Videos: reviewed

A Time Remembered. The Terminal Island Story. Van Nuys, CA:
Audiographic Films and Video, 1994. 42 min. Color. Preview available. Junior high and high school.

This video examines the aftereffects of the Japanese bombing of Pearl Harbor, which caused the United States to become involved in World War II. A group of Japanese American fishermen living and working on Terminal Island in the Los Angeles Harbor were torn from their homes "for security reasons." The men were removed from the island, then the women and children were given 48 hours to gather whatever they could carry with them and were loaded on trucks to be taken to relocation camps where they stayed for four years. These scenes evoke memories of Jews being loaded into trains and taken to the death camps at the same time. When the war was over, these people were not able to regain their homes, businesses, and property. A hard look at one of the most embarrassing times in United States history. Good for history and sociology classes.

Act of War: The Overthrow of the Hawaiian Nation. Produced by Na Maka o Ka'Aina in association with the Center of Hawaiian Studies, University of Hawaii, 1993. Distributed by Na Maka o Ka'Aina. 57:42 min. Color. High school and up.

This compelling history of Hawaii is told from the native Hawaiian point of view, using both male and female voices. As was said by one tour guide on Waikiki, "The missionaries came here to do good. And they did *great*." After the missionaries came white businessmen who conspired with the descendants of the missionaries to overthrow the Hawaiian government and imprison the queen for several years. Although the move was condemned by President Grover Cleveland, this act was only the first of many which resulted in the annexation of other nonwhite territories such as the Philippines, Samoa, and Puerto Rico. The song, "Blue Hawaii" plays in the background as native Hawaiians protest the conquest of their land and the suppression of their culture, religion, and language. Suitable for social studies classes; units on Pacific Americans, colonialization, and racism; and for public library collections.

Anatomy of a Springroll. New York: Distributed by Filmmakers Library, 1993. 56 min. Color. Preview available. High school and up.

Paul Kwan was born in Vietnam and now lives in San Francisco. This film describes his experiences in the United States and how his family has blended their traditional Vietnamese culture with that of the United States. The title is derived from scenes of Paul and his mother cooking—a visual feast of colorful vegetables and spices. When Paul returns to Vietnam to find his old family home abandoned, the viewer sees that memory, family, and culture are an important part of the immigrant experience. Appropriate for units on Asian Americans and multicultural units. Good for all young adult collections.

The Art of Japan. Educational Dimensions Group, 1977. 30 min. Color. High school and up.

Starting from the prehistoric era, this program shows the gist of Japanese art history of 1,500 years in thirty minutes. The pictures of art works are clear and well-matched with the narration. The narration is easy to understand. The history is explained from the point of view of Chinese influence and the process of its adaptation and its development as Japanese art. This focus clarifies the long history and makes it easy to understand. The relationship between arts and its social and historical background of each period is explained well. Although it focuses more on the traditional arts and not on more recent periods, it is a good introduction to the Japanese culture in relation to the art and history.

Bara Bara / Scattered. Produced by Dick Jones and Walter Hatch for The Market Oral History Project, August 1979, at Evergreen State College. University of Washington Libraries, 1979. 28 min. Color.

A brief history of the South Park Japanese American farming community around World War II. Most of the documentary consists of interviews with Japanese Americans who were farmers at South Park who recall their memories and feelings about the past. Although the content is unique, there are some distracting problems with video technique such as excessive background noise during the interviews. Also, it would be more informative if the interview also included the experience of female members of the families.

From East to West: The Asian-American Experience. Bohemia, NY: Produced by Video Dialog, 1993. Distributed by Rainbow Educational Video. 224 min. Color. Preview available. Junior high.

This video is presented in two parts—a description of the countries comprising the continent of Asia including Japan, China, the Philippines, Korea, and Vietnam and an exploration of the reasons for the two major waves of immigration to the United States, one in the mid-1880s and the other after the Vietnam War. The Chinese were first, followed by the Japanese. They gained the reputation of being excellent workers, which caused many Americans to fear for their jobs. Fear and discrimination caused the implementation of the Chinese Exclusion Act of 1882, the establishment of "Asiatowns," and the internment of Japanese Americans during World War II. The second wave was after the Vietnam war when war, famine, political oppression, and atrocities forced many Southeast Asians to seek safe haven in the United States. The video goes on to describe the contributions made by Asian Americans in the United States. Should be used in conjunction with a history curriculum since there are many historical references that younger students and viewers will not understand.

How to Fold a Paper Crane. Santa Cruz, CA: Produced by Informed Democracy, 1994. 30 min. Color. Includes teacher's guide. Junior high and up.

Excellent video instructions on how to fold the traditional Japanese crane. Even younger students will be able to follow these directions with a minimum of assistance. A complete set of instructions accompanies the video. The story of *Sadako and the Thousand Paper Cranes* by Eleanor Coerr is told at the beginning of the video. Teachers using the book will want to use this video along with it. There are easier ways to fold the traditional crane, but they might not be as easy to demonstrate on camera. The male narrator folds the crane, but all the viewer sees is his gloved hands. He "talks" to the audience in mime, using a kazoo for expression. Amusing even if you don't fold the crane. Can also be used by art teachers and in conjunction with units on Japan and Japanese Americans. Highly recommended for school and public libraries, but less expensive films can be ordered from Origami, USA in New York City.

Japan Bashing. Produced by WCBS–TV, 1992. New York: Distributed by Carousel Film and Video. 22 min. Color. Preview available. High school and up.

Japanese Americans reveal how they have been treated by others because they are of Japanese descent. Many of the interviewees' parents were interned during World War II. One man tells of a Chinese man who was beaten to death by American auto workers because they thought he was Japanese and was taking jobs away from Americans. Good for Asian American, multicultural studies, and units on prejudice and racism.

The Killing Fields. Produced by David Puttnam, Burbank, CA. Distributed by Warner Home Video. 1984. 142 min.

This award-winning movie depicts the actions of a journalist and his native translator during 1975 when the Khmer Rouge captured the Cambodian capitol. This period was a nightmare for the Cambodians. Over three million people would die as a result of the turmoil. The story concentrates on the struggle of the translator, Dith Pran, and his four years in labor camps before he escapes to Thailand.

Swimming to Cambodia. Producers Spaulding Gray et. al. Irvine, CA: Distributed by Lorimar Home Video. 1988/1987. 85 min. High school and up.

This is a unique "concert film" of Spaulding Gray's off-Broadway monologue detailing his thoughts and experiences in Southeast Asia during the filming of "The Killing Fields." Gray is an excellent storyteller and touches on the political history of Cambodia, somehow turning serious subject matter into hilarious comedy.

Tae Kwon Do for Kids, Volume I—Beginners. Produced by Dogwood Productions. Distributed by Tapeworm, 1994. 25 min. Color. Junior high.

Master Edward G. Robinson, black belt and certified instructor, demonstrates stances and kicks. Importance of exercise and warm-up are emphasized and suitable exercises are shown to music. The philosophy of Tae Kwon Do, which includes respect, humility, perseverance, self-control, and honesty, and the history of Tae Kwon Do are given. More emphasis should have been placed that watching the video is not an adequate substitute for attending classes and practicing under a licensed instructor. Shows children sparring—something beginners do not do. Will be interesting to those interested in the martial arts.

Videos: Not reviewed

Chan Is Missing. New York: New Yorker Video. 1989/1981. 80 min. Junior high and up.

A middle aged Chinese American cab driver must find his friend who has disappeared in San Francisco. American Independents Series.

The Girl Who Spelled Freedom. Burbank, CA: Walt Disney Home Video. 1987/1985. 90 min. Junior high and up.

A family is forced to flee from Cambodia and find refuge in the United States. Here they must adjust to a new lifestyle and overcome cultural and language barriers.

Hiroshima Maiden. Chicago, IL: Public Media Video. 1988. 58 min. Color. Junior high and up.

Badly scarred in the bombing of Hiroshima, Miyeko Matsuda comes to the United States in 1955 for plastic surgery. The Bennett family welcomes her into their home for the duration of her stay—all except Johnny, who is convinced that she is a spy. Part of Wonderworks PBS television series.

Yankee Samurai: The Little Iron Man. Oak Forest, IL: MPI Home Video. 1985. 50 min. Junior high and up.

While the United States government was keeping their families in internment camps and denying them the rights of other Americans, 4,800 Japanese American men gave their lives in the line of duty fighting in the United States armed forces. This video is their story. The Nisei 100–442nd regiment.

The Year of the Dragon: A Young People's Special. Princeton, NJ: Films for the Humanities, 1988. Distributed by Zenger Media. 24 min. Color. Junior high.

Jimmy, who is Irish, and Hua, who is Chinese, must go work to overcome prejudice and antagonism when they are sent off together to hunt for game for the laborers building a railroad in the Sierras in the 1860s. Near tragedy strikes, changing their attitudes and bringing them together as friends.

❈ MULTIETHNIC MATERIALS ❈

Reference and Scholarly Works

Encyclopedia of the Third World. Fourth edition. Three volume set. George Thomas Kurian. New York: Facts on File, 1991. 2,432 pp. ISBN 0–8160–2261–5. LC 84–10129. High school and up.

This set from Facts on File is made up of three volumes covering 122 countries of the world. Each section provides a map and a basic fact sheet. Information given describes systems of each country. Also included is a glossary of terms, a recent chronology and a bibliography of additional sources. Useful for world cultures units and multicultural units.

The Ethnic Almanac. Stephanie Bernardo. Garden City, NY: Doubleday, 1981. 560 pp. ISBN 0–385–14143–2. LC 78–14694. Junior high and up. Out of print.

A witty potpourri of useful information about numerous ethnic groups, this unusual volume covers inventions, comic strips, folk medicine and cures, food, racial stereotypes, slang, and superstitions. Interesting to compare with a more current work to see how such things as humor and stereotypes have changed.

Ethnic Film and Filmstrip Guide for Libraries and Media Centers: A Selective Filmography. Lubomyr R. Wynar and Lois Buttlar. Littleton, CO: Libraries Unlimited, 1980. 277 pp. ISBN 0–87287–233–5. LC 80–18056. Professional use. Out of print.

This excellent volume annotates 1,400 films and filmstrips which treat 46 American ethnic groups as well as general studies of immigration and related topics. A more up-to-date version would be useful to librarians serving a multiethnic population.

Harvard Encyclopedia of American Ethnic Groups. Stephan Thernstrom, Ann Orlov and Oscar Handlin, eds. Cambridge, MA: Harvard University Press, 1980. 1,102 pp. ISBN 0–674–37512–2. LC 80–17756. High school and up.

This scholarly tome, invaluable in all types of libraries, includes authoritative information on 108 American ethnic groups from African Americans to Yankees. The essays, many of which are lengthy, treat the historical, cultural, religious, and socioeconomic aspects of each group. Some entries, however, are thematic essays on topics such as intermarriage, labor, and politics. Eighty-seven maps and tables support the volume. Useful for studies on cultural diversity. Illustrated.

Index to Collective Biographies for Young Readers. Fourth edition. Karen Breen, ed. New York: R. R. Bowker, 1988. 494 pp. ISBN 0–8352–2348–5. LC 88–19410. Junior high and up.

Access to the collective biographies is possible through either the alphabetical or subject listing of "biographies." This is an inclusive rather than selective listing, and as a result the quality of the resources has not been evaluated. This is potentially useful but awkward to use. First one must locate the individual by name or by subject, then turn to the first section of the book to determine what books the location codes refer to (this section is alphabetical by author), then turn to the back section (alphabetical by title) to get complete title information. Be sure to have pencil and paper handy so you won't get lost translating, as most entries have multiple title codes. Of possible use as a secondary source of biographies for young adults.

Minority Student Success in College: What Works. Carolyn Brewer. Olympia, WA: Minority Student Success Project, 1990. 45 pp. ISBN N/A. LC N/A. High school and up; professional use. Out of print.

Compilation of pertinent statistics with commentary, key elements of effective programs, what doesn't work, and descriptions of model programs in Washington and in the rest of the nation. The model programs are in the areas of early intervention and recruiting programs, college student and academic support programs, transfer and articulation programs, instructional programs with integrated student support services, and curriculum and pedagogy. Each model program includes full contact person information. A list of conferences and references is also included. This report is valuable, because "minority student success programs are relatively new and few have undergone systematic evaluation or scholarly analysis accessible through a traditional literature search." Useful for counselors, teachers, and professionals working with minority students.

Multicultural Student's Guide to Colleges: What Every African-American, Asian-American, Hispanic-American, and Native-American Applicant Needs to Know. Robert Mitchell. New York: Farrar, Straus & Giroux, 1993. 839 pp. ISBN 0–374–52362–2. LC 93–21749. High school and up, professional use.

Mitchell gives minority students needed information on applications, requirements, enrollment figures, retention rates of non-white students, remediation programs, support programs, and number of minority faculty members for more than 200 colleges. Each college is described in a chatty style describing the academic and social life of the school and how minority students are received. Weakness: This book focuses on the nation's most well-known colleges and universities and leaves out lesser-known ones that offer outstanding programs. A must for minority students, school libraries, public libraries, and high school counsellors.

Refugees in the United States: A Reference Handbook. David W. Haines. Westport, CT: Greenwood Publishing Group, Inc., 1985. 243 pp. ISBN 0–313–24068–X. LC 84–12794. High school and up.

This is a valuable source for overviews of the refugee situation in the U.S. Presented in an essay format, the book is divided into two parts. The first part provides general information about the refugee programs and initial adjustment and integration of refugees into American society; the second part focuses on refugees from specific countries, including Cambodia. An annotated bibliography to the literature on these subjects included as well as a subject index. The easy-to-read format makes it appropriate for many age levels and useful for a variety of purposes and needs.

Nonfiction

The Challenge of Immigration. Vic Cox. Springfield, NJ: Enslow Publishers, 1995. Multicultural Issues Series. 128 pp. ISBN 0–89490–628–3. LC 94–34645. Junior high and up.

Cox tackles issues of immigration such as the sides of those who support and those who oppose strict immigration laws, the laws themselves, whether or not immigrants take jobs away from Americans, whether immigrants take advantage of the welfare system, whether or not the spread of Spanish threatens the English language, the impact of immigration on education, and the impact on crime. Limited index. Limited number of uninteresting photos. Fine resource for reports.

Coping with Interracial Dating. Renea D. Nash. New York: Rosen Publishing Group, 1994. Coping Series. 159 pp. ISBN 0–8239–1606–3. LC 93–6895. Junior high and high school; professional use.

Written in a style designed to appeal to teens. Nash presents the pros and cons of interracial dating, showing through fictionalized accounts what some of the pitfalls can be. She takes a realistic view, urging teens considering interracial dating to consider such factors as their motivations for entering such a relationship, potential for biased reactions from both families involved and from society, sensitivity to cultural differences, and the importance of communication, honesty, trust, understanding, and empathy in any relationship. Useful for counselors of junior high and high school students, parents, and units on family relationships.

A Different Mirror: The Making of Multicultural America. Ronald Takaki. New York: Little, Brown and Company 1994. 508 pp. ISBN 0–316–83111–5. LC 92–33491. Young adults.

A major focus of this work is racism. Takaki deals with the history of African Americans, Native Americans, Hispanic Americans, Jewish Americans, Chinese Americans, Irish Americans, and Japanese Americans. He chronicles some of the major instances of racism such as the Trail of Tears, the Triangle Shirtwaist Factory Fire, the Harlem Renaissance, and the internment of Japanese Americans during World War II. He then addresses America's changing climate and echoes Rodney King's plea, "Can't we just all get along?" A good starting point for a social studies, history, or political science unit.

Discrimination: Prejudice in Action. Scott Gillam. Springfield, NJ: Enslow, 1995. Multicultural Issues Series. 128 pp. ISBN 0–89490–643–7. LC 94–38962. Junior high and up.

This series explores discrimination of several types, including race, sex, age, gender, and disability. Each chapter describes a particular act of discrimination, why it is discrimination, and suggests ways in which to overcome that particular type in the future. Includes black-and-white photos, chapter notes, short bibliography, and lists of activist organizations. Useful for discussions and units on racism.

Going Where I'm Coming From: Personal Narrative of American Youth. Anne Mazer, ed. New York: Persea Books, Inc., 1995. ISBN 0–89255–205–0. (Paper: ISBN 0–89255–206–0). Junior high and up.

A number of non-Caucasian writers, some well known and some obscure, tell their stories of growing up in the United States. Their recollections speak of racism, prejudice, discrimination, loss of identity, love, abuse, the necessity of learning to think and speak in two different languages, and overcoming stereotypes. Authors include Gary Soto, Naomi Shabib Nye, Susan Power, Graham Salisbury, Luis Rodriguez, Lee Daniels, Judith Ortiz Cofer, and Lensey Namioka. Useful for multicultural studies, racism studies, and lives of notable minority Americans.

Hate Groups. Deborah Able. Springfield, NJ: Enslow Publishers, 1995. Issues in Focus Series. 104 pp. ISBN 0–89490–627–5. LC 94–33429. Junior high and up.

Hate groups are not new in the United States. Able's book, while cursory rather than comprehensive, gives the reader some food for thought while covering the causes behind the foundation of such groups and their appeal to young people. Includes black-and-white photographs, and reproductions. Readable and accessible. Useful for discussions of racism and bigotry.

Immigration: Newcomers and Their Impact on the United States. Tricia Andryszewski. Brookfield, CT: Millbrook Press, Inc., 1995. Issue and Debate Series. 112 pp. ISBN 1–56294–499–1. LC 94–21834. Junior high.

Well researched but dully written. Andryszewski shows why the subject of immigration has been controversial for over 200 years. The first half of the book traces the reasons for emigration patterns to the United States, while the second half deals with the current impact of streams of immigrants to the United States. Includes black-and-white photos. Use to supplement better-written material.

Makers of America. Wayne Moquin, ed. Encyclopaedia Britannica Educational Corporation, 1971. 10 volumes. ISBN 0–87827–000–0. LC 74–129355. High school and up, research. Out of print.

An extensive collection of source materials on 85 ethnic groups who have contributed to national development, this set includes selections from letters, diaries, newspaper editorials, magazine articles, poems, and documents. More than 1,000 photographs and drawings illustrate the text. Of use to researchers who need primary material.

Melting Pot or Not? Debating Cultural Identity. Paula A. Franklin. Springfield, NJ: Enslow Publishers, Inc., 1995. Multicultural Issues Series. 112 pp. ISBN 0–89490–644–5. LC 94–37945. Junior high and high school.

The author suggests that the United States is not a melting pot or a mosaic, but a kaleidoscope. She explores the histories of various ethnic groups and treats their various problems with tact, sensitivity, and subtlety. Index. Clear design with subheadings and black-and-white photos. Good chapter notes. Useful for units on multicultural studies and racism.

Migrant Farm Workers: The Temporary People. Linda Jacobs Altman. Danbury, CT: Franklin Watts, Inc., 1994. Impact Book Series. 112 pp. ISBN 0–531–13033–9. LC 93–11921. Junior high and high school.

Altman offers a well-documented, sympathetic, chronological overview of migrant workers in the United States. This work concentrates on Mexican farmworkers, but covers other nationalities as well. Contains black-and-white photos, reproductions, lists for further reading, index, and notes. Stands well alone and complements existing titles. Useful for minority studies.

Minorities: A Changing Role In American Society. Alison Landes, ed. Wylie, TX: Information Plus, 1994. 172 pp. ISBN 1–878623–83–4. LC N/A. High school and up, research.

This reference source provides a compilation of statistics on minorities in the U.S. published by various federal agencies including the Bureau of Census, National Center for Health Statistics, Bureau of Labor Statistics, U.S. Department of Education, and the U.S. Department of Justice. The chapters are arranged by subject area, such as demography, labor force participation, and occupations. Within each chapter are bold headings for information on the different minority groups. It includes a brief index, tables, graphs, and charts. Much of the information and statistics is on broad categories of minorities such as African American, Hispanic, Asian, and Native American; however, there is also information on more specific minorities. Useful for statistics on minorities for reports and research.

Multicultural Monologues for Young Actors. Craig Slaight and Jack Sharrar, eds. Lyme, NH: Smith and Kraus, Inc., 1995. 112 pp. ISBN 1–880399–47–4. LC 94–44188. High school and up.

Multicultural Scenes for Young Actors. Craig Slaight and Jack Sharrar, eds. Lyme, NH: Smith and Kraus, Inc., 1995. Young Actors' Series. 256 pp. ISBN 1–880399–48–2. LC 94–44187. High school and up.

Excellent material for drama students and coaches. Explores the lives and conflicts of today's youth. These two collections provide 21 pieces for women, 23 pieces for men, and considerable material for groups and pairs. Strong language and mature themes. Not recommended for classroom performance.

A Multicultural Portrait of the Civil War. Carol Ann Piggins. Tarrytown, NY: Marshall Cavendish, 1994. 80 pp. ISBN 1–85435–660–7. LC 93–10319. Junior high and up. Out of print.

Piggins presents the contributions of several cultures, ethnic groups, and women during the Civil War. Her coverage of the war itself is rather perfunctory, but the book is well written and contains a treasury of interesting facts. Includes black-and-white and full-color illustrations. Useful as an addition resource.

Respecting Our Differences: A Guide to Getting Along in a Changing World. Lynn Duvall. Minneapolis: Free Spirit, 1994. 208 pp. ISBN 0–915793–72–5. LC 94–7164. Junior high and high school.

Duval covers stereotypes, controversies over U.S. immigration policies, cultural diversity, theories about race, and racism. "Time Out" sections can be used to start classroom discussions. Extensive resources are provided for students who are interested in the problems of racism and discrimination. Good for social studies units, discussions of racism. Illustrated. Edited by Pamela Espeland.

The Splendor of Ethnic Jewelry: From the Colette and Jean-Pierre Ghysels Collection. Frances Borel and Colette Ghysels; translated by I. Mark Paris. New York: Harm N. Abrams, Inc., 1994. 256 pp. ISBN 0–8109–4453–7. LC 94–8417. High school and up.

An index, illustrations, and color photographs by John B. Taylor enhanced by text lead the reader through an amazing collection of jewelry worn by peoples in Africa, Asia, Oceania, and the Americas. For art students, multicultural units, and general interest. Contribution by Colette Ghysels.

The Story of English. Robert McCrum, William Cran, and Robert MacNeil. New York: Viking Penguin, 1993. 400 pp. ISBN 0–14–015405–1. LC 85–41070. High school and up; research.

A study of the English language balancing historical aspects with its present use all around the world. The book's basic theme is the changing nature of English and includes its cross-cultural spread to places as diverse as China, Singapore, India, and the West Indies. Written as a companion to the extremely popular PBS television series with the same name, the book is able to stand entirely on its own. Chapters of particular interest to readers who want to know about the non-Anglo expressions of English include "Speaking of English," "An English Speaking World," "Black on White," "The New Englishes," and "Next Year's Words," as well as "Pioneer's! Oh Pioneers!" and "The Echoes of the English Voice." The book's readability is enhanced by tables of its 156 color and black-and-white illustrations and 34 maps, illustration credits, good indexing, well-documented notes and sources, and interesting examples throughout of word origins and usage. Useful for linguistics students and language students. Suggested for high school, academic, and public libraries.

Strangers To These Shores: Race and Ethnic Relations in the United States, fourth edition. Vincent N. Parrillo. New York: Macmillan Publishing, Co., Inc., 1994. 556 pp. ISBN 0–02–391741–5. LC 93–012047. High school and up.

This book, arranged in textbook format, presents a conceptual and theoretical overview of immigration from all points in the world. The book is divided into five major parts, providing treatment to each separate ethnic group. Within each chapter, firsthand immigrant accounts and text summary highlights are given, as well as extensive maps, photos, and line art illustrations. Also included are key terms, review questions, an annotated bibliography at the end of each chapter, and an appendix. Useful for units on immigration.

We the People: An Atlas of America's Ethnic Diversity. James Paul Allen and Eugene J. Turner. New York: Macmillan Publishing Co., Inc., 1987. 315 pp. ISBN 0–02901420–4. LC–87–28194. High school and up.

This atlas contains information about the social geographic makeup of America. It is divided into several sections, grouping races by a U.S. map pinpointing population distribution of the group. It also includes three appendixes breaking each group into geographic distribution more specifically by counties. It contains an index of places and an index of ethnic populations. This could be used at the high school level for multiethnic studies.

Videos
Multicultural Videos: Nonfiction, reviewed

America's Multicultural Heroes. Five videos. Distributed by Society for Visual Education, 1993. Approximately 20 min. each. Color. Includes teacher's guide. Preview available. Junior high.

Series includes "Susan B. Anthony Tells Her Story," "Harriet Tubman Tells Her Story," "Chief Seattle Tells His Story," and "Frederick Douglass Tells His Story." Each contains reenactments of historical events, photos, illustrations, and live action detailing the lives and times of these famous Americans. Good addition for an American History unit.

Multicultural Peoples of North America Video Series. Fifteen videos. Produced by Schlessinger Video Productions, 1993. Distributed by Library Video Company. 30 min. each. Color. Junior high and high school.

Each video discusses a particular culture that emigrated to the United States—their reasons for leaving their homeland, their cultures, customs, traditions, history, transition to life in the United States, and leaders within each culture. Each contains interviews with historians about the contributions and impact of each group in American society. One family from each culture is profiled to add a personal touch. Cultures included are African Americans, the Amish, Arab Americans, Central Americans, Chinese Americans, German Americans, Greek Americans, Irish Americans, Italian Americans, Japanese Americans, Jewish Americans, Korean Americans, Mexican Americans, Polish Americns, and Puerto Ricans. Based on the *People of North America* series from Chelsea House. Useful for multicultural units.

The Possible Dream? The Quest for Racial and Ethnic Harmony in American Schools. Littleton, MA: Convergent Media Systems, 1993. 58:16 min. Color. Junior high and up; faculty, administrators, and counsellors.

Five months after a racial brawl at Medford High School in Massachusetts on December 12, 1992, a group of students concerned about and involved in the altercation met for a discussion with psychiatrist Dr. Alvin Poussaint. This video focuses on their discussion of the brawl, the events leading up to the brawl, the students' concern with growing racial tension and unrest, and its effect on tourism and foreign trade. The students then break up into smaller groups to discuss how similar situations could be handled in the future and how to promote understanding and tolerance. Could be used in faculty or professional development sessions or in social studies classes.

Power Surge: Racism. Glendale, CA: Distributed by Media International, 1993. 16 min. Color. Junior high and high school.

"Getting to know each other is the best weapon against racism" is the message of this brief video featuring rock music, colorful graphics, and notable sound effects. Footage of the Los Angeles riots is shown along with comments from students. A diverse group of students is interviewed. Matt is a college student from Georgia who was raised as a racist but changed his mind when he became friends with an African American roommate. Ruby is an African American music teacher from Los Angeles. Susie is a Korean girl whose best friend, Karen, is white. James is a young African American from south central Los Angeles where the riots occurred. Erin is a white teenaged girl who is opposed to racism. The program emphasizes the importance of communication and getting to know other people rather than relying on the opinions of others. Excellent for facilitating discussions on racism and for social studies.

Prejudice: Answering Children's Questions. Oak Forest, IL: Produced by ABC News, 1992. Distributed by MPI Home Video. 75 min. Color. All ages and education levels; professionals.

Peter Jennings moderates this video on the implications of how race, sex, religion, and disability affect how we see and treat people. Answers questions about prejudice and its effect on our lives. Includes information on skin color and the different ways a young black man and a young white man are treated by strangers. One segment covers experiments on separating people by eye color and how "oppressed" and "oppressors" act differently toward each other when so identified. Especially good for school libraries and programs on prejudice.

Reducing School Violence Through Ethnic Harmony. Chatsworth, CA: Produced by the Foundation Payal. Distributed by Aims Media, 1994. 26 minutes. Color. ISBN 0–8068–8745–1. High school and up; professional use.

Well-edited video opens with footage of a racial fight at a school in Medford, Massachusetts, then shows a racially mixed group of students discussing issues which lead to the altercation. The group is ethnically mixed, including some Hispanic and Asian American students, but consists of predominantly African American and white students. More males than females participated, and the males dominate the discussion. The group then breaks up into smaller groups to do some problem solving on relieving racial tension. Good for training students, teachers, administrators, and community leaders on how to discuss racial issues rationally and how to address the underlying causes.

Working in the U.S.A. San Francisco, CA: Copeland Griggs Productions, 1986. Distributed by Encyclopedia Britannica Educational Corporation, Chicago. 31 min. Color. High school and up; professional use.

This video is geared to the newcomer to the United States who is here to work for a corporation and it assumes that the viewer has proficient English language skills. The video is not a celebration of diversity, as the main aim is to help a business person succeed by understanding the corporate culture and fitting in. Individuals who have come to the United States to get their "B.T.A." (Been to America) give their impressions and suggestions for success, such as "finding a buddy who knows the lay of the land." The competitive and aggressive approach required in many American companies is stressed, as well as the importance of schedules, deadlines, and the bottom line. The most illuminating section of the video contrasts the qualities of a valued employee in Japan with the qualities of an American employee, presented in a convincing role-play situation. The observations that industries have subcultures and that there are regional differences within the United States are noteworthy. Although it is stated that one can keep his or her individuality and that various styles can accompany success, the overall message is that fitting in is extremely important. The video is not inspiring, but it is realistic, informative, and well directed. It packs a lot of information into a half hour and the pace mirrors the pace of business in the United States.

INDEX

Title Index

Author Index

✵ INDEX ✵

Subject Index